saur

**Violence and Peace-Building
in the Middle East**

VIOLENCE AND PEACE-BUILDING IN THE MIDDLE EAST

Proceedings of a Symposium
held by the Israeli Institute
for the Study of
International Affairs (I.I.S.I.A.)

Edited by
Mari'on Mushkat

K·G·Saur München·New York·London·Paris 1981

The Israeli Institute for the Study of International Affairs gratefully acknowledges research grants from the Menachem and Mrs. Weiss Foundation and the H. M. Schleyer Foundation which helped to hold the symposium and prepare its publication.

★ ★ ★

The Institute gratefully acknowledges also the grant from the Deutsche Gesellschaft fuer Friedens und Konfliktforschung, which made possible the printing of this book.

Violence and Peace-Building in the Middle East: Proceedings of
a Symposium held by the Israeli Institute for the Study of
International Affairs (I.I.S.I.A.).
Ed. by Mari'on Mushkat. — München; New York; London; Paris;
Saur, 1981

ISBN 3—598—10355—7

NE: Mushkat Mari'on (Hrsg.)

© Copyright 1981 by K. G. Saur Verlag K.G., München
and the Israeli Institute for the Study of International Affairs
P.O.B 17027, Tel Aviv 61170, Israel

ISBN 3—598—**10355**—7

Printed by "Yeda-Sela" Ltd. P.O.B. 25051
Tel-Aviv 61250, Israel

To the renowned International lawyer
Louis M. Bloomfield, Q.C., Ph.D., D.C.L., L.L.D.

Contents

Introduction

The Israeli Institute for the Study of International Affairs (IISIA) has recently organized a Symposium on "Some Issues of Violence and Peace-Building in the Middle East." About 25 scholars from different countries as well as numerous Israeli politicians and researchers from all Israeli universities and many research institutes delivered their papers and/or participated in the discussions. They represented various political views and scientific outlooks.[1]

Among the Israeli politicians who took part in the Symposium were Prof. M. Arens, Chairman of the Foreign Affairs and Security Committee of the Knesset, Mr. A. Eban, MK, one-time Israeli Foreign Minister, Mrs. Sh. Aloni, Head of the "Human Rights Group" in the Israeli Parliament, Mr. M. Savidor, MK, Dr. Z. S. Abramov, former Deputy Speaker of the Knesset, Mr. G. Hausner, MK, former Attorney General and Chief Prosecutor in the Eichmann Trial, Prof. A. Harel, former Israeli Ambassador to Moscow and Bucharest, other members of the present government coalition and opposition parties, of the Labor Movement and the Histadrut (the Israeli Trade Union Central Organization), Mr. Sh. Lahat and Dr. M. Peled, mayors of Tel Aviv and Ramat-Gan, and other personalities.

The different Arab positions were presented by Y. Chamis, a veteran Arab politician and parliamentarian, and Prof. H. Tuma, a Palestinian scholar.

The Symposium's organizers received messages of good will from the presidents of Israel, Egypt, Mexico, the USA and from other leading figures in political and academic life in many countries (a complete list of these messages, their text, as well as a report on the Symposium's proceedings and the list of all participants were published in the IISIA's journal, *International Problems*, (Nos. 3–4 (36), vol. XVIII, Fall 1979).

Only several main papers are published in this collection, since they seem to have a lasting scientific and political merit. Their importance has even increased nowadays, in spite of the recent changes in the political situation in the Middle East and in the international arena.

The main purpose of the Symposium was not only to present different points of view—optimistic and pessimistic, realistic and

1

future-oriented trends—but, above all, to focus on problems which will need additional research, clarification and completely new solutions for the sake of progress and the peace process in the Middle East, which started with the Israeli–Egyptian Peace Treaty. This process is still very new: we are still very far from the day when there will be no more wars in the area and from a final transition from the political, economic and military confrontations to a comprehensive normalization of relations among all nations living here, and to their peaceful cooperation to the benefit of all parties.

Taking into consideration the Arab rejectionist front and the USSR's opposition to the beginning of the peace process in the Middle East (issues dealt with in this volume by Dr. A. Yodfat and Dr. A. Zaremba), the majority of the Symposium speakers were of the opinion that this fact alone might prevent any illusions that the region has already ceased to be a focus of tensions and dangers to world security and that it has entered a definitive stage of peace-building.[2]

The recent occurrences in Iran, in Afghanistan and elsewhere confirm not only this thesis but also the contention that the Israeli–Palestinian conflict is not the main cause of turmoil in the region.

Even some Soviet bloc researchers and scientists of the various Arab countries whom we contacted on matters of the Symposium and who, for various reasons, were prevented from participating in it, share this point of view (we have mentioned this in a summary of the proceedings published in *International Problems*, No. 36, 1979).

The Civil war in Lebanon, the growing opposition to Assad's regime in Syria, the deterioration of relations between the latter and Iraq, between Iraq and Iran, Egypt and Libya, Gamal Abdel Nasser's wars and subversive activities in Yemen and elsewhere, the attempt to overthrow the regime in Saudi Arabia following the occupation of the Holy Shrines in Mecca by religious fanatics in the fall of 1979, Khomeini's rule in Iran or the recent Soviet occupation of Afghanistan, and many other foci of tensions and armed encounters in the area—all this have nothing to do with the Israeli–Palestinian controversy. Some of them have been influenced by the superpower's rivalry, others are chiefly rooted in internal causes of religious, tribal, political or socio-economic character.

Most of those present at the Symposium have also refused the thesis that the Arab fight against Israel has anything to do with the decolonization process.

The study of the Nigerian scholar, Dr. O. Ojo, published in this volume, proves how meagre, sometimes even negative, was the Arab contribution to the decolonization of Black Africa.

The paper of another African scholar, Dr. S. K. B. Asante, shows how the Organization of African Unity was manipulated into adopting an anti-Israeli position by pressures which have little to do with the genuine interests of the Black Continent. It may be worthwhile to recall in this context that as long as the territories occupied by Israel in 1967 were under Jordanian and Egyptian rule the idea of creating the Palestinian state was never raised by anybody.

Other theses rejected by the majority of the Symposium participants were concerned with the assumption that the Egyptian–Israeli Peace Treaty is a failure because it has not immediately effected a radical change in the situation, and with another assumption, namely that the Middle East Confict is rooted in national controversies only. They are so deep that they nullify any prospects for reconciliation through compromise and, moreover, supposedly have nothing to do with the East–West rivalry and will grow following the growth of Muslim fanaticism and the Third World's militarization.

By and large, the Third World strives to establish an International Military Order as an instrument in the struggle for a New International Economic Order. This struggle is financed by the Arab oil magnates who push all developing nations to the anti-Israel front by promises of financial help.

It is true that some Israelis, as well as Egyptians and other Arabs and politicians outside the region, have already become impatient with the slow progress of the peace process. After all, it is still limited to two partners only, albeit the strongest and most important, but nevertheless surrounded by a sea of hatred, intolerance and militaristic tendencies.

Those pressing for quick solutions forget that no peace treaty in human history was reached quickly and was perfect or yielded fruit immediately.

The Bible, the holy scriptures of other religions, as well as the sages of ancient China, India and other nations, all speak about year-long negotiations, often interrupted by outbreaks of hostilities.

The Westphalian Peace Treaty of 1648 was concluded after years of bargaining. The last stage of negotiations took place in Osnabrück and Münster. This role is played today in the Middle East by Jerusalem and Cairo, Geneva and Washington, Ismailiya and Beersheba, Asswan and other places.

The American War of Independence, which started in 1775, finally terminated only 40 years later, if we take into account the impact of the Napoleonic expeditions of 1812–1818 on its outcome. For years London refused to recognize the US and regarded its recognition by other states as a *casus belli*.

Spain, too, was sometimes willing to recognize her former South American colonies only after many years of confrontations.

Peru was recognized by Spain 40 years after her declaration of independence.

The Versailles peace negotiations which formally put an end to the First World War in 1919 lasted for many years. They did not simultaneously relate to all parties. The peace settlement was actually arranged by the victorious allies who did not feel it was necessary to make a deal with the former enemies.

The negotiations for peace treaties with Hungary, Rumania and other former Nazi allies started formally in Potsdam in 1945 after earlier arrangements of armistices; they were concluded only in 1947. Again, in principle, the settlement was made possible by the agreement of the victorious allies.

The negotiations for the reestablishment of Austrian independence lasted for ten years, from 1945 to 1955.

Japan till now, 35 years after the end of WWII, has not yet succeeded in concluding a comprehensive peace treaty with all her former adversaries. She had to make separate arrangements with the West and the USSR, because the latter has refused to return to her some of the Japanese territories still occupied by the Soviet army.

There is no peace treaty with Germany. Germany (and Korea) has become divided into two different states, a situation breeding permanent friction.

Peace and the unity of Vietnam were restored after more than thirty years after the end of WWII. Almost in the aftermath of this peace Vietnam has become involved in a new clash in the Indo-Chinese peninsula, Cambodia now being its main victim.

Therefore we should not be too pessimistic because of the slowness of normalization of the Egyptian–Israeli relations and the slow progress in solving the complicated Palestinian problem. Nor should we fear the postponement of final decisions on this and some other matters for five years, or the continuing stubborness of the "rejectionist" camp and the Soviet opposition to the peace process.

The claim of some politicians and researchers that the decision to make peace with Israel is Sadat's manoeuvre for regaining the lost territories and preparation for a new war, and that Begin is trying to mollify Egypt in order to have a free hand to continue the conquest of all the other Arab lands, was regarded by all participants in the Symposium as groundless and bordering on pathological.

It is true, however, that the road to the realization of the Palestinian right to self-determination and the shape of its proper forms are extremely complex. (Ch. Boasson's paper throws more light on this difficult problem.)

Some Israeli, Egyptian and other Arab and non-Arab lawyers who regard themselves as eminent experts have been probably hurt by the fact that they have not been consulted by the decision-makers who succeeded in contributing to the breakthrough in the Middle East stalemate.

It is difficult for them to understand that the law of nations of today is not merely a collection of unchangeable principles and procedural directives, rather, it is an instrument for changing and for adapting them to realities in a constant process of metamorphosis — proposing solutions to ever new problems. Practice is changing old theories filling them with new content or replacing them by new doctrines and norms. The latter are concerned with human and national rights, development assistance, ecological problems, outer space and ocean exploration, peacekeeping and other operations and issues and, above all, with the highly diverse questions of conflict solution.

We must recall that in the past, too, peace treaties were not always concluded, borders not always changed and sovereign rights of different communities sometimes not recognized by an absolute consent of all parties involved or by usucapio, that is, the prescription of unquestionable possession, as claimed by some old-fashioned, dogmatic lawyers. Is not this true with regard to changes in sovereignty and territory after WWI and even earlier? And what about the border changes after WWII, the reestablishment of Poland, of the Baltic and other states in the aftermath of WWI, the new borders in Eastern Europe after WWII, the rebirth of Israel, the decolonization of many territories which started in the sixties? All this has little to do with the parties' consent, the laws of prescription or the right to self-determination, especially in Africa where the nation-building processes are still at the beginning and tribal confrontations shake the foundations of the new states.

Some of the African and other new nations based their rights on ius postliminii, the Roman law of return to freedom, other on the decisions of the former colonial metropolises or of international organizations.

Several Israeli lawyers cling to the Alon Plan which has long been dead because Jordan has refused to be a partner in negotiations on a repartition of land previously annexed by it.

The late Mr. Alon himself finally supported the autonomy plan for Palestinians, and rightly so, because the dynamics of its realization will pave the way for their complete freedom where they will be able to shape their own destiny. It will also make easier their peaceful coexistence with the Jewish state, both Jewish and Palestinian entities having to exist within the former mandate territory.

After all, the Palestinian Arabs already have their own sovereign state, although for the time being it is ruled by the Hashemite dynasty.

Israel does not need to rule over Arab centers in the West Bank to assure her security and development. In fact, this rule over Arab centers can endanger her national character, hurt her democracy and even threaten her existence. To oppose the creation of another Palestinian state and to continue the search for other solutions to this painful problem (in fact, not only some Israelis, but foreign politicians too, are against the creation of the Palestinian state) does not mean a denial of the Palestinian Arabs' right to self-determination. The West Bank and Gaza Palestinians themselves will finally have to decide what form of ties, federal, confederal or other should they have with their compatriots to the east and partly to the west of the river Jordan, and with the Jewish state. Israel has formally consented to this view, commiting herself already at Camp David to respect the legitimate rights of the Palestinians and frequently repeating that she is willing to uphold this engagement according to the principle of *pacta sunt servanda*.

That is why it is not so important to assume, if the final arrangement with regard to sovereign powers and borders is to be reached, whether the West Bank was legally or illegally conquered and ruled over by Jordan and whether Israel has therefore occupied a foreign or non-ruled territory, which means she has legitimately "liberated" it. What is important is to acknowledge that Israel occupied the said territories in a defensive war when she fought for survival and that her military government in the occupied territories is of temporary character. Hence, time is ripe to determine the conditions (in this way also paying respect to the Hague and Geneva Conventions, to UN Resolution 242 and to other specific commitments) for a peaceful coexistence of Jews and Arabs — rather contrary to the proposition of Prof. F. Ansprenger, but according to considerations of the Arab scholar, Prof. E. Tuma — in the frames of formally separate entities within the former mandatory territory of Palestine. Not less important is to secure the access to all Holy Places — administered by their own authorities — to the adherents of different religions by avoiding a new partition of Jerusalem (as proposed, i.a., in Dr. R. Barkan's paper). This, however, will not suffice; it is essential to determine conditions for the constructive cooperation of the Jews and the Palestinian Arabs that quite possibly would lead in the future to a federal or other common framework or associative ties.

Not a few Israelis recall when they consider the Palestinian issue that according to an old Roman maxim nobody is entitled to exercise his right if in this way he damages or endangers similar rights of others.

The "Palestinian Charter" denies the right of Jews to independence even in a part of their historical homeland. Its adherents propose to replace Israel by another "democratic and secular state" where the Arab majority will rule according to basic principles of democracy.

Needless to stress, Israelis even when they merely consider the status of Jews in Syria and Iraq cannot rely on such a proposition. However, it is mostly their traumatic past which compels them to cling desperately to their independence. The Shemtov–Yariv formula, a proposal of two former members of the Israeli government, Shemtov representing the Labor movement, Yariv, the Liberals, calls on Israel to recognize and negotiate with any Palestinian who would renounce terrorism and recognize Israel. This scheme seems also to overcome the difficulties mentioned by the adherents of the above-mentioned Roman maxim.

Prof. Perelman's paper on violence is not only an important theoretical contribution to peace research but it also helps to understand some aspects of the Palestinian problem.

It is quite possible that in order to extend and strengthen the peace process in the Middle East it might be useful not to press for an immediate comprehensive solution, but to prefer interim arrangements with Syria, Jordan and the Palestinians. This scheme does not exclude the beginning of Palestinian self-rule, but it pays respect to the rights of all parties on the basis of equality and justice. According to this scheme, these rights must be realized in a peaceful way and the step by step arrangements will ease the rapprochement of the foes.

Unfortunately, the PLO, certain parts of the Palestinian population in the occupied territories and a few small Israeli groupings still do not accept such solution. It is very bad that the governments and diverse movements of all parties often act under pressure of these groups and even share their irrational motivations, giving priority to questions of prestige, historical traditions, disbelief in reconciliation and territorial considerations over security and development needs, so important for the well-being of all nations of the region and the whole world.

Many Symposium participants have strongly criticized not only the above-mentioned dogmatic position of some lawyers and politicians who stubbornly cling to *Realpolitik* or irrational approaches, but also some of their fellow scholars, primarily, the modern, so-called "orientalists-mizrahanists." They were of the opinion that with all their impressive knowledge of various Middle East countries, none of these scholars was able to work out a worthy synthesis or to predict the October War, the ruin of Lebanon or the Israeli–Egyptian peace initiative, and, as we know today, they also failed to predict the fall of the Shah's regime in Iran, the rise of the tyrannical theocratic rule there, its war with Iraq, or the occupation of Afghanistan by the Soviet army.

Some of them have for many years taught that our destiny is to live in a state of war on all fronts for many generations more, if not for ever. Others have stressed that the Arabs understand, only the language of force and lies and that the Israelis cannot rely on any formal arrangements with them or on outside guarantees, but only on their military might and "secure" boundaries.

Almost all of these scholars remain pessimistic. They deny the prospects of peace-building because of the deficiencies of the Israeli–Egyptian peace, as if there ever was a peace treaty which was perfect and agreed upon immediately by all parties involved. They even ignore all aspects of Egypt's and Israel's negotiating experience that quite possibly might even be of importance for other attempts of conflict resolution (see J. Bercovitch's paper). By and large, the Egyptian–Israeli experience, like any other experience of negotiating peace, is not limited to the given case. It is also relevant to the philosophical perception of means of ending violence by discourse, as dialectically intertwined and existing at the base for the struggle of men seeking the reasonable; and (as persuasively argued by Dr. Mortimer Becker and Dr. William Kluback) at the base of the hope that peace is possible even in the worst of all possible situations.

Many contemporary "orientalists" do not even accept the concept of the Orient as an enchanted cultural region, as it was for Goethe, Mickiewicz or Byron. Nor have they drawn any conclusions from the German–French, French–Algerian, German–Jewish and, although still fragile but important, Egyptian–Israeli reconciliation, or from the Chinese–American or East Germany–West Germany rapprochement. Too often they pass over in silence the signs of successive decay of the Third World's ranks (which in fact have never been united) and ignore the emergence of the Fourth World of the poorest. This decay multiplies the difficulties of the Arab "rejectionist front" and oil-producers that try to uphold their alliance with the Fourth World; it is directed not only against Israel, but is also important to their attempts to build a New International Economic Order (NIEO). The "rejectionists" and oil-producers claim that building of a NIEO is of common interest to them and the Fourth World, but even today one can see that relevant steps towards this aim are evidently profitable (at least for the time being) only to the rich and relatively advanced partners of the Third World and of the so-called non-alignment camp, currently led by Cuba, a prominent Soviet ally. Many "orientalists," who focus on specific problems, underestimate the superpower impact on what happens in the region, namely, the role of the US in promoting peace and the Soviet policy of sabotaging it and the ensuing involvement of both superpowers in the region. Moreover, some of the "orientalists" are of the opinion that Islam is currently growing in strength and is on the offensive. They view the Khomeini revolution not as a transitional atrocious reaction to a tyrannical and corrupt regime, but as an expression of growth.

Actually, with the decay of post-revolutionary Iran, with the Soviet occupation of Afghanistan, Soviet threats to Pakistan and Iran, the internal frictions in Syria, Iraq and elsewhere (and the inter-Arab controversies), Islam has suffered a stroke, quite probably it might even accelerate the decrease of its influence on the world arena, and, as in Afghanistan and South Yemen, result in surrender to Soviet influence and rule.

Almost all participants of the Symposium strongly criticized the contentions of many "orientalists" that there are very few (if any) prospects for the implementation of the Camp David agreements. The prevailing opinion was that this initiative, although it may know pitfalls, is hopeful, if not irreversible. That is why the scenarios for peace in the Middle East were regarded utopian only in the sense that there was a serious chance of transforming them into realities not today, but only tomorrow (see, for instance, M. Mushkat's paper).

It is true that there will be many obstacles on the road to peace and it will be necessary to take risks and to elaborate entirely new models of cooperation and international assistance (see the papers of Prof. F. Ginor, Dr. J. Reuveny and Prof. L. Hamon). However, one should not exclude the possibility that fruitful solutions to the Middle East conflict might be even reached sooner than expected in consequence of the dynamic metamorphosis of the situation in the Middle East and in the entire world.

The Symposium unanimously condemned the attempts to see deterrence policies as a contribution to peace and adopted the assumption that neither the Israeli–Arab, nor any other regional conflict may destroy our planet, but the global arms race may (see Dr. M. Thee's paper).[4]

As regards more real prospects for renewal and progress of détente and rapprochement in the Middle East as in other parts of the world, the general opinion of the Symposium participants was that not to a small extent they depend on strengthening democracy, individual and national freedom and the realization of human rights (see the papers of Prof. M. Kriele and Prof. M. Maneli.)[5]

It is clear that the discussion of violence and security-building issues in our nuclear era could not ignore the crop of contemporary peace research. The discussion of this matter was initiated by Prof. O. E. Ozempiel, one of the founders and most distinguished students of this discipline, which is still in the making.

H. Lamm of Paris, Prof. Salvador M. Dana Montano of Santa-Fe, Dr. G. Douglas Young, the director of the American Institute for

Holyland Studies, Prof. Ch. Bloch, Prof. M. Mushkat and Prof. S. Somekh of Tel Aviv University, Prof J. Ben-Dak of the University of Haifa, and other participants discussed different problems related to the science of peace with a special reference to its postulates of peace education and to its analysis of the ME issue.[6] However, the general feeling was that this discipline had to be seriously reassessed before its contribution to constructive action for war-prevention would become genuinely important.[7]

Prof. Maneli said in his concluding remarks that the latter conclusion seems also to be one of the positive results of the Symposium.

The organizers and participants believe that the reader will share their view that the Symposium papers, some published in this collection, others — elsewhere, would be helpful not only to students of the ME question, but also to any person interested in acquiring more knowledge and in participating in the efforts to extend and strengthen the peace-building process in the Middle East and the whole world.

April 1980   M.M.

Notes

1. For the "dovish" tendencies in Israel, see, i.a., the Symposium addresses of Dr. A. Silfen, D. Rothfield, Y. Gotthelf and J. Majus, published in *International Problems* (IP), vol. XVIII, No. 3–4 (36), Fall 1979, pp. 36–7, 39 and 43; in the same issue see also the references to the speeches of A. Eban, MK, Dr. M. Vardi, M. Savidor, MK, Dr. Z. Sh. Abramov, former deputy speaker of the Knesset, Dr. J. Lador-Lederer and the mayors of Tel Aviv and Ramat-Gan, Sh. Lahat and Dr. N. Peled. For the contrary trends see in the same issue the theses of Prof. M. Arens, Prof. A. Harel, Prof. P. Riebenfeld and attorneys G. Margalit and B. Garber.

2. The dangers to international security and peace in the ME, created by social and international violence, were mainly discussed in the paper of Prof. Perelman of Bruxelles and in the papers of Dr. W. Kluback and Dr. M. Becker of New York.

3. For some aspects of the Third World's position as exemplified by its approach to the issues discussed at the recent conferences on reconstructing the law of the seas, see i.a., the paper of Dr. A. D. Martinez of the WHM University in Silver City, which will be published in the *1981 Israeli Yearbook*. Also see another Symposium paper entitled "National Sovereignty: The Case of Israel" by Dr. V. Belfiglio of the TUW University in Denton, USA, published in the *1980 Israeli Yearbook*.

4. This problem was also analyzed by Amb. H. Aynor of Jerusalem (although he mainly discussed the Israeli contribution to projects of development in Africa) and in some of my studies presented elsewhere. See, for

instance, M. Mushkat, "The Diffusion of Economic and Military Power and Its Impact on the ME Conflict," in *Arms Control and Technological Innovation*, ed. by D. Carlton and C. Schaerf, Croom Helm, London, 1977, pp. 247–254 and M. Mushkat, "The Socio-Economic Malaise of Developing Countries: The Case of Egypt and Israel," *Co-Existence*, (Glasgow), vol. 15, No. 2, 1978, pp. 135–145.

5.   The issues of human rights and humanitarian law with regard to the ME were thoroughly dealt with at the Symposium by Prof. F. Kalshoven of Leyden, A. J. Tsur of Jerusalem and Mrs. Sh. Aloni, MK.

6.   For a summary of the relevant observations by Prof. Salvador M. Dana Montano of Santa Fe, Dr. G. Douglas-Young of the USA, Prof. M. Czarny and Dr. G. Tamarin of Tel Aviv, see *IP*, vol. XVIII, No. 3–4 (36), Fall 1979, pp. 36–37, 39 and 43. See also the Symposium papers of Hamon, Vashitz, Boasson and Bercovitch, in *International Problems*, vol. XIX, issue No. 1–2 (37), 1980.

7.   For more details on this proposition, see, i.a., M. Mushkat, "Peace Research Reassessed," *IP*, vol. XVIII, No. 1–2 (35), Spring 1979, pp. 11–46 and M. Mushkat, "Die Ost-West und Nord-Sued Konflikte sowie einige Probleme der Friedensforschung," 7 *Die Dritte Welt*, No. 3, 1979, pp. 325–355.

8.   See *IP*, No. 36, quoted above, p. 50.

Peace Research and the Policies of Peace in the Nuclear Age

Ernst-Otto Czempiel

The difficulties of peace research clearly originate in the difficulties of peace itself. Nobody knows precisely what peace means, what conditions and situations are covered by the term. What is even worse, nobody seems to be able to define whether a certain process will lead to war or peace. This is amply demonstrated by the discussion about SALT II. Will the treaty diminish the arms race, stabilize détente, initiate an era of peace? Or will it lead to de-stabilization, increased armaments or promote the possibility of aggression? These are two completely different assessments of one and the same fact. The concept of peace poses as many intellectual problems as the reality of peace poses analytical ones. No wonder then, that peace research does not come to grips with the policies of peace, that politicians are left alone in their endeavours to muddle through the challenges of the day.

Given the complexities of peace as a concept and a political problem, is there nothing that can be done? This is too pessimistic a view. We will neither be able to solve the problem of peace theoretically, nor the political conflict in the Middle East. It should be possible, however, to indicate the approach peace research should take in order to explore both of these problems. The first suggestion is that peace research resume the discussion of peace as a concept. This discussion was abandoned a couple of years ago because it had proved to be extremely difficult. During the last few years no book, or article has appeared which has dealt with the concept of peace. The result is that there are as many peace concepts as there are authors writing on the subject. You cannot deal with a subject whose meaning is not clear. Therefore, the question of the meaning of peace should be re-opened. Certainly, there will be no unified concept of peace. Peace has a single meaning, but it means different things under different conditions. Peace is not a static pattern, but a dynamic one. It evolves through time. Peace means different things when it is applied to, say, Western Europe or

13

to Central Africa. To be more precise: it always means the same thing but it looks different according to the respective situation. Peace is not indivisible, as the political saying goes. Peace is divisible. Or, again, to be more precise: peace is spread over the world in different degrees. There may be war, not peace at all, in one portion of the world as/was the case in Indochina. There may be détente in Europe, integration in Western Europe. There is cooperation within the American–European relationship. There is high tension in the Middle East with elements of war included. There is, now, open expansion in Indochina, and war-prone situation in Southern Africa. In other words: there exist various degrees of peace in different parts of the world, but in what way can they be measured? The yardstick of peace is always the same, but it is not clearly defined. The main task of peace research, therefore, consists in defining peace as a political concept and drawing analytical consequences from it.

If this requirement is fulfilled it will help with the second task. Peace research should abandon its tendency either to purely speculate about, or to purely describe, political conflicts. On the one hand we have very interesting and stimulating theories about conflict and cooperation,[1] about deterrence,[2] or integration.[3] On the other hand we have very interesting descriptions about the various conflicts in the world, for instance in the Middle East.[4] There is no in-between, no amalgamation of theory and analysis. Both fall apart. Theories do not reflect the reality, and the empirical analyses go on without being guided by a theoretical concept. Both miss the focus of peace research. It must concentrate on the societal structures that generate violence and/or justice. In order to evaluate these structure one must have a theoretical concept of peace as a combination of non-violence and social justice, and one has to apply this concept to the political situation concerned. Only with such a specific concept that is used for empirical analyses can the task of peace research be fulfilled. We will then be able to analyze a situation unequivocally because one can relate political processes to the underlying struc-tures and interpret the processes accordingly. Certainly, this task is not easy, it poses many obstacles and problems. But it can be solved adequately when we have an explicit concept as a yardstick. A political situation can then be analyzed systematically and this is what matters.

With such a perspective, peace in the nuclear era does not seem substantially different from peace generally. It has become more urgent because arms have become more destructive. But the underlying causes which produce tension, conflict, and war are not necessarily different from causes that have produced those phenomena in former times. Whether men kill each other by throwing stones, firing rifles or by exchanging nuclear missiles is less important than the question of why they attempt to kill each other. The answer cannot be found in the instruments of war but in the societal structures which produce the intention to go to war.

Instead of sticking to such structural problems peace research very often has attempted to tackle the actual phenomena. Unable to cope with them on this basis peace research has been frustrated very easily and quickly. It did not persist, but shifted its attention to new and different subjects. It behaved like the young Henry Stimson, former American Secretary of War, in his manner of peace-making: "You begin by bringing...in a small handful of able men who believe that the achievement of peace is possible. You work them to the bone until they no longer believe that it is possible. And then you throw them out—and bring in a new bunch who believe that it is possible." This, obviously, is the fate peace research is facing. It occupies itself with one problem, cannot solve it, becomes disillusioned, changes its focus of interest to another problem and the same story repeats itself.

In the meantime, policies are formulated, tension mounts, and peace is damaged, or at least not promoted. To correct this situation peace research should turn to the structual aspects of peace and conflict. It should determine what peace is all about and should analyze the societal structures under such a defined concept.

Again this task cannot be fulfilled here. What is possible is a look into some recent results of peace research, particularly as far as the East–West conflict and the North–South conflict are concerned and to draw some conclusions for the conflict in the Middle East. They will seem rather distant from the actual situation in the Middle East, but they might be at the very centre of this situation.

1.   Political conflict in the Middle East as elsewhere is characterized by high armament levels. This is true for the nuclear era in general. East and West confront each other militarily and the arms race goes on and on. One is tempted to relate armaments to the conflict in question. There is no denying the fact that this relation does exist. On the other hand, armament accumulation is a well-known traditional phenomenon. There was an arms race before the First World War,[5] and there have been arms races throughout the history of mankind. The use of arms has characterized political behavior practically in every era of human history. It is important to note this fact because it saves peace research from the misunderstanding that arms and armaments are of a contemporary nature only. If they are typical for the behavior of political units generally then they must have at least some general causes. From this point of view some results of modern European (and American) peace research appear somewhat short-term oriented. For example they relate the defense policies of the Western power to their economic

interests. Coined by President Eisenhower in his farewell address, the term of the military-industrial complex has become very famous.[6] Its arguments appear very convincing. There is an arms industry and there is the revolving door between this industry and the government, particularly the Defense Department. There is the economic importance of arms production. Nobody would deny these facts. The question is: do they explain the defense policies of the Western states?[7] Or at least: what part of the variance do they explain? Is it true that economic interests produce armaments? Empirical analyses prove that the opposite is true: the governments are interested in armaments and urge the industry to produce them. Only after this production has begun industry is interested in its continuation.[8] If those interests, nevertheless, do explain part of the variance they do not explain all parts, not even the important parts.

This is also valid for the other theories that have been developed in order to explain armaments and defense policies. There are many of them, relating arms races to technological constraints or the tendency of bureaucrats to follow their standard operation procedures.[9] Already Richardson has developed the theory that arms races are fed by actions and reactions,[10] so that they can be analyzed by mathematical equations. On balance, peace research has not given a convincing answer to the question of what causes the arms race, particularly the contemporary East–West arms race. It has produced partial explanations, but not a general one. As a consequence, we do not know what causes the arms race in the Middle East. Obviously, there isn't a military-industrial complex neither in Israel nor in the Arabian countries. If we include in our observations the above-mentioned fact that arms races have existed before capitalism, industry, and bureaucracy came into being; if we add to this the fact that the rearmament levels of the Soviet Union and the socialist states since 1972 are remarklably higher than in the West, it becomes obvious that the theories which peace research has developed are not comprehensive enough. They explain some modern causes of armaments behavior but obviously not the basic ones. They must be more deeply inbedded in the fabric of societies and must be of a more general character. A phenomenon which occurs through all human history cannot have only particular and specific causes.

There are some theories within the traditional international relations discipline which offer interesting explanations. Raymond Aron has pointed to the "situation hobbésienne," to the open situation in the world which makes defense necessary and initiates arms race.[11] John Herz has developed the more specific theory of the security dilemma which makes armaments inevitable and again initiates the unavoidable arms race.[12] These are very interesting explanations stemming from the analysis of the systemic situation. If there is complete insecurity within an international system, armaments and the reaction to it are inevitable. This situation exists in the Middle East on both sides. The societal goal of security is such a dominant one that it overrides all other goals. Nations strive for the attainment of security because insecurity means destruction and the end of the society as such. If this is true than one condition of peace is the elimination of insecurity. It is impossible to point out all the consequences which will stem from such a result. Some may be mentioned in passing. To eliminate insecurity means to develop a new understanding of conflict. The natural reaction towards conflict is defense. The pertinent reaction to conflict might be to enhance cooperation in order to avoid insecurity. This does not and will not resolve the conflict, but it will transfer the conflict to a different niveau of solutions. Furthermore, the traditional diplomatic behavior is at stake. At present it seeks benefits for the respective unit. In order to strike out insecurity it should be directed toward mutual benefits.

It is, as mentioned, impossible to enumerate all the consequences that come from a more comprehensive analysis of the causes of war. But they are important and provocative. It is impossible to analyze peace intensively and stick to traditional behavior. Like the young man in the famous poem by Friedrich Schiller (*Das Bildnis von Sais*), the researcher as well as the politician who seriously tries to discover the secret of peace will never be the same as before.

2.   If the situation of complete insecurity in the international system is one of the basic causes of war, conflict, and tension, then the other large complexes of causes are of a domestic societal nature. Arms are produced and used not only for defense purposes, but also for the purpose of domination. There is an aspect of power behind all defense posture. To be mighty in military terms means also to be mighty in political terms, to influence, if not to dominate others. These relationships can be clearly seen in the Soviet Union. Its rearmament since 1962 obviously is related to defense requirements. At the same time it is motivated by the goal of improving the political power of the Soviet Union in the world and particularly in Eastern Europe. The defense buildup is also used to quell domestic demands for more consumption. Since these demands could potentially disturb the rule of the Communist Party in the Soviet Union, they must be kept at bay with the demonstrated necessity to rearm against the enemy.

Armaments and domination, therefore, are related manifold. There is the externally oriented domination, even in the form of territorial expansion. There is the drive for power and influence in the world. There is the interest to stabilize domestic rule by absorbing capacities, which otherwise could stir up the demand for a change, for armaments purposes. There is, finally, the tendency to concentrate the degree of domination and the distribution of power within a society. Schumpeter has pointed toward this fact[13] and he has ably demonstrated the role armament and conflict traditions play for this concentration.

For the analyst, the relationship between armaments and rule is obvious, not only in the Soviet Union but everywhere. The relationship varies in degree, at some places it tends towards zero. But generally speaking it can be found everywhere, even in Western societies. The discussion within the United States regarding SALT II can be understood only as a discussion concerning the future configuration of the American society. The opposition against SALT consists of those who want to preserve the traditional outlook of American society. The protagonists of the treaty are interested not in a revolutionary change but in a new distribution of power and inlfuence. If the dispute in the United States (as elsewhere in the Western World) is interpreted in these terms, it explains why people who are genuinely interested in a fair treaty and a watertight defense for the United States come to completely different assessments of the same treaty.

It is very much worthwhile to look into this relationship between domestic rule and external conflict. North Vietnam, for example, for more than 30 years of its existence has had to fight against different enemies. The society of North Vietnam has been organized correspondingly. Now the war is over, but the organization of the society has not changed. As a result, it can be expected that North Vietnam for a long time to come will produce the environment which is appropriate for its domestic organization. In order to conserve the present distribution of power and influence in North Vietnam the elites have to produce the external conflict which legitimates their elite role. Vietnam policies towards Cambodia are a first case in point. Others might easily follow.

It could be interesting to look for the same relationship within the Middle East conflict. It has continued now for more than 30 years and the societies have changed its structure accordingly. It can be assumed that the structure will continue to produce traditional conflict attitudes. Since interests in power and domination are involved, there might exist a direct relationship between conflict goals and these interests. To a certain, if unknown degree, the conflict consists of divergent interests in external power and domestic domination.

If taken seriously, this result again has interesting and provocative consequences. If there does exist a relationship between the degree of domestic domination on the one hand and the use of the military for purposes of external power or influence, then the concept of peace demands the decline of domestic domination. Democratic rule with a high degree of participation would serve the purposes of peace in so far as it diminishes the causes of conflict and war which stem from the interest in domination. This is not to say that a completely democratic society will be completely peace-loving. History teaches us that this does not need to be the case, although one must add that history up to now has not seen a completely democratic society. Nevertheless, the diminishing of power would eliminate all those causes of war and armament which serve the continuation of power.

Again, the East–West conflict offers some insights into this relationship. Comparing the conflict attitudes of the Soviet Union with those of the United States it strikes the mind that the Soviet Union always has been more interested in high tension than the United States. This is true even for the German Democratic Republic compared with the Federal Republic of Germany. The GDR cannot afford to have a high degree of détente because the ruling party would lose the legitimating source of tension. On the other hand, the Federal Republic of Germany cannot only afford détente but is genuinely interested in it, because the degree of domination is so much lower. The two governing parties are so democratic, serve so many useful functions for the society, that their legitimacy has a natural political base. It need not be artificially enhanced by demonstrations of external power.

These are examples, they are not results of systematic analyses. But they add value to the hypothesis that one important domestic source of conflict and war lies in the degree of domination and participation. If this should prove to be true the consequence would be to enlarge democratic participation. The images of war and conflict would change considerably, the degree of tension could be diminished.

If one detracts from some of the causes of war those which have been provoked by the security dilemma and/or by the degree of domestic dominations, how many are still left? This is a very important question and it is extremely difficult to answer. It can be assumed that there are substantial and valid reasons for conflict. There cannot be an Israeli and Arabian State at the same time on the same piece of territory. There might be no possibility for a compromise or an arrangement between liberalism and communism. The Nazi regime in Germany did not deserve any other reaction than outright opposition. History offers more examples in this category. There are individual, specific causes for conflict which do not have any systemic or societal origin. But even the treatment of those might be influenced if the two other causes of conflict behavior and armament have been eliminated. This is not more than a hunch. But it deserves attention and, perhaps, a systematic exploration.

For the time being, peace research does not offer conclusions of this sort. It seems as if the impetus behind peace research has come to a certain normalization, "without any striking new ideas or new lines of development."[14] In Europe, and particularly in West Germany, peace research in a large part has turned towards development research. It has abandoned the East–West conflict and has taken on the North–South conflict. Along the traditional lines of theories of imperialism, and enhanced by a certain input of Marxist thinking, German peace research has strengthened its interest in North–South relations.[15] Led by Johann Galtung who pointed the way and, influenced by Latin American thinking, West Germany's peace research has analyzed, and continues to analyze problems of exploitation and dependence within the present international economic order.[16] Certainly, involved here are manifest and important conflicts, short of war. Dependence and development are legitimate subjects of peace research. On the other hand one has to note that problems of development are being treated also within other disciplines, in political science as well as in economics. The great problems of peace and war are treated nowhere except in peace research. If peace research abandons this subject no one else will deal with it.

It is a fact that peace research does not tackle the contemporary dangerous international conflict in the world. There are exceptions, of course. But there are no systematic analyses, done by peace research, dealing with the conflict in the Middle East, the conflict between Greece and Turkey, and between China and the Soviet Union — to name a few. In West Germany, peace research has begun to analyze the East-West conflict, to offer analyses and suggestions for the conferences on security and cooperation in Europe.[17] Peace research in general, however, has evaded the most obvious and dangerous international conflicts and has occupied itself with the exploration and treatment of new fields of conflict. It has thus avoided the great subject of peace and war in the nuclear era. Again, there are exceptions. The discipline of peace research originated around the opposition towards atomic weapons; the problems of mutual deterrence, the contemporary arms races, and the dynamic of arms production and armaments have been dealt with extensively.[18] As mentioned, these studies seldom reached the structural layers within the societies involved, not to speak of systemic causes. Having exhausted its small personal capacities, peace research became quickly frustrated with those subjects and switched over to other points of interest. As a consequence, politics goes on as usual., But it goes on more dangerously because its instruments have been improved tremendously. The sources of foreign policy behavior probably are the same as they used to be in the past. Its consequences are, because of nuclear weapons, tremendously more dangerous.

It is all the more important that peace research returns to the great problems it is facing. They can be handled only in a systematic, comparative way. It might seem to be a contradiction to look into history in order to find answers for contemporary problems. But it is only logical. If it is true that the reasons for war and conflict to a very large part are not different in different societies and times, then attention should be primarily given to them. It might be useful to study in a comparative manner the history of the Middle East, in order to find clues for the solution of the contemporary conflict. It might be equally useful to analyze the balance-of-power politics of the European countries in the 19th century, in order to better understand what is happening between the Soviet Union and the United States. Only on the basis of reliable systematic insights into those causes of war and conflict is it possible to study the individual, specific issues at stake in a particular conflict.

Notes

1. K. E. Boulding: *Conflict and Defense*, New York 1967. Cf. the new approach of W. Link: "Zum Begriff 'Konflikt' in den Internationalen Beziehungen," in: *Politische Vierteljahresachrift* 20 1, May 1979, p. 33.

2. D. M. Snow: "Deterrence Theorizing and the Nuclear Debate: The Methodological Dilemma,," in: *International Studies Notes* 6, 2, summer 1979, p. 1.

3. See E. B. Haas: "Turbulent Fields and the Theory of Regional Integration," in: *International Organization* 30, 2, 1976, p. 173.

4. See, for example, Y. Evron: *The Role of Arms Control in the Middle East*, Adelphi Paper, no. 138, London 1977.

5. K. J. Gantzel, et. al. (eds.): Konflikt—Eskalation—Krise, sozial-wissenschaftliche Studien zum Ausbruch des Ersten Weltkriegs, Düsseldorf 1972.

6. St. Rosen (ed.): *Testing the Theory of the Military-Industrial Complex*, Lexington, Mass. 1973.

7. For a critical review see G. Krell: "Zur Theorie der Rüstungs-dynamik in Ost—West-Konflikt," in: *Politische Vierteljahresschrift* 17, 4, December 1976, p. 437.

8. Cf. M. Medick: *Waffenexporte und auswärtige Politik der Vereinig-ten Staaten*, Meisenheim 1976.

9. M. H. Halperin: *Bureaucratic Politics and Foreign Policy*, Washington 1974.

10. L. SD. Richardson: *Statistics of Deadly Quarrels*, Chicago 1960.

11. R. Aron: *Paix et guerre entre les nations*, Paris 1962.

12. J. J. Herz: *International Politics in the Atomic Age*, New York 1959.

13. J. A. Schumpeter: "Zur Soziologie der Imperialismen," in: Schumpeter: *Aufsätze zur Soziologie*, Tübingen 1953, p. 72.

14. K. E. Boulding: "Future Directions in Conflict and Peace Studies," in: *Journal of Conflict Resolution*, June 1978, p. 342.

15. D. Senghaas: *Weltwirtschaftsordnung und Entwicklungspolitik. Plädoyer für Dissoziation*, Frankfurt 1977.

16. H. Hermann Pfister u. A. Walter: *Friedensforschung in der Bundesrepublik Deutschland*, Waldkirch 1975.

17. Sponsored mainly by the Deutsche Gesellschaft Friedensund Konfliktforschung, cf: its periodical: *DGFK-Informationen*, Bonn.

18. See the publications by the Stockholm International Peace Research Institute and the Hessische Stiftung Friedens und Konfliktforschung, Frankfurt.

Persuasion et Violence

Chaim Perelman

Les notions "persuasion" et "violence" peuvent être définies de différentes façons, mais elles gagnent en précision si on les oppose l'une à l'autre. En effet, il apparait que l'on ne peut utiliser la violence qu'à l'égard de ceux que l'on n'aurait pu chercher à persuader...C'est ainsi qu'on ne dira pas qu'on a eu recours à la violence en comprimant un lingot de fonte dans un laminoir, ou bien que l'on est accusé de violence à l'égard d'objets, mais la violence n'existe que dans la mesure où l'on s'en sert comme d'un instrument d'action à l'égard de personnes. Celui qui donne des coups de pied à un poêle qu'il ne parvient pas à allumer, nous semble colérique et déraisonnable.

Mais les menaces, et les promesses d'ailleurs, sont-elles un moyen de persuasion ou un recours à la liolence? Les américains du *far-west* ont qualifié le revolver de "persuader." Et quand un prédicateur nous promet le paradis et nous menace de l'enfer, ne se sert-il pas de moyen de persuasion?

Il est vrai que ces moyens sont incongrus quand il s'agit de questions purement théoriques, quand il s'agit de prouver des faits ou des théries. On ne conçoit pas que, dans une discussion scientifique, on cherche à corrompre ou à menacer des juges pour influencer leur décision.

Il 'y a des situations mixtes où une thèse qui apparait scientifique à l'un des interlocuteurs se présente pour l'autre comme une atteinte à l'autorité. C'est l'ambiguïté du procès de Galilèe, dont on a obtenu, par des menaces une rétractation, l'admission de l'immobilité de la terre. Mais cette soumission à l'autorité ne changeait pour lui rien à la véracité de la thèse que la terre se meut, quoi qu'il ait pu dire sous contrainte.

Quand il s'agit d'attitude pratique, on admet que des concessions et des menaces soient chose normale dans les négociations. Si Clauzewitz a pu écrire que la guerre est la continuation de la diplomatie par d'autres moyens, l'inverse est également vrai, et l'on peut chercher à obtenir par la persuasion et la négociation ce qu'on n'a pas réussi à se procurer par la violence et par la guerre.

23

Pourtant, en renonçant même temporairement, à la guerre pour passer à la négociation et à la persuasion, quelque chose de fondamental a changé: l'ennemi est devenu un interlocuteur et, si on veut le persuader, obtenir son accord à certaines concessions demandées, c'est en utilisant, comme levier, les valeurs fondamentales pour l'interlocuteur, le respect de son existence, de sa survie, de sa sécurité. C'est la tactique utilisée par le président Sadate lors de sa mémorable visite à Jerusalem et du discours qu'il a tenu à la Knesset.

Il accordait à l'ennemi d'une guerre de trente ans le respect, la reconnaissance, une négociation tenant compte de ses préoccupations légitimes de sécurité, mais en demandant en échange le retrait des territoires occupés après la guerre de 1967.

Il n'offrait que des paroles, des promesses, en échange de territoires, mais cela a suffi pour provoquer un choc dans tout le monde arabe qui a qualifié le président Sadate de traître et l'a mebacé de mort.

Pour comprendre cette réaction du monde arabe, il est important de dire qualques mots des rapports entre la rhétorique, comme thérie de la communication persuasive et la politique.

La condition préalable à toute argumentation, c'est la reconnaissance de la qualité d'interlocuteur. Nous savons combien, après la dernière guerre et la décolonisation qui a suivi, les peuples d'Afrique ont lutté pour être reconnus. Nous avons assisté à des manifestations de noirs, de femmes, d'étudiants, de jeunes, même de prisonniers, qui manifestai pour être entendus. Le recours à la violence est fréquent, et même indispensable parfois, c'est une condition préalable à l'argumentation, à la persuasion, à la négociation.

C'est par la persuasion que l'on forge une communauté politique ou religieuse. En me référant à la rhétorique d'Aristote, qui est encore aujourd'hui un classique pour l'étude de la communication persuasive, je rappelle qu'il a distingué trois genres oratoires, le délibératif, le judiciaire et l'épidictoque.

On comprend très bien les deux premiers genres qui concernent les discours que l'on prononce, dans un débat politique ou judiciaire, pour gagner l'adhésion de l'auditoire à l'une des thèses en présence, pour obtenir de lui qu'il choisisse une ligne d'action, pour qu'il adopte l'une ou l'autre des thèses opposées. Mais le genre épidictique est celui, où un orateur est seul, sans aucun adversaire à combattre, et se propose simplement d'exalter les valeurs communautaires. Ce sera l'élige funèbre prononcé par Périclès des soldats athéniens morts à la guerre, ce sera le célèbre discours de Gettysburg prononcé par Lincoln pour célébrer les valeurs de la démocratie américaine, ce seront les discours de Churchill ou de de Gaulle, qui ont galvanisé les Anglais et les Français devant les épreuves qui les attendaient.

Comme les exemples indiqués le montrent, les discours épi-
daictiques, qui consistent dans la mise en valeur des valeurs, sont
essentiellement éducatifs, visant á créer une communion des esprits
autour des valeurs exaltées. Ils oréent une disposition à l'action, un
esprit communautaire indiquant les valeurs à protéger, les fins à
atteindre, auxquelles tout le reste sera subordonné. Les valeurs
exalées, une fois reconnues, tendent à se confondre avec ces valeurs
religieuses, deviennent sacrées. Les chefs charismatiques acquièrent
une qualité divine, qu'ils soient eux-mêmes divinisés, ou qu'ils
so'ent considérés comme les représentants de Dieu sur la terre. Les
valeurs unanimement reconnues seront représentées par des sym-
boles, religieux ou patriotiques, la croix, le drapeau, et des rites
auxquels il faut se conformer. Il ne s'agit plus de discuter, mais de se
conformer aux prescriptions; ici, il faut se lever, là il faut se
découvrir, marcher en cadence ou s'agenouiller.

Il est notoire que cette unanimité, on l'obtient le plus facilement
quand on s'unit face à un ennemi commun. Les valeurs négatives,
l'ennemi commun, constituent le lien le plus efficace pour cimenter
une communauté et surtout une alliance. C'est le rôle rempli par
l'Etat d'Israël, comme élément d'union et de communion de la
nation arabe. Sans lui, les Etats arabes deviennent une mosaïque de
peuples et de régimes qui se combattent, ayant des ambitions et
des valeurs diamétralement opposées, chacun voulant imposer sa
domination à d'autres, chacun complotant contre le régime de son
voisin. Mais la haine commune envers l'Etat d'Israël, leur désir
commun de l'anéantir est le seul lien vraiment efficace. C'est
pourquoi d'ailleurs nous avons vu dans le passé, et verrons encore
dans l'avenir, l'assassinat de ceux qui étaient prêts à reconnaître
l'Etat d'Israël et à négocier avec lui.

En effet, en reconnaissant l'Etat d'Israël, on admet que le conflit
israélo–arabe est passé d'un plan quasi religieux, de l'opposition
fanatique et inconditionnelle, à un plan politique, permettant de
négocier afin de sauvegarder ses intérêts. On abandonne le plan
d'une hostilité quasi mystique, où Israël était le pestiféré, dont il
fallait nier l'existence, même s'il s'était affirmé victorieux pendant
une guerre de trente ans, pour reconnaître qu'il a le droit à l'existence, en lui demandant des concessions en échange de la coexistence
pacifique.

C'est le grand mérite du président Sadate d'avoir transposé les
relations avec Israël du plan religieux, dans lequel communiait toute
la nation arabe, au plan politique qui permet des négociations.

Mais ce nouveau plan, tout en présentant un progrès indéniable
par rapport à la situation de guerre, ne va pas sans ambiguïte, sans
équivoques pouvant déboucher sur des nouveaux conflits. Qu'il me
suffise de signaler deux aspects par lesquels toute négociation, tout

effort de persuasion donne lieu à des possibilités d'interprétations différentes et même opposées. La première résulte de ce que toute communication persuasive utilise le langage; la deuxième de ce que toute situation argumentative peut être interprétée d'une façon statique ou dynamique.

Les problèmes posés par l'ambiguïté du langage et les divergences d'interprétation qui en résultent, sont connus de tous les juristes. Il suffit de prendre comme exemple la Déclaration universelle des Droits de l'Homme adoptée par les Nations-Unies en 1948. Comment les Etats constituant les Nations-Unies ont-ils pu se mettre d'accord sur un texte alors que leurs régimes et leurs idéologies sont diamétralement opposés? C'est que chaque Etat s'était réservé la faculté d'interpréter les textes à sa façon. Mais le jour où un certain nombre d'Etats reconnaît à une Cour de Justice le droit d'interpréter cette déclaration, celle-ci devient un texte juridique, qui s'impose à tous les Etats qui reconnaissent la compétence de la Cour en question. La création d'une Cour Européenne des Droits de l'Homme a transformé la nature de la déclaration, et tous les termes ambigus et équivoques qu'elle contient n'ont fait qu'accroître les pouvoirs des juges qui auront à les interpréter et à les appliquer dans des situations concrètes. De même, les éléments ambigus de n'importe quel accord indiquent que l'on a reporté à plus tard ou abandonné à quelqu'un d'autre la solution des difficultés résultant d'interprétations divergentes.

La deuxième ambiguïté résulte du fait que tout accord peut être interprété d'une façon statique ou dynamique. Quand deux parties négocient et que l'un veut amener son interlocuteur d'un point A à un point B, il se peut que le second s'y oppose nettement, mais accepte pourtant de passer de A à B. Il se rendra en B affirmant que c'est la seule concession qu'il soit prêt à admettre. Mais une fois qu'il sera en B, peut-être obtiendra-t-on de lui plus facilement qu'il passe en C, et puis enfin en D. Car chaque fois qu'il a fait une concession, la situation s'est modifiée quelque peu. Il en est de même d'ailleurs de son interlocuteur chez qui une concession peut en amener d'autres.

Nous voyons cette divergence d'interprétations déjà dans la concession faite par Israël en ce qui concerne le Sinaï. En rendant à l'Egypte l'entièreté du Sinaï, le gouvernement israëlien a insisté sur les différences fondamentales qu'il voit entre le Sinaï et la Judée-Samarie, qui font, d'après lui, partie intégrale de l'Etat d'Israël. Mais l'Egypte n'a pas hésité à envisager le retrait du Sinaï comme un prcédent qui devrait s'appliquer de la même façon à tous les territoires occupés par Israël après la guerre de 1967.

Ces divergences d'interprétations peuvent rester non-résolues mais il se peut que l'un des interlocuteurs désire imposer son propre point de vue par la force, si c'est nécessaire. C'est pourquoi, chacun doit, dans le négociation, conserver une position de force, pour que son interlocuteur ne soit pas tenté de remplacer la persuasion par la menace, ou même la violence.

Alors que, à première vue, persuasion et violence semblent des antithèses, il s'avère de l'analyse que, quand il ne s'agit pas de la solution de problèmes théoriques, les deux sont dans un rapport dialectique, car le cas échéant, elles peuvent servir de substitut l'une à l'autre.

Peace and Freedom

Mieczyslaw Maneli

I

Let us first reflect on the mutual interdependency of freedom and peace from a traditional source of our understanding, Aristotle's *Politics.*

> The tyrant is also very ready to make war; for this keeps his subjects occupied and in continued need of a leader. Friends are a source of protection to a king but not to a tyrant; it is part of his policy to mistrust them as being potentially more dangerous to him than the rest.[1]

Aristotle had plenty of empirical data upon which to base this conclusion. He had already analyzed the histories of various states. His evaluation of despotism, oligarchy, and tyranny as forms led him to his conclusion that despots were interested in promoting international tension and wars in order to reinforce their arbitrary rule inside their own countries. War, and even the mere possibility of war, justifies all kinds of emergency measures and especially the continued necessity for a supreme leader.

Aristotle did not develop his own coherent theory of how permanent peace might be secured. He did not connect peace with democracy and we know his reservations concerning certain forms of democracy. But he put his finger on the most significant factor: tyranny and oligarchy are pushed by the logic of their own internal development toward war.

At the beginning of the modern era, at the end of the eighteenth century, this idea was taken up once more and elaborated.

Two hundred years ago, three Western thinkers connected these two ideas, of peace and freedom. They were Thomas Paine, an English-American political theorist and statesman; Immanuel Kant, a German philosopher; and Stanislaw Staszic, a Polish universalistic scholar, scientist, and politician.

Kant's ideas in *Perpetual Peace* became world-famous while the thoughts of Staszic have even been forgotten in his own country. Thomas Paine is practically unknown as a theorist, although he is highly honored as a patriot in the United States.

29

II

According to Kant, there are six "preliminary articles" and three "definitive articles" of perpetual peace among nations. Let me note two of them. "No state shall violently interfere with the constitution or administration of another," and "The civil constitution of each state shall be republican."

The independence of any nation, explained Kant, includes the right of its citizens to struggle through their own nation's diseases; nothing justifies the "scandal" of outside interference even the pretext of eradication of an "evil example." On the contrary, writes Kant, a bad example may act as a desirable warning.

When Kant wrote about the "republican state" or the "republican constitution," he meant, using modern terminology, a democratic form of government, elected by and responsible to the people, based on natural law and due process; he meant a state of free citizens treated like human beings.

According to Kant every despotism not only constitutes a danger to perpetual peace, but the mere existence of despotism anywhere is a violation of the state of peace everywhere. This was also the idea of Staszic, an eminent representative of the European and of the Polish Enlightenment. He was an original and creative philosopher of the Polish progressive and patriotic movement, a friend of the most eminent leaders of the Polish 18th-century upheaval, and one of the leaders of the "camp of reforms."

Staszic wrote a creative Polish version of the French philosophers' theories of reform and progress.[2]

The laws of nations, wrote Staszic, are "the rights of man generally considered." Every man should use his reason and strength to defend himself and not to oppress others and acquire their rights. The same rules also apply to nations. They have the same rights of self-defense as any individual! War as the defense of a country should have one purpose only: the defense of the rights, freedom, and property of its citizens.

Every despot has a standing army and every standing army can only serve "to defend slavery and despotism." Compare these words with Kant's "preliminary article" of perpetual peace: "3. Standing armies shall be abolished in time." Why? Because their mere presence is a threat to peace. Armed soldiers of despotism incite fear and induce other states "to emulate one another" in numbers of soldiers; and to the number of soldiers, "no limit can be set."

Two philosophers, one from an oppressive, despotic state and the second from a declining democracy, weak and internally fragmented, drew the same general political and practical conclusions: tyranny and freedom cannot "peacefully" coexist for long.

Some decades later, the German and Polish philosophers were joined by a Russian, Alexander Herzen. Herzen, especially during the Polish Uprising in January 1863, was one of those who saved Russian honour; he supported the Poles against the Czar, against the cloudy ideology of Russian patriotism which was no more than Great-Russian chauvinism. Herzen called his compatriots to fight against despotism and the Czarist "prison of peoples." Based on Russian history, he developed a theory that internal freedom is inseparable from international peace' respect for the rights of other peoples must be accompanied by respect for the rights of one's own people. It was Herzen who consciously elaborated the famous maxim of Karl Marx: A nation which oppresses another nation cannot be free itself.

Modern history offers innumerable examples in confirmation. There was historical logic in the fact that those who condemned Israel in 1967, invaded Czechoslovakia some months later and suppressed the newborn freedom symbolized by the "Prague Spring."

Peace is inseparable from freedom; freedom is in constant danger when despots, oppressing their own nations, are preparing wars, interventions, and aggression.

III

The ideas of Kant and Staszic were greatly extended by Thomas Paine, one of the greatest pamphleteers of the American Revolution.

In his *Common Sense: The Call to Independence* he had already argued that the cause of freedom was endangered in America because of political oppression all over the world.[3]

In *Common Sense*, Paine tried to connect the idea of freedom with the American struggle for freedom against English domination. In his next book, *The Rights of Man*, he exposed tyranny as a perpetual source of war and tried to lay theoretical foundations for perpetual peace.[4]

At the same time he expressed a broader and more profound idea: America should support the cause of freedom in the world, because otherwise her own freedom would be endangered in a "world overrun with oppression."

At the dawn of American independence, the far-sighted thinker argued that any political system which could use tax revenues for war and private profit would be dangerous to peace and freedom. The only remedy, once such a system was instituted, was extirpation, reverse, or abolition; such a system could by no means be reformed.

We do not deal with separate war-longing governments, but, as Paine concluded, with "the system of government" which is identified with "the system of war." Every war commences with new taxes and it terminates with the addition of taxes. Every new revenue increases the power of governments which have "a distinct interest to that of Nations."[5]

This system of government and war, argued Paine, is also the source of the animosity among nations. Each government accuses the other of perfidy and intrigue, inflames the imagination of the respective nations, and incites them to hostilities. Paine declared solemnly: "Man is not the enemy of man, but through the medium of a false system of government."[6]

On the other hand, experience shows that whenever we have a truly republican, democratic government, war is absent. Even Holland, which, as Paine stressed, was an ill-constructed Republic, existed nearly a century without war. When the government in France was changed, then instantly "the republican principles of peace and domestic prosperity and economy arose with the new Government."[7]

The great and unforgettable, although forgotten, contribution of Thomas Paine to political theory was his explanation that despotism had many faces, that it could hide itself even behind the facade of parliament. According to him, despotism is a system of government, of war, of animosity among nations, and of tax revenues being misappropriated by the system of war.

In order to win peace, one should act against the *principle* of such governments.

Benjamin Franklin was no utopian pacifist: he did not recommend "peace" without any qualifications: he recommended peaceful settlements "without cutting throats."[8]

And now a final remark concerning Paine.

Paine authored one more peace proposal.

In *The Rights of Man* he made a suggestion almost entirely forgotten in connected with this philosopher. Paine extolled Henry IV of France for his toleration and for his plan of 1610 for abolishing war in Europe. Henry IV wanted to establish a European Congress, a Pacific Republic, in which delegates from the several nations were to act as a Court of Arbitration.

Why did the plan of the European Pacific Republic fail? Paine answered: because of the vested interests of those who made money from war and tax revenues. The forgotten idea of peace through freedom and international congress, was strangely revived in the works of a forgotten European thinker, of Jewish origin, Ian Bloch.

During the second half of the 19th century, and especially after the Franco-Prussian war of 1870, many efforts were undertaken to put a permanent end to war. Many proposals were made by statesmen, businessmen, authors, and philanthropists. The best elaborated of them all was that advanced by Ian Bloch (1836–1902), author of a fundamental, six-volume treatise, *The Future War —from the Technical, Economic and Political Viewpoints*.[9] The original text was written both in Russian and in Polish and this *opus magnum* was almost immediately translated into French, German, and English.

Let me at first give a little information about Ian Bloch himself. He was born to a Jewish family in Poland. As a child he was baptized a Calvinist by his own parents, but when he grew up he rejoined the Warsaw Jewish community and regularly paid the prescribed membership fees to it. As a non-Jew, officially, he became a high ranking official in the Czarist Russian administration of railroads and supervised the construction of the line between Warsaw and Moscow. Bloch was an eminent engineer and economist, a successful banker, the author of one of the most amazing encyclopaedic treatises on political and military affairs, and one of the early proponents of institutions like the International Court of Justice and the League of Nations. He is possibly the first author who proved, not just preached, that nations must either live in peace, or face mutual annihilation. This prediction was made at the end of the 19th century.

The purpose of Bloch's treatise was to demonstrate that future war had to be avoided unless mankind was either prepared to commit suicide or open a Pandora's Box of revolutions or other violent social and political upheavals. Bloch presented a complete and unique analysis of the art of war of his time and of all kinds of weapons then in use and their impact on the fabric of the societies of his time. He mastered military affairs to such an extent that a special commission of military experts appointed by the Russian Minister of War recommended his treatise for study by present and future officers. They also added that no book could contribute more to the success of a future peace conference.

The unusual additional importance of this treatise is that it was a civilian who had made such a penetrating and exhaustive analysis of military affairs as well as their bearing on economic, technical, and political relations. He challenged military specialists with a greater understanding of their own speciality than they had.

Bloch's economic analysis supported by statistical data represents one of the finest and deepest analysis of the economic aspects of the armaments race ever written.

Bloch tried to prove that not only war, but even an "armed peace" including an arms race, would be economically and socially ruinous.[10]

Ian Bloch worried as a man and a prosperous banker, not as a revolutionary socialist, who did not want society to collapse because of mindless militaristic fury. He predicted that war and war preparations would depreciate the value of the currency and the value of all securities, especially governmental securities. The accompanying inflation would ruin the middle class while the nobility would panic.[11]

Bloch's most important conclusion concerning the evolution of modern weaponry was that modern weapons will become less deadly on the battlefield because they will become more deadly generally. Bloch agreed with the prediction of Lord Lytton who in his novel *The Coming Race* attributed the disappearance of war to the discovery of a weapon so deadly that an entire army could be annihilated "by the touch of a button by the finger of a child."[12]

Perhaps this is the first reference in modern history to technological "deterence" and "the balance of fear." Bloch also understood that the prospect of total annihilation would not by itself influence the imagination of the people.

The general predictions of Bloch, concerning the results of an armed peace, an arms racee war, and "increased slaughter," were not prophecies, but conclusions deduced from empirical data. The events of two World Wars have proved how correct Bloch was.

•   •

In 1899, Bloch participated in the first International Conference at the Hague as a member of the Russian delegation. During the Conference, he met Theodore Herzl, the founder of modern Zionism. We know from diaries which Herzl kept what the relations and discussions between these two statesmen were.

Baroness Berta von Suttner, who was active in the world movement for the preservation of peace, helped to arrange the first meeting between Herzl and Bloch.[13] There is no doubt that they were mutually compatible from the very beginning.

On June 17, 1899 Herzl and Bloch had a substantial talk about Zionism. Herzl chronicled that Bloch did not raise any great objection to it.[14]

Herzl left The Hague shortly after his conversations with Bloch. They remained in touch and in July of 1899, Herzl received a wire from Bloch which he mentioned in his diary without any elaboration. In December they met once more and discussed their common project of mediation between the English government and the Boers. Bloch wanted to persuade the English to submit their dispute with Transvaal to arbitration, and envisioned himself active as an intermediary. Herzl remarked that Bloch was looking forward to this function "which promises him *La beau rôle*" (the starring role).[15]

Bloch's relations with Herzl are very significant in assessing Bloch's personality and philosophy. We have mentioned that he was baptized a Calvinist by his parents; all his life he moved in a non-Jewish milieu. Obviously, no Jew could have been the Czar's Counsellor, have the ear of the Czar, and be able to persuade the Czar to undertake important international initiatives.

There is no doubt that Bloch was a great humanitarian; the ease with which he operated in the international arena proves that he was also a cosmopolitan. And at the same time he preserved deep feelings and strong spiritual ties with the Jewish nation. His co-operation with Herzl and his efforts to persuade the Czar to issue a pro-Zionist manifesto are even more significant than his assertions made before his death that he was Jewish his entire life. Although his Jewishness was peculiar, he could be described as a secular Jew. In this capacity, he tried to combine general humanitarianism, efforts for peace, and the rebirth of the Jewish state. Especially today, when certain old Czarist Russian traditions are being selectively revived, it would be advisable to remember the idea of one of the Czar's counsellors, an idea approved by the Czar's ambassador to The Hague Conference: the cause of peace could be better served by connecting it, among other things, with the cause of Zionism. It is significant anyway that young Bloch being a son of a stateless nation, was able to elaborate a prophetic structure for cooperation between Zionists and states within the framework of well-conceived international organizations and international law. In his search for predecessors, Bloch presented a concise history of peace efforts, peace initiatives, and philosophies of peace, and peaceful coopera-tion throughout history. His personal philosophy is a continuation of these traditions, both religious and secular.

One should observe that Bloch agreed with the basic ideas of Kant and praised him for being even more practical than the Frenchmen. Why? Because, according to Bloch, Kant understood that the point of departure for peace endeavors should not be an abstract idea of peace, or a well-composed peace proclamation, but the process of securing peace should start with the gradual transformation of international relations. According to him, peace will be a result, but not a beginning, of the process of change. The International Court of Justice will not be the only institution on the road to the humanization of the human race although it will be very important. Mankind has to create more organizational forms in order to move successfully towards eternal peace.

This is an illustration of how Kant's concept of how peace should be attained was developed in Bloch's philosophy; the stages are the following:
- Demonstration that war is "impossible";
- Elaboration of the concept of the International Court of Justice, as indispensable for peaceful settlements;

- Support for Zionism as an element of the humanization of the "civilized world."

At the turn of the twentieth century, Bloch was one of the last representatives of the optimism and naivete so characteristic of progressive authors of the preceeding two hundred years.

V

The good and bad experience of our century confirms the philosophies born at the dawn of our era concerning the relationship between peace and freedom.

The rise of totalitarian governments after World War I produced an entirely new situation and compelled the traditional Western democracies to face new choices which could be narrowed down to the following dilemma: to what extent can democracy cooperate with one totalitarian system in order to fight another? After the second World War this problem became even more important and complicated, and it was dealt with simplistically. There was a period when any anti-Communist dictatorship was automatically regarded as an ally of the West.

Practical experience shows that it is democracy and respect for human rights which are the only true antidotes against the cancer of totalitarianism. Whenever the West uncritically supported little or great tyrants pledging anti-communism, whenever the West was prepared to forgive their crimes in exchange for their alleged anti-revolutionary services, it was communism not liberty that was the gainer. The most graphic examples are the communist victories in China, Cuba, and Vietnam. The revolution in Iran is also very significant from this viewpoint. The situation in that country as we know is far from stable, but we can already make the following observation: unqualified Western support for the previous regime, without criticism or advice extended to it, paved the way for another breed of political despot and bigot who was able to deceive the people, to seize power, and direct the country toward a temporary mixture of religious theocracy and ill-conceived radical leftist tendencies.

If the Western democracies, and especially the United States, do not learn lessons from the experience of recent decades, they will suffer more such painful disappointments. The lesson is: attempts to use one despotic or totalitarian regime against another are only of limited value. There is only one such country in the Middle East—Israel. If Western politicians try to exchange the hard indestructible value of democracy for the ephemeral coin of local despots, crowned and uncrowned, the result might be the same as in Munich in 1938: shameful capitulation. When it comes to a trade between ethics and politics every petty tyrant is better equipped than the best parliamentary government to profit from the affair.

This is true, let me stress, in this half of our century. Perhaps it was not the rule in the period of the European colonial empires. But their heydays have passed and today the rules of the game are different. We live in a period of new tyrannies and new concepts of human rights. Today it is the consistent defense of human rights which is only reasonable and the only Realpolitik. Whoever tries mechanically to apply the principles of Realpolitik from the era of Louis XIV or Bismark at best shows naiveté of an honest player who seeks to outsmart the professional card shark.

We have entered an era in which the support of democracy and human rights is the best, surest, and safest policy for democratic states. We have entered an era in which democracy breeds either democracy or, in case of wrong policy, can produce a monster; *tertium non datur*. In this era the value of freedom and democratic rights should not be narrowly interpreted as a security against external aggression or regarded as empty moralism or Kantian phraseology. Human rights have become a juridical fact, an integral part of positive international law, and in one way or another, a part of the internal law of every nation which signed the Charter of the United Nations. Most governments do not observe these laws, although they are not only morally, but also legally, bound to respect them.

Thus democratic states have the upper hand whenever and wherever they appeal to the world to respect human rights. Despots can try to evade and to deceive, but are unable to reject the requirements of human rights as non-existent. They are hypocrites, it is true. But let us not forget that hypocrisy is the tribute which vice pays to virtue, as de la Róchefoucould observed. The power of democracy, which it is often unable and unwilling to exercise, lies in the mere fact that it can legally demand from the new despots and totalitarians to respect what they themselves hypocritically acknowledge.

In the 18th century when the philosophy of freedom and peace was developed for the first time to such a degree, there was an insurmountable chasm between the sphere of "ought" and "is" between *sein* and *sollen* in morality and politics. But today democracy has a chance to overcome this gap, because morality has now become a political force and a virtue in itself. Everything depends on the understanding and determination of the world democracies to achieve their basic politically feasible aims. The alternative could only be tragic.

The Western democracies must either approach and slowly accomplish the once impossible dream of making the world safe for democracy, or they will be going, in their own way, to a gigantic Massada.

Notes

1.   Aristotle, *The Politics*, Book V, Chapter 11 (Great Britain: Penguin Books, 1970) translated and with an introduction by T. A. Sinclair, p. 226.

2.   *Warnings to Poland* was republished after the Second World War in the series "Library of Philosophical Classics," volume 8 in 1954. It is this edition which I have used.

3.   Thomas Paine, *Common Sense: The Call to Independence* (Woodbury, N.Y.: Barron's Educational Series, Inc., 1976) p. 101.

4.   Thomas Paine, *The Rights of Man* (New York: London Everyman's Library—Dutton, 1979) p. 58.

5.   *Op. cit.*, p. 137.

6.   *Ibid.*

7.   *Ibid.*

8.   Ralph Ketcham, ed. "The Political Thoughts of Benjamin Franklin" (New York: Bobbs-Merrill Co., 1975). Exerpt from the letter to Sir Joseph Banks, July 27, 1783, p. 335.

9.   I. S. Bloch, *The Future of War*, "Preface: Conversations with the Author," W. T. Stead (New York: Doubleday and McClure Co., 1899) p. xii.

10.   *Op. cit.*, p. 351.

11.   *Ibid.*, p. 354.

12.   *Ibid.*, "Preface . . ." p. xv.

13.   *The Diaries of Theodor Herzl* (New York: Dial Press, 1956) p. 313.

14.   *The Complete Diaries of Theodor Herzl*, ed. Raphael Patai, vol. III (New York and London: The Herzl Press, Thomas Yoseloff, 1960) p. 1016.

15.   *Ibid.*, p. 1016.

Reason and Violence

Mortimer Becker and William Kluback

Western European civilization has remained forever loyal to the concept of the rational and has subordinated the concept of the irrational to a less distinguished position, and even less has this tradition made serious attempts to understand the nature of violence. In one of the grandest philosophical systems — Hegel's — the role of violence, the rejection of coherent discourse, was not considered worthy of philosophical consideration. Nevertheless, a serious understanding of the Hegelian system is hardly possible, unless we are willing to admit that underlying the search for coherency and meaning lies the possibility of its denial and rejection and even the refusal to be heard. The prejudices that have been developed in favor of rationality, the easy and not deeply considered definition of man as a rational being, have been accepted without thought because philosophy finds it very difficult to deal with anything but rationality.

The reasonable is born out of the awareness. The reasonable is a search for meaning which is already aware that what is discovered is only possibility. If the rational sought to eliminate possibility as a threat to its existence, so the reasonable seeks possibility as the realization of its essence. Possibility is differentiated from the self-evidency of rationality in that its discourse is not a search for abstract truth or *necessarily* its attainment.

Both rational and reasonable discourse are at any time threatened by violence. If violence is conceived as negation, it is no longer a disruptive but, rather, a positive power. It is in this sense that Hegel and Marx understand violence.

It has been proverbial in philosophy to define man either as political, or rational, or economic or religious, inter alia. Be these definitions accepted or not, their comprehension of reality is one-sided and unhistorical. Whatever we may say of man can only be grasped in his history and through his power to negate the reality which surrounds him and transform it. The freedom of man lies neither in definitions nor in analyses of his needs, but in his power to negate the reality which confronts him.

On the other hand, violence can also be expressed as the language of non-sense which is different from nonsensical. To speak of non-sense, means at the same time, to speak of truth, to be aware of the duality of non-sense and truth.

There are three major figures, Eric Weil, Hannah Arendt and Chaim Perelman, whose philosophical writings have dealt with the problems of rationality, reasonableness and violence. It is to their works that we turn to elucidate what we assume to be the dialectical interplay between the rational, the reasonable and the violent.

The works of Eric Weil constitute a systematic description of the human experience from three interrelated aspects: Logic, Morality and Politics.[1] Underlying each human experience is the dialectical relationship between discourse and violence. No contemporary philosopher has made us more aware of the fact that violence is both at the origin of philosophy and the discourse which it attempts to enunciate. He makes us realize that violence can threaten or destroy discourse at any moment. Eric Weil is the philosopher of the reasonable. It is the contribution of Eric Weil's thought to have placed the dialectic of universal and particular within the reasonable which expresses the human need to make sense of the struggle with nature. It is in this struggle that all the categories of human thought are born.

Another philosopher who has attempted to give the reasonable its proper perspective and value is Chaim Perelman, who has devoted most of his writings to the study of the dialectic of discourse and to the reasonable. He has opposed all philosophic attempts to reduce the philosophic experience to the abstract, the self-evident and the mathematical. It is not because he has failed to appreciate the abstract as an important element of man's thinking, but it is because he believes that the criterion of the reasonable, and pluralism which results from it, is the necessary and sufficient means to understand that vast field of human concern which deals with decision-making, judgment and opinion to which the abstract can make little contribution. In a concluding paragraph to one of his articles, "Disagreement and the Reasonableness of Decisions," Perelman says: "In a political community or before a court we may have to choose between several equally reasonable eventualities; the criterion for the decision can be recognized by everyone as involving opportune considerations, but this does not in the least imply that the solution that has been rejected is unreasonable."[2]

Perelman's ideas have elucidated more clearly than other thinkers of our age the deliberative quality of the reasonable. It is this quality which has made Perelman the foremost exponent of the pluralistic society and has brought philosophy into the world of human activity. It is in this world, however, that violence threatens the very deliberative activities which Perelman describes.

No article dealing with the significance of violence can ignore one of the most important essays recently written on this theme by Hannah Arendt called "On Violence." Miss Arendt sets the theme for her consideration of violence by saying " . . .I shall argue in what follows that violence is neither beastly nor irrational whether we understand these terms in the ordinary language of the humanists or in accordance with scientific theories."[3] Miss Arendt's position is not widely different from that of Weil or Perelman. What is different is the perspective. While Weil spoke from the viewpoint of the logic of philosophy and Perelman from the inseparability of dialectic and rhetoric and their pluralistic implications, Arendt speaks from the viewpoint of political theory and from the history and development of political institutions.

The rage which is born in our reaction against the unjust is not to be dismissed as a meaningless emotional outburst. It has positive political and social consequences. It is an expression of our humanity and is stimulated by the age-old desire to belong to the fabric of a free political and social order. We witness this today in the writings of the Soviet dissidents, to cite only one example. This rage must lead to something beyond itself. It must lead to discourse on " . . .the ability to begin something anew."[4]

These views of Hannah Arendt are in contrast to those of Eric Weil and Chaim Perelman only insofar as Miss Arendt's interests are concerned primarily with an analysis of the nature of politics, whereas Eric Weil is concerned with violence as a dialectical moment in the realization of reason, and Chaim Perelman is concerned with the reasonable as the bulwark against all the manifestations of violence.

• • •

No discussion of violence and reason would be complete without reference to the situation in the Middle East. With the failure of Arab states and Palestinian militants to accept the existence of the State of Israel, and the organization of the PLO in 1964 with bases in neighboring territories, there began a series of attempts to create disorder and unrest through hijackings, border infiltrations and attacks on Jewish and Israeli personalities and offices at home and abroad. Peculiar to this movement is the wide financial support that is obtained from Arab governments and other terrorist movements.[5] With these facts in mind, we turn back to philosophy and ask again about the dialectic of philosophy and violence. The philosopher does not refuse violence outright, he knows that the struggle against violence requires the use of violence, for without defence against violence the goal, which is also the starting point of philosophy, of non-violence would be unattainable. If dialogue is the means to reduce violence to non-violence, then the choice held before us must be that between discourse and violence. Violence for the philosopher is a necessity only because we are still living under the law of violence. It is this law of violence which still rules in the Middle East and as long as it is not renounced we are conditioned by its demands.

Violence as a technical necessity must be comprehended as violence against violence. It is this violence against violence which gives to life its coherency and reason. Knowing that violence is a means to bring about the possibility of non-violence is the only imaginable philosophical justification and legitimacy which reason and coherency can confer. Philosophers who are so given to non-violence, because it is the essence of philosophy, must never lose sight of the fact that the non-violence of philosophical discourse is at every moment threatened with violence. If the philosopher is not the politician, he is nevertheless a man who thinks about politics and morality, his search for non-violence should be rooted in his understanding and awareness that the origin of the struggle for meaning is inseparable from what is meaningless and senseless. Coherent language is the consequence of silence or the language of coherent incoherency. The interrelationship and interdependency of one upon the other is at the core of philosophical thinking. If we may now ask again what does this all have to do with the struggle against violence in the Middle East and a symposium dedicated to peace, let me at once say that philosophical and political thought are hardly separable; the understanding that is in one is in the other. Violence and discourse are at the base of the struggle of men seeking the reasonable and meaningful.

Notes

1. Weil, Eric, *Logique de la philosophie* (Vrin, Paris, 1950); *Philosophie morale* (Vrin, Paris, 1961); *Philosophie politique* (Vrin, Paris, 1956).

2. Perelman, Chaim, "Disagreement and Reasonableness in Decision," *Droit morale et philosophie* (Paris, 1968), pp. 106–109. (Translated by W. Kluback.)

3. Arendt, Hannah, "On Violence" published in *Crisis of the Republic* (Harcourt Brace, Jovanovich, Inc., New York, 1972), p. 160.

4. *Ibid.*, p. 179.

5. See Walter Laqueur, *Terrorism* (Little, Brown & Co., Boston, 1977), 191.

Human Rights and Peace Policy

Martin Kriele

The relationship between human rights and peace policy is a complex problem of which a one-sided judgment can seriously endanger human rights as well as peace. Many elements that at first glance seem to contradict one another must be brought together in a balanced relationship.

On the one hand, foreign policy must respect the states' exterior sovereignty, which is based on the efficiency of the ruling power, even when that power rests on the principle of interior (absolute) sovereignty and neglects human rights. Respect for exterior sovereignty is the basis for the universality of international law, and this is the basis for world peace. Assurance of world peace means the survival of humanity and thus is the first precondition above all others for the realization of human rights.

On the other hand, we must make a distinction between the political claim for fulfillment of the contract and its realization. To demand the fulfillment of a treaty does not mean that the universal validity of international law is being questioned: on the contrary, it is evidence of its confirmation. This holds particularly true for the claim for fulfillment of human rights agreements. Today the realization of human rights is no longer merely a domestic matter of nations, but thanks to international agreements has become a matter of concern for all of humanity.

An attempt to apply pressure to this claim up to the limit of what is legally permitted according to the treaty is an intervention in domestic affairs. This concept was described precisely in Article VI of the final Helsinki Agreement: the participating countries are mutually bound to refrain from "any armed intervention or threat thereof," "any military, political, economic or other pressure," as well as activities for the purpose of "the direct or indirect support of terrorist, subversive" or other forcible overthrow of the government. It is important here to note three things:

1. "*The countries*" are bound;
2. to refrain from force or *pressures* (not information, the public expression of opinion and its dissemination through radio and other means of publication);

3. "Subversive activity,.." whose support is forbidden, is that which is directed "toward the *forcible overthrow* of a government"—thus not civil rights movements that demand from their government the observation of human rights agreements or the final Helsinki Agreement. However, support from the East for western Communist parties, organizations or propaganda institutions whose goal is the forcible overthrow of democracy is intervention in domestic affairs, contrary to international law.

Of course, not everything that is legally permitted is politically wise. Diplomatic restraint, for instance, allowing the other party to save face can under certain circumstances, accomplish more than public demands. The yardstick of politically sound behavior is the contribution that it made to the broadest possible realization of human rights. Even politically and economically powerful countries like the United States and the Federal Republic of Germany can achieve the realization of human rights only through negotiations. Mainly they can bring about an increase in the number of exit permits, and they can promote mutual person-to-person contacts. That is one of the main goals of the "Third Basket" of the final Helsinki Agreement. The easing of human contacts by dictatorships are not human rights, but toleration: somewhat more liberality, somewhat less use of instruments of terror, somewhat more formal legality and security. The main thing is, in time, to raise the Communist dictatorships at least to the niveau of the constitutional monarchies of the 18th and 19th centuries.

The demand for real and complete realization of human rights— that is, the demand for the replacement of a dictatorship by a constitutional democracy—cannot be the object of practical foreign policy. That would be merely a moral demonstration. How empty this would be was demonstrated by the helplessness with which we stood by and watched when the attempts at self-determination by the Hungarian, Polish and Czech people were crushed by force. This helplessness is based on the view that world peace can only be based on mutual recognition of the territorial status quo. Since this view is the basis for détente politics, western governments should not give the misleading impression that they could help the peoples of Eastern Europe in similar situations.

Communist dictatorships fear public knowledge of the violation of human rights. The collection and publication of such information is therefore one of the more effective ways of helping those who are affected. Progress in human rights is the result of an intellectual and political fight and not diplomatic pleas. Only unceasing indignation about violation of human rights can help human rights to be fully realized. Of particular importance, therefore, is the distinction between the Western governments themselves and other political and social institutions. Under certain circumstances a government must exercise diplomatic reserve in matters of human rights. Once diplomatic reserve becomes a pattern of behavior for society, human rights become a matter of relativity. Members of Parliament, the parties and their youth organizations, the unions, and above all the media do not have to act like little foreign ministers and stand up for human rights merely in the form of polite diplomacy. That does not help foreign policy, and it endangers people in the East Bloc, especially the civil rights activists. Now our problem is that relativism then becomes a pattern of social consciousness in Western Europe.

External behavior forms internal conviction.

If in the general consciousness of the West the political systems are moored to relativism, then that is an indication that political reason and morality and the western democracies' political instinct for self-preservation have begun to waver.

It is therefore necessary for Western governments, despite their external diplomatic restraint, never to have doubts about their fundamental right to become politically involved in human rights. It must be obvious to the public that restraint is based purely on diplomatic and pragmatic grounds. Behavior when dealing publicly with Communist rulers is therefore important: symbols of friendship used by Western officials towards representatives of Eastern governments (i.e. Brezhnev-kissing) could reinforce the tendency toward relativism in the systems of social consciousness.

There remains the question of whether relativism would at least contribute to the stabilization of peace. This widespread assumption is based on an insufficient analysis of the conditions of peace. On the contrary, peace can only be maintained when our commitment to human rights retains sincerity, determination, and political and moral passion. Only then will we be able to compromise, because only then will we be in a position to partially give up our goals.

The politics of peace can only be the piecework of broad-based politics; it cannot become the decisive substance of politics. It is true that peace ranks above realization of human rights because without peace the precondition for any realizations of human rights would be eliminated. But if as a result of this priority the will for peace were to destroy the political substance and peace were to become the decisive substance of politics—in effect, peace at any price—then we would become the victims of coercion and blackmail from the opponent who continues to follow substantial politics. The opponent would need only couple demands with threats: the peace politician would have no other choice but to retreat in order to avoid a conflict. Continuous repetition of this game would lead to the step-by-step surrender of one position after the other to the opponent. And then it would be repeated again. There is a kind of horror vacuity also on the political scene; when peace is made the decisive political substance, an intellectual and moral vacuum is created that actually encourages the opponent to political agression.

Eastern Bloc politicians are realistic enough in this connection and work with the following formula: coexistence with other countries, but with intensified ideological confrontation—although only from their side. Détente would be at stake if the Western democracies were to take the offensive with their political substance—human rights. The agreements with the Eastern Bloc countries could be interpreted to mean that we would be one-sidedly obligated to assume at least spiritually and morally, political relativism. The government and the lawmakers would be bound to take steps to influence the media, education, and free political activity along these lines. That is already the political claim to power from across the border for our territory: Our acceptance of that claim is the first step to the Self-Finlandisation of Western Europe.

Let us look at the mirror-image of this process; let us imagine that the Communist countries, for the sake of peace, forgo expounding about the ideological basis of their system at home and abroad; let us suppose they acquiesce to the relativism of the systems, and the more they do this, the more the western democracies go on the spiritual offensive and support the dissident movements in the Eastern Bloc financially and politically. This would be seen as an extraordinary political success of the West, and the Communist bloc would not have much chance of survival; the band-wagon effect would accelerate the erosion of Communist dictatorships.

Dictators are technicians in the assertion and expansion of power; they do not make that kind of mistake. The new Soviet Constitution of 1977 expressly acknowledges an offensive ideological confrontation even in its foreign policy. According to Article 28 (II) of the Constitution, the Soviet Union calls for "strengthening of the positions of world socialism, support in the fight of peoples for national liberation and social progress, and the prevention of aggressive wars"—all concepts that the Soviet Union understandably interprets according to its own purposes.

As paradoxical as it may sound for unenlightened ears: the precondition for peace is that the substantial enmity that confronts us is recognized as such and not lied about; furthermore, this enmity must not cause fear, adaptation, gnawing doubts, and the creation of fellow-travelers but must be rejected with spiritual clarity and moral inflexibility. Only then is there a balance of political strengths that would lead to mutual recognition, foresight and moderation, to compromise and its contractual security, to civilized coexistence secured by treaties and above all to adherence to the treaties. The alternative would not by any means be that we could live in peace, but that we would be despised objects of political manipulation and blackmail.

For example, from the beginning of détente the Soviet Union tested from time to time whether our will for peace had consumed our political substance: it put President Kennedy to the test by installing nuclear rockets in Cuba; its answer to the German *Ostpolitik* was an increased number of sophisticated weapons in Europe that far exceeded its defense needs; it interpreted clearly stated provisions of the Berlin Agreement according to its own whims and tolerated obvious treaty violations by the German Democratic Republic—all of this to test whether the priorities we have of securing peace could be exploited for political blackmail. Nothing is more dangerous to world peace than when the Soviet Union casts doubt over the West's defense readiness and tests it. Sometimes these tests will reach the limits of our substantial political will. The West is inviting the Eastern Bloc to make a dangerous political miscalculation if it does not make it clear that the tests are futile. The Cuban missile crisis demonstrated the risky mechanism of such an entanglement. It was the inflexibility of the West that created the real basis for détente.

The policy of agreements makes peace more secure only on the basis of solid compromises. The preconditions for these compromises is that will against will, power against power existed and that the pre-existing balance is not changed thereafter. On this basis, both sides have an interest in entering balanced agreements and in retaining interest in their observance. Therefore, restraint in matters of human rights must be recognized as only pragmatic, diplomatic behavior, and it must be limited to those involved directly in foreign policy matters; it cannot become a model for behavior of a free society committed to human rights, without endangering human rights as well as peace.

On the Nature and Dynamics of the Contemporary Arms Race
Some Remarks on the Internal and External Determinants of Armaments
Marek Thee

1. The Indices

A number of indices point to and emphasize a growing intensification and acceleration of contemporary armaments.

- Global military expenditure today runs at the rate of approximately 1.25 billion US dollars daily. The annual costs of world armaments — 400–550 billion US dollars — are equal to the annual gross national income of about half the world's population in the poorest countries of Asia and Africa.
- In the last three decades world military expenditures, in constant prices, have more than trebled.
- The nuclear stockpiles in the armouries of the great powers, by conservative estimates, surpass at present the explosive power of about one million bombs that destroyed Hiroshima, i.e., one Hiroshima bomb may be earmarked for every four thousand people on the globe.
- The arsenals of tactical and strategic nuclear weapons contain tens of thousands of warheads, by far exceeding any imaginable target — military installations, industrial complexes and population centers.

As stated by President Carter in this 1979 State of the Union address:

> ...Just one of our relatively invulnerable Poseidon submarines — less than 2% of our total nuclear force of submarines, aircraft, and land-based missiles — carries enough warheads to destroy every large and medium-sized city in the Soviet Union ...

Similar capabilities are at the disposal of the Soviet Union.

- The sophistication and destructiveness of both nuclear and conventional weapons have reached levels unparalleled in history. Usability was always designed in nuclear weapons. Yet originally, in their crude form, these weapons were meant to serve deterrence purposes only. But today, with their abundance and third-generation technology, they have been streamlined for an enhanced ability to actually wage nuclear war. Decision-makers in East and West are induced to think the unthinkable, and in times of crisis nuclear catastrophe may be imminent, whether by miscalculation or design.

- There is also a rapid horizontal proliferation of modern arms. The number of Third World countries which acquired supersonic aircraft between 1955 and 1975 has grown from 1 to 43. The number of Third World countries which acquired modern missile systems between 1954 and 1977 has grown from 2 to 42. The number of Third World countries which acquired advanced fighting vehicles of post–1945 design between 1950 and 1977 has grown from 1 to 62. Major weapons are today imported by 75 Third World countries.

By whatever indices we try to measure the escalatory trend in contemporary armaments — military expenditures, the nuclear stock-pile, lethality, warfighting capability or the spread of modern weapons around the globe, the drift into an ever more dangerous international military environment is alarming. The arms race has become a global phenomenon and has acquired a momentum of its own, almost impervious to political and social control.

2. The New Armaments Dynamics

Various new elements in the arms race tend to increase the armaments dynamics and make efforts at arms control and disarmament extremely difficult.

First, the arms race today is no longer a competition in quantities only. It is predominantly a race in modern technology — in product improvement, refinement and breakthrough accomplishments. Implicit in this race is a rapid rate of change and a constant disruption of presumed conditions of strategic stability. There is a perpetual fear of destabilization which in turn fuels the race. Military balances, however construed, become difficult to quantify, and their assessment invites subjective and arbitrary judgements. The outcome is a proneness to worst-case scenarios and over-reaction.

Second, with technology the focal point in armaments, the arms race achieved a qualitatively higher level of intensity. Past static notions of the arms race with customary step-by-step arithmetic augumentation of arsenals do not fit anymore the new reality. Armaments today channelled into an exponential curve — steep, fast and unpredictable.

Third, traditional assumptions of quantitative arms race dynamics based on the theory of even action-reaction behavior tend in conditions of the technological race to lose their validity. Past action-reaction theory assumed that (a) the increase in a nation's armaments is positively proportional to the opponents armaments expenditures, and (b) that the rate of armaments acceleration is negatively proportional to the level of existing armaments. However, because of the race in technology, the action-reaction effect has a much stronger and wider impact than in the past. The technology race generates a propensity to reach far into the future so as to pre-empt possible moves by the adversary, and this in turn stimulates over-response—a reaction becomes a permanent condition. At the same time, the rate of innovation in technology tends to subdue any inhibitions which may arise because of the attained level of armaments. The process of acceleration, mainly of a qualitative nature, is inherently part of the current arms race.

Fourth, present-day military doctrines such as deterrence, balance of power schemes or worst-case contingency planning generate inner-directed hostile impulses and a threat system which fuels the arms race. The main assumption of deterrence is that the foe can be held in check by the threat of devastating retaliation. It thus requires a constant augmentation of armaments so as to enhance the retaliatory power and to inflict ever greater damage on the enemy. The outcome is a state of constant war-preparation. Growing military capability by one side is interpreted by the other as political and military intent, and the race for superiority, i.e., to "win" the arms race, is perpetuated.

Last but not least, there are today powerful socio-political forces in society with vested interests in sustaining the arms race. It was President Eisenhower who in his farewell Presidential address first drew attention to the new phenomenon of the "military-industrial complex" with a "potential for the disastrous rise of misplaced power." Speaking from a position of personal experience, Eisenhower was deeply concerned about possible consequences. In fact, in the context of the subsequent US Indochina involvement, his words had a prophetic ring. A close analysis of Eisenhower's statement shows that he had in mind not only the military and industry but also the role of the state bureaucracy "in every State House, every office of the Federal Government," as well as the new position of power captured by the military "scientific-technological elite." Thus Eisenhower's "web of special interests" can well be defined as the military-industrial-bureaucratic-technological complex forming a competitive alliance of interests behind the arms race.

I need not add, and this is easy to prove, that the military-industrial-bureaucratic-technological complex is not a purely

Western phenomenon. It exists both in East and West. Together with the other structural elements energizing the arms race, it is a formidable force which tends to block any efforts at disarmament.

3. *The Military R&D Establishment*

Within the driving forces behind armaments special attention has to be given to military research and development (R&D). The growth and role of military R&D is a relatively new international phenomenon, reflecting the impact on armaments of the second technological revolution. Whereas before World War II military R&D consumed less than 1% of military expenditures, it now absorbs 10–15%. The investment in military R&D has increased 4–5 times quicker than the general rate of growth of global armaments expenditures. Given that current global military expenditures amount to 400–450 billion US dollars annually, one can safely estimate that annual world investments in military R&D today reach the sum of 40–60 billion US dollars. It is also estimated that the military R&D establishment counts up to half a million employees—almost one-half of the world's best qualified physical and engineering scientists. Naturally, such an enormous investment and effort must produce dramatic results. It is from the mode of operation of military R&D—its structure, institutional set-up and way of functioning—that armaments get to date its strongest autonomous impulse. McNamara called it "a kind of intrinsic mad momentum of its own." Analyzing the mode of operation of military R&D, we may detect some regularities which have a powerful impact on the arms race. Four of those regularities are of basic importance:
1. The impulse to technological competition;
2. The stabilizing and invigoriating effects of the long lead-times;
3. The follow-on imperative and growth propensity;
4. The block-building and cross-fertilization effect.

The impulse to technological competition derives from the very size, expansion and goal-setting of military R&D. It is only natural that the hundreds of thousands of scientists and engineers dispersed in thousands of research plants and laboratories, and working on parallel problems, should be competing among themselves in inventing, developing, and perfecting new arms and weapons systems. Incentives to this competition do not lie only in the material and intangible fields. They are reinforced by the demands of excellence: the end product must respond to the highest technological standards and must exceed any mark achieved by the adversary. The race is thus both on national and international levels.

The stabilizing and invigorating effect is linked to the long lead-lines—up to 10–15 years—needed for the development of modern arms. This has several consequences. *First*, it assures stability, constancy and continuity to the armaments phenomenon. *Secondly*, long lead-times intertwine with bureaucratic inertia strengthening commitments and making it difficult to withdraw from planned new weapons once an initial investment has been made. *Thirdly*, long lead-times act as a time pressure for early decisions in order to pre-empt the adversary and make the new weapons available in time. *Fourthly*, long lead-times act also as a technological imperative to improve the performance of both military R&D and the armaments effort.

The follow-on impetative and growth propensity reflects the very urge—in conditions of the technological race—to go ahead and expand. Preservation or the winning of the lead in technology is today crucial for the goals of the military establishment, and the position of power on the international scene. The completion of one weapons system requires a follow-up by a new one, the development of offensive arms required a response in the development of defensive weapons, and *vice versa*. The highly specialized manpower mobilized for military R&D must be maintained on a constant footing and extended. Thus military R&D, as a very specific case of the Parkinson law on the spontaneous growth of bureaucratic institutions, tends to swell and expand, and in turn tends to invigorate the arms race.

Finally, *the block-building and cross-fertilizing effect* in the functioning of military R&D results from the meeting of many projects, initially unrelated, but complementary in technology and leading very often to breakthrough discoveries. This was for instance the case with the development of the multiple independently targeted re-entry vehicles—the MIRVs. The abundance of different weapon development projects generates building-blocks for entirely new technologies.

In sum, military R&D has grown to become the main backbone of the armaments effort and the strongest impulse to the arms race. To bring military R&D under control is the curcial task if arms control and disarmament should become a reality.

4. Arms Control and Disarmament

From the above short review it is evident that powerful blockages and barriers of a socio-political and structural-technological nature stand in the way of arms control and disarmament. One should therefore not nurture illusions that genuine arms control and disarmament can be easily achieved.

True, objectively seen, the overwhelming majority of people in all corners of the world are losers in the arms race. Not only that armaments represent a tremendous waste in human and material

54 • *Violence and Peace-Building*

resources. Not only are they repellent on ethical grounds. The contemporary arms race is also counterproductive as far as security is concerned. The greater the arms build-up, the larger looms the danger that the weapons will finally be used. And unlike in the wars of the past, in a future world military conflagration the very human survival is at stake.

Simple reason and human rationality should then generate sufficient political will to bring about change.

Unfortunately, we are still far from such a change. This is not the place to develop concrete strategies for disarmament. At the present stage, the most important task is perhaps to educate people on the perils of the arms race, to raise the general awareness of the predicament caused by armaments, to make armaments dynamics more transparent and mobilize public opinion to take a stand and speak out against the mad drive to self-destruction. It lies in the self-interest of every human being, nation and the international community to find ways to halt the arms race and ensure that disarmament works.

Selected Source Materials

World Armanents and Disarmament, SIPRI Yearbook, vols. 1977, 1978, 1979. Stockholm International Peace Research Institute.

Marek Thee (ed.): *Armaments and Disarmament in the Nuclear Age. A Handbook.* Stockholm International Peace Research Institute, 1976 (available also in French, German, Serbo-Croatian, Finnish and Norwegian).

Ruth Leger Sivard: *World Military and Social Expenditure*, vols. 1976, 1977, 1978. WMSE Publications, Leesburg, Va.

Documents on Disarmament. Washington: United States Arms Control and Disarmament Agency, yearly editions.

World Military Expenditure and Arms Transfer 1967–1976. Washington: ACDA, 1967.

Randall Forsberg: *Resolurces Devoted to Military Research and Development.* Stockholm: SIPRI, 1972.

Herbert York: *The Origins of MIRV.* Stockholm: SIPRI, 1973.

Marek Thee: "International Arms Control and Disarmament Agreements: Promise, Fact and Vision," *International Social Science Journal*, vol. XXVIII, no. 2, 1976.

Marek Thee: "Arms Control: The Retreat from Disarmament," *Journal of Peace Research*, vol. XIV, No. 2, 1977.

Marek Thee: "Militarism and Militarization in Contemporary International Relations," *Bulletin of Peace Proposals*, vol. VIII, No. 4, 1977.

Marek Thee: "The Dynamics of the Arms Race, Military R&D, and Disarmament," *International Social Science Journal*, vol. XXX, No. 4, 1978.

Quelques observations et vues françaises sur la manière de réaliser la paix

Leo Hamon

La paix durable est en effet le souhait, le rêve des hommes mais c'est la guerre qui est leur destin et la réalité de leur histoire. Y a-t-il une chance de voir ce cycle des guerres prendre fin, existe-t-il une chance de généraliser et de consolider la paix? C'est à cette interrogation que nous voudrions consacrer quelques réflexions en partant des choses telles qu'elles sont et non telles que nous voudrions les voir. A cet effet rappelons d'abord quelques traits de ce que l'on appelle l'âge nucléaire.

(A) Un premier trait est l'absurdité manifeste d'une guerre nucléaire qui amènerait évidemment l'anéantissement des différents adversaires; alors qu'on a pu considérer (avec de moins en moins de raisons d'ailleurs mais enfin avec quelques illusions) que la guerre par armes classiques pouvait, si elle était gagnée, constituer une bonne affaire, la guerre nucléaire ne peut elle être une semblable affaire, elle ne peut qu'être un suicide commun. D'ou les guerres limitées. C'est nouveau: Sans doute a-t-on connu des guerres limitées au 18éme siècle et même auparavant en ce sens que les conflits étaient limités dans le temps, dans le nombre des participants et dans ce que les armées de métier échangeaient des coups prédéterminés — et rien que cela sur des objectifs eux-mêmes limités. Il y avait bien lá ce que l'on pourrait appeler, pour reprendre un terme anglais, un "self-restraint" mais ce qui est nouveau par rapport aux guerres qui ont précédé la Révolution française et l'Empire c'est qu'à présent la limitation est essentiellement volontaire.

(B) Un second trait de notre ère nucléaire peut être marqué ainsi: La peur de l'entrée dans la guerre nucléaire par la voie de l'escalade est si grande qu'entre des puissances nucléaires il n'y a même pas de guerres classiques tant elles craignent de n'être plus à un moment donné maîtresses de l'escalade et de se trouver, à partir d'hostilités classiques, entraînées dans une guerre nucléaire.

55

(C) Donc pas de guerres entre puissances nucléaires, mêmes par armes classiques; mais qu'en est-il des autres puissances, non nucléaires? Le droit international public, la loi internationale ne sont pas, je pense, un moyen d'empêcher la guerre. Je ne crois pas aux pactes qui mettent la guerre hors la loi. J'entends bien qu'il y a l'opinion mondiale, des Nations Unies es des autres organisations mondiales. Mais considérons si vous voulez bien le résultat pratique. Il y a eu des guerres, Israël le sait mieux qu'aucun autre pays, seulement ces guerres ont été très rapidement arrêtées et, un cessez-le-feu du Conseil de Sécurité étant destiné à intervenir assez rapidement. Le cessez-le-feu est un compromis qu'entérine le Conseil de Sécuritécette limitation dans la durée est renforcée par le progrès même des armes classiques, car le progrès technique n'est pas seulement celui des armes nucléaires, il est aussi celui des armes conventionnelles. Les puissances belliqeuses épuisent leur stock d'armement rapidement et doivent s'en remettre pour leur renouvellement à leurs grands fournisseurs et protecteurs. Si ces grandes puissances refusent de renouveler leur "aide," force est bien aux belligérants— dont les armements sont épuisés grâce à la vitesse accrue de consommation— de s'incliner devant la volonté d'arbitrage, de compromis exprimée par leurs fournisseurs. La guerre du Kippour tn4est à cet égard significative: même si les belligérants égyptiens et israéliens avaient voulu la poursuivre, même s'ils avaient voulu passer outre aux pressions diplomatiques de leurs protecteurs respectifs, ils n'auraient pu le faire, car le combat aurait cessé faute non pas de combattants mais d'armes de combat. Ainsi Israël et ses voisins— l'ensemble du Proche-Orient— sont entrés avec la guerre du Kippour, plus encore qu'auparavant, dans l'orbite des relations des puissances mondiales et ont même connu une situation comparable d'une certaine manière à celle des puissances nucléaires. Israël et ses voisins ne seraient-ils pas arrivés au temps où la guerre classique est sinon impossible du moins vouée à être courte?

(D) Mais tout cela qui est l'absence de guerre n'est pas encore la paix. Ce qu'on ne peut plus obtenir par une guerre ouverte, on le demande à des hostilités sub-nucléaires et même infra-classiquesnous pensons à la guérilla, au terrorisme et nous pensons aussi au boycottage économique, aux propagandes hostiles, conduites avec intenfiorté grâce aux moyens modernes de diffusion, plus généralement, les raisons de l'absence de guerre chaude que je viens d'évoquer laissent subsister la guerre froide qui dure parce qu'elle ne peut conduire à la défaite de l'un des partenaires (Israël ne connaît que trop cette situation qui dure depuis trente ans).

"On ne peut en rester là," s'écriait un jour le Général de Gaulle, pour caractériser la situation de mutuelle défiance entre l'Est et l'Ouest, qui avait succédé au paroxisme de la guerre froide. Il fallait, pensait-il, aller plus loin vers la paix. Peut-on donc et à plus forte raison faire mieux que cette absence de vraie guerre et de vraie paix que nous avons esquissée? Pour répndre à la question ainsi posée je voudrais énoncer quelques idées et règles d'action commandant la réflexion qui va suivre, idées et règles d'action dont procède en France l'analyse dominante de la situation contemporaine.

En premier lieu les nations sont et demeurent les principaux personnages de l'histoire et la reconnaissance de leurs Etats n'est par conséquent que la simple reconnaissance de la réalité. Les idéologies passent mais les nations demeurent. La Russie soviétique n'est certes pas identique à la Russie tzariste mais comment ne pas remarquer qu'elle reprend un certain nombre de ses positions et revendications, comme la Chine communiste fait valoir un certain nombre de préoccupations que sans doute la Chine d'autrefois, trop faible, ne pouvait imposer aux autres Etats mais qui étaient déjà cependant celles de ses empereurs. Ainsi sommes-nous dans notre rôle en assumant le destin de nos nations et nous ne pourrions faire autre chose sans manquer au devoir et à la raison. Mais à la différence de ce que les nationalistes ont fait trop souvent, il faut considérer non seulement notre droit d'être une nation et un Etat au service de notre nation — mais aussi le droit des autres nations à pareille existence. Si le nationalisme est naturel et légitime chez nous, il ne l'est pas moins chez les autres. Exiger la reconnaissance de notre nation et de son Etat implique que nous reconnaissions nous-mêmes les nations et les Etats des autres.

Une autre constatation est l'apparition de nouvelles nations: au temps de la colonisation il n'y a pas en Afrique une nation guin- éenne, une nation centrafricaine, une nation soudanaise véritable; il y a des peuplades qui sont séparées par des rivalités tribales, des différitable' il y a des peuplades qui sont séparées par des rivalités, tribales, des différends locaux; c'est la colonisation elle-même et ensuite la décolonisation qui assurent l'apparition d'Etats, souvent antérieurs à une conscience nationale que ces Etats s'attachent d'ailleurs très vite à créer chez leurs gouvernés. Ainsi, non seule- ment les anciennes nations subsistent, mais de nouvelles nations apparaissent. Ainsi, réalité des nations et de leurs Etats, apparition de nouvelles nations et de nouveaux Etats, volonté d'empêcher l'établissement d'hégémonies qui seraient comme un refus d'in- dépendance, telles peuvent nous apparaître les données de la réalité contemporaine. De là se déduit une démarche dont vous me per- mettrez de relever un certain nombre de traits dans la politique de la France sans prétendre d'ailleurs pour cette politique une perfection qui n'est jamais de ce monde.

Je relève d'abord une manière réaliste d'aborder les problèmes; quand la 5éme République reconnaît la République Populaire de

Chine, alors que les Etats-Unis obtiennent encore chaque année des Nations Unies un vote hostile à l'admission de Pékin dont le siège reste tenu par le gouvernemnt de Chang Chai Chek, replié à Taiwan, quand la France, dis-je, rompt avec cette consigne atlantique et cette majorité à l'ONU, elle le fait en estimant qu'elle doit reconnaître le gouvernement réel du pays et non pas un gouvernement fictif. De la même manière nous considérons que la reconnaissance diplomatique est acquise à un Etat et non pas à son gouvernement, en sorte que lorsque le gouvernement en place vient à être chassé par un autre, même si c'est à l'origine illégalement et que l'autorité du nouveau venu s'installe effectivement dans l'ensemble du pays et de manière durable, la reconnaissance de la France qui est acquise à l'Etat et non à un gouvernement donné, profite au nouveau pouvoir. Ensuite le refus des hégémonies a pour conséquence la lutte contre les blocs. Mais qu'est-ce qu'un bloc et qu'est-ce qui caractérise le bloc dont nous ne voulons pas par rapport aux alliances que nous continuons d'avoir et que nous pratiquons? Le bloc auquel s'oppose si volontiers la diplomatie française, semblable en cela aux nations non-alignées, se caractérise selon moi par trois traits. Le premier est l'identité systématique des positions puises: on agit "comme un bloc" en ce sens que chacun des Etats composant le bloc prend d'office les mêmes positions. Ainsi pendant longtemps là où la France, la Grande-Bretagne et les Etats-Unis étaient associés avec l'URSS par exemple pour l'Allemagne. les trois puissances apportaient un soin et même une ostentation dans la remise à Moscou de trois notes non seulement semblables quant au fond mais identiques quant aux mots mêmes employés. Mais—second trait qui se relie au premier—cette unité de position ne peut être assurée que par une hiérarchie dans le pouvoir de décision, sans quoi il faut bien penser que tous les Etats membres du bloc n'arriveraient pas á la même conclusion par une harmonie spontanée, en sorte que le bloc n'est maintenu que par une hiérarchie de fait dans l'influence: théoriquement les différents Etats-membres se détermiment librement mais en fait ils considèrent comme un mal (j'allais dire un mal absolu) l'absence de positions communes et sont en fait disposés à accepter que l'un, le plus puissant, impose sa manière de voir à l'autre. Il y a donc une puissance dominante qui tend très vite à généraliser la manière de penser comme elle et sur laquelle on s'aligne: c'est le troisième trait. L'identité de positions, la hierarchie dans le pouvoir de détermination, l'uniformié dans la manière de penser, caractérisent donc ces blocs auxquels il convient selon nous de mettre fin afin que subsistent seulement des alliances par lesquelles on se promet assistance mutuelle dans le respect des souverainetés des divers Etats membres de l'alliance, comme cela s'est toujours fait.

Une troisième orientation génerale — qu'il faut rapprocher de la démarche réaliste et de l'opposition aux blocs — c'est la volonté d'avancer dans une sorte d'escalade de la confiance: éviter d'abord bien entendu la guerre chaude et tàcher ensuite de substituer à ce qu'on a appelé la guerre froide ce qui s'est bien vite appelé la détente, réduire encore après les tensions et dans ce processus de réduction vouloir aller au-delà de la détente. "De la détente à l'entente et de l'entente à la coopération" avait pu dire le Général de Gaulle à propos des rapports est-ouest. Il s'agit de parvenir entre des nations aux intérêts et aux idéologies différents et qui ont parfois des sujets de conflits, non seulement à éviter les tensions mais encore à permettre des coopérations intellectuelles par échanges de vues, de livres, d'hommes, d'enseignements, de recherches en laboratoire ou sur le terrain et aussi des coopérations purement techniques par la réalisation de grandes entreprises communes, nucléaires, satellites, lanceurs, productions d'énergie nucléaire.

Si ces objectifs sont atteints et que l'on avance dans la co-opération, comment concevoir de manière réaliste le désarmement à l'âge nucléaire? (a) Observons d'abord qu'il n'y a pas de recette magique pour réaliser le désarmement. Quand certaines armes ont été découvertes il serait illusoire de croire qu'on pourrait les détruire à tout jamais: Si une catégorie donnée d'armement redoutable est condamnée et même si la condamnation s'accompagne d'une destruction effective — qui ne voit que le jour même où éclateraient des hostilités où s'engagerait une guerre par les seuls moyens tenus pour légitimes, le premier acte d'un gouvernement responsable serait de reprendre au plus vite la fabrication des armes détruites en pensant d'ailleurs que son adversaire se hâte d'en faire autant, et bien entendu, les Etats, les savants, les techniciens qui avaient découvert le moyen de fabriquer certaines armes et qui ne l'auront pas oublié sauront très vite refaire ce qui a été détruit. On ne reviendra plus à l'état d'innocence nucléaire pas plus qu'Adam et Eve, après avoir mangé le fruit défendu, n'ont pu, malgré leur renords et peut être leur effroi, retrouver l'état d'innocence antérieur au péche.

(b) Il faut reconnaître et proclamer le droit à la sécurité pour tous; car la sécurité ne doit pas être un privilège réservé aux plus puissants mais autant que possible assurée à tous les Etats. Remarquons tout de suite que cette garantie donnée aux différents Etats est la condition ou la conséquence de leur sortie des blocs, car qu'est-ce donc qui fait accepter par un Etat les contraintes d'un bloc sinon le sentiment qu'on ne le défendra pas suffisamment en dehors des acceptations, des disciplines et des rigidités d'un bloc? L'Etat qui sort d'un bloc doit donc posseder les instruments de cette sécurité propre. La France, même en demeurant sept ans dans l'Alliance, a lié sa sortie de l'Organisation de l'Atlantique Nord, constitutive d'un bloc, à l'acquisition d'une arme nationale de dissuasion. Sans doute n'y aura-t-il pas universalisation de l'existence d'une dissuasion nucléaire et le plus grand nombre des Etats restera des puissances non nucléaires mais l'idée à retenir ici est que les arrangements intervenus doivent assurer pour la part la plus grande la sécurité des Etats non nucléaires et ceux-ci doivent même conserver les armements classiques nécessaires pour pouvoir rejeter une agression ou en tout cas faire payer aux agresseurs éventuels le prix d'une victoire si élevé qu'ils renoncent à l'agression. Dès lors, le désarmement doit être équilibré, ce qui est difficile alors que la tendance naturelle de chacun est de s'attacher surtout au désarmement de l'autre pour asseoir notre sécurité avant de penser aux inquiétudes que nous pouvons nous-mêmes suggérer. Le désarmement ne peut donc avoir d'effet que pour autant qu'il est contrôlé pour l'essentiel. On sait combien les possibilités de contrôle varient avec les développements techniques au moins autant qu'avec les arrangements diplomatiques.

Un rôle particulier doit donc être joué—une importance particulière s'attache à ce que l'on a appelé "les mesures de confiance." Le fait pour un Etat de signaler aux autres ses déplacements de troupes, d'inviter les attachés et les commandements militaires étrangers à nos manoeuvres nationales—ne constitue certes pas un système de contrôle complet, total, mais peut suggérer l'invention de méthodes plus hardies et surtout développe une confiance qui prépare à l'acceptation du contrôle.

Quand il y a hostilité, tension, méfiance entre des Etats et que ceux-ci se sentent par conséquent menacés dans des exigences essentielles, il n'y a pas, il ne peut y avoir de désarmement. Celui-ci ne commence qu'avec une certaine détente et il la suit bien plus qu'il ne la précède. Sans doute, à partir du moment où une certaine détente, un certain sentiment de sécurité dû à l'apaisement des conflits ont permis de réaliser quelques accords de désarmement ou, plus modestement, de limitation des armements, ce désarmement, cette limitation interviennent à leur tour comme une confirmation, une consolidation du sentiment de sécurité.

Voici donc à la fois des traits de la période nucléaire et quelques conséquences de ces traits et voici aussi, pour essayer d'aller de l'avant, quelques propositions pour analyser les exigencex en présence comme aussi quelques propositions de règles à suivre.

Peut-on conclure sur quelque philosophie des problèmes de la paix en notre temps? Je proposerai alors les réflexions suivantes: Ce que le Président actuel de la République Française a souvent appelé la mondialisation des problèmes est une réalité en ce sens que les différents pays sont de plus en plus souvent aux prises avec des problèmes semblables; les problèmes de l'énergie ou des fonds sousmarins, pour ne prendre que ces deux exemples sont en effet des problèmes mondialisés; et chaque pays est concerné par ce qui se passe d'important dans l'autre. Mais cette mondialisation des problèmes n'est pas une mondialisation de la décision et c'est une caractéristique de notre temps que des problèmes mondialisés y sont traités par une série de décisions nationales: entre la mondialisation des problèmes et le caractère national de la décision il y a une manière d'antinomie qu'on peut déplorer mais qu'il faut bien constater.

J'insisterai en second lieu sur la valeur du principe d'équilibre. Les négociateurs, les chercheurs de paix doivent s'attacher à maintenir un certain équilibre entre les puissances et si l'on veut faire accepter une modification substantielle il faut que cette modification comporte une similitude sinon une égalité d'avantages ou · de compensations pour les parties en présence. Autrement la négociation n'a pas de chance d'aboutir sans guerre (et nous ne voulons pas traiter ici des négociations, bien souvent semblables à des capitulations, qui interviennent après une victoire sanglante). La négociation antérieure à la guerre est une négociation qui est à la recherche d'un équilibre. D'où il suit que si l'équilibre existant a été très profondément modifié par un gain d'influence d'une des puissances, considérée au détriment des autres, il en résultera de nouvelles tensions; le pays qui s'estime lésé ne voudra pas consentir de nouveaux arrangements mais retrouver d'abord l'équivalent du désavantage qu'il a subi. Des évolutions se produisent sans doute mais pour pouvoir être acceptées il faut qu'elles soient lentes. Vouloir changer rapidement un équilibre c'est accroître les tensions.

Une autre réflexion générale concerne la dimension du temps: Toujours il faut préparer l'avenir. Tout négociateur doit aussi rechercher pour son propre pays un meilleur environnement, une situation régionale et mondiale meilleure, moins grosse de périls de crises, un meilleur climat international: Ce doit être là l'objet d'un effort continu et cet effort exige que chacun des acteurs se réfreine lui-même, pratique une manière de self-restraint — une auto-limitation de ses propres exigences, de ses propres revendications et même des gains qui sont peut-être immédiatement à portée de mains mais qui recèlent la possibilité, la probabilité de contestations ultérieures, de recherches de revanches etc. Un constant contrôle de sa propre expansion est ainsi la contribution de chacun et il faut rapprocher de ce contrôle de soi l'étalement dans le temps dont chacun saura jouer en pensant que cela même qui est impossible aujourd'hui sera possible demain. On doit donc considérer le résultat obtenu aujourd'hui non seulement par ce qu'il apporte et qui est le moins mauvais possible mais encore par la chance de faire mieux pour l'avenir. C'est pourquoi je tiens la paix séparée intervenue entre Israël et l'Egypte comme un événement, particulièrement à cause de la dimension de temps incluse dans cet instrument; c'est dire combien j'ai apprecié le discours de haute qualité qu'a prononcé hier devant nous Monsieur Abba Eban; ce qui me frappe le plus dans le traité israélo-égyptien—quant à la technique même des diplomaties et des accords internationaux, c'est bien cet étalement dans le temps qui, réglant un certain nombre de problèmes immédiats, se donne un délai pour en régler d'autres, par ce que l'engrenage mis en train est ce qui procurera à la fois un meilleur environnement et pour plus tard de meilleurs arrangements. Ainsi l'ère nucléaire nous oblige à éviter la guerre et la terreur fait ici davantage que la raison, mais parce que cela n'est pas encore la paix nous allons lentement de l'absence de guerre réelle à la réalisation d'une vrai paix. Parlant du Tiers Etat au début de la Révolution Française Sièyes disait dans une brochure célèbre: Qu'est-ce que devrait être le Tiers Etat? Tout. Qu'est-ce qu'il est ajourd'hui? Rien. Que veut-il être? Quelque chose. Remplaçons le mot de "Tiers Etat" par celui de "paix." Qu'est-ce que nous devrions avoir? Une paix générale dans un monde désarmé. Qu'avons-nous? La défiance et l'hostilité. Que voulons-nous? Une certaine paix, car il n'y a pas d'autre solution de rechange que le compromis, car il n'y a pas d'autre chemin vers la paix que le compromis. Apprenons donc à mobiliser pour notre entreprise le temps qui rendra possible ce qui est encore impossible aujourd'hui. Le tournant a été chez vous la visite de Sadate à Jérusalem et le traité israélo–égyptien. Ainsi pourra-t-il se faire que la paix séparée qui a été conclue soit une paix générale commencée.

Se restreindre soi-même et savoir apaiser ses inquiétudes et ses exigences en faisant entrer dans sa démarche la considération du temps ce sont des traits qui me paraissent s'imposer dans la recherche de la paix—et que l'état présent de la connaissance du monde et de la pratique internationale nous permettent de reconnaître avec une particulière netteté.

Il y a 130 ans un homme dont on peut dire en ce pays d'Israël qu'il était un juif quelque peu antisémite, Karl Marx lançait le mot d'ordre célèbre "prolétaires de tous les pays unissez-vous." Au lendemain d'un traité qui fait l'objet ici et là de critiques de la part des extrémistes, sachons qu'en matière de paix, le mot d'ordre qu'il faut lancer est celui-ci: "Modérés de tous les pays unissez-vous!"

"Self-Determination" and Violence

Charles Boasson

The expression "self-determination" is widely used, sometimes thoughtlessly but often maliciously for the purpose of abuse.

The term conveys many different meanings and it is not difficult to make it into a slogan for purposes remote from its original idealistic aims.

The word itself, according to the Shorter Oxford Dictionary,[1] made its entry into the English speaking world almost three hundred years ago, in 1683. The same dictionary asserts that, in the particular sense of the "independent determination by a state of its own polity" the word only appeared on the scene in 1925. This is misleading, as the expression had already in the 19th century acquired that explosive meaning of the desire, perhaps the claim, of a "people" (another word that can be interpreted in divergent ways and a "people" is always a unity of a mysterious character) to be recognized as a state-like entity which should determine its own polity.

The earlier use of the word "self-determination" stressed rather moral philosophical ideals and personal aspirations "to become who we are," as Nietzsche defined it. This personal idealistic aspiration re-emerged in the demand for the *collective* right to strive towards becoming who we are.

Such a collective ideal has been expressed at its best in Leon Pinsker's appeal to a Jewish national rebirth under the title "Auto-Emancipation"[2] where the appeal to individual and inner-spiritual efforts is still supreme.

George Scelle, one of the foremost international lawyers and thinkers of the first half of this century, made a well-balanced analysis in favour of the right of self-determination ("le droit des peuples a disposer d'eux memes") which is a pioneering marvel of clear and creative thinking. He traced the historical and doctrinal evolution of this right to the earliest Jewish idealistic phenomena of nationalism, "in the face of powerful and cruel neighbours."[3] It is very much to be regretted that Scelle's perceptive, wise and humane chapter is so little referred to.[4] The more the political stress has come to prevail the more the element of malicious abuse of the claim

63

has become part and parcel of it. This was most conspicuously so when Hitler and the Sudeten "Germans" insisted on the right to wreck Czechoslovakia's existence. There is no need to particularize malicious examples in the discussions on Middle East politics.

There exists a popular mistaken belief that the first politician on the international scene to clamor for self-determination on behalf of subjected colonial populations or suppressed minorities has been Wilson. As President of the U.S.A. he indicated in his famous Fourteen "Principles" what should be the moral basis for peace-treaties at the conclusions of the First World War. Self-determination, however, was not one of Wilson's fourteen points mentioned in his most famous speech of January 8, 1918. It is not enough to say that,[5] without indicating that the idea of "self-determination" did figure prominently in Wilson's equally important, if less famous, speech of a few weeks later (February 11). Even there the word itself does not appear in the actual text of his summarized "Four Principles," but the prior discussion of these principles deals extensively with Wilson's concept of self-determination and makes use of that term. Indeed, in the full text (preceding the enumeration of the "Four Principles") Wilson said: "Self-determination is not a mere phrase. It is an imperative principle of action which statesmen will henceforth ignore at their peril."[6]

Wilson, however, had clearly understood that one cannot use the word "self-determination" as if it is a *right which is sufficiently clear and well defined in itself*. The principle always needed further elaborate definitions and, above all, restrictions. This holds to the present day.

Temperley[7] had already noted in 1920 that it was not always recognized how carefully Wilson expressed the relevant principle in his speeches (v Principle *four* of speech of 11 February 1918): "that all well-defined national aspirations shall be accorded the utmost satisfaction that can be accorded to them without introducing new, or perpetuating old, elements of discord and antagonism that would be likely in time to break up the peace of Europe, and consequently of the world." Temperley emphaticaly added: "The limitations here implied on the application of the principle are considerable."

Many reproaches made against Wilson are therefore invalid. He did not "re-introduce" the idea of "self-determination" into world politics towards the end of World War I. At that period Lloyd George had preceded him, with much greater emphasis even, e.g., in a speech at Glasgow on 29 June 1917, again in the House of Commons on 20 December 1917; and once more, still over a month earlier than Wilson's February speech of that year, in the House of Commons on 5 January 1918: "The general principle of national self-determination is, therefore, as applicable in their cases (namely: the German colonies) and, as would soon appear, the Turkish empire as in those of occupied European territories.[8]

Wilson was certainly not responsible for the many subsequent misuses of the slogan nor for the social misery they caused.

Since the flag of "self-determination" is popular with persons who do not consider carefully what it stands for, abuse is so easy. It is forgotten that the most serious supporters of self-determination made the principle's validity depend on many restrictions and demanded to apply it cautiously, so that it should not inflame[9] a sensitive situation. Many erstwhile supporters therefore came to regret its political misuse. President Wilson, for example, had already said in 1919 in the U.S. Senate Committee of Foreign Relations: "When I gave utterance to these words ('that all nations have a right to self-determination') I said them without the knowledge that nationalities existed, which are coming to us day after day . . . .You do not know and cannot appreciate the anxieties that I have experienced as the result of many millions of people having their hopes raised by what I have said."[10]

If we take a few other adherents — and I limit myself to adherents, not mentioning opponents — of the principle of self-determination, we again find their repeated warnings that the principle needs restrictions and cannot be applied indiscriminately.

Discriminate use of technical terms with delicate implications is, of course, not to be expected from the floor of the General Assembly of the United Nations. It is enlightening therefore to compare their resolutions with the writings of the earlier champions of the principle; it is also helpful to refer to later objective comments on those U.N. Resolutions which, as drafted, purport to change the classic principle of self-determination into a modern positive right.

Much can be learned from Inis Claude's book on national minorities, which surveys this international problem up to the mid-fifties[11] that is to say up to the time before the U.N. Resolutions. His overview of political approaches from before the First till well after the Second World War is comprehensive. Claude makes a relevant distinction between two kinds of self-determination. One kind refers to colonial or ex-colonial groups struggling to shape their own political, economic and cultural future, free from the fetters imposed by the colonizing power. Quite another kind of self-determination is claimed for national minorities. Here the element of abuse is by no means restricted to the glaring example of Hitler and the Sudeten Germans.[12] It has become almost inherent in this second kind of claim, and its present day use is simply suspect.

This distinction between self-determination for a colonial or ex-colonial entity and self-determination for a national minority is most important, because quite different material conditions as well as quite different logical theories are involved, even though the existence of some exceptional borderline cases may have confused both politicians and theorists.

The fact that some de-colonization kind of self-determination can be readily assented to has brought about the existing confusion as to the desirability of self-determination for national minorities. In colonial occupation a small ruling minority, hailing from a different ethnic and culturally developed people *settled elsewhere*, usually technically skilled and unified, governs the subjected local majority. The interests of that majority need by no means be entirely neglected, but the interests of the rulers and of their home country prevail over those of the local population. The local majority instinctively prefers "self"-government, even of doubtful quality, to "foreign"-government.

In practice "the morning after" achieving independence may bring bitter disillusions.[13] Nevertheless such movements for "self-determination" as liberation from colonial suppression, seem both understandable and logical and in this light U.N. Resolutions seem acceptable.

After independence of large, none too stable, colonial units has been won, however, their own minorities may thereupon become subjected to cruel repression from which they were reasonably protected before. "Self-determination" is then appealed to by the suppressed minorities, but such sub-divided "self-determination" for ex-colonial ethnical minorities is hardly ever consented to in political practice.

The de-colonization processes have often brought about a pseudo-self-determination rather than *self-reliance*, a new term which may to some extent clarify the issue, namely: "the right to pursue one's own route to development."[14] It is well to remember that the most boisterous claims for self-determination are often made by or on behalf of minority groups, who are not only lacking in, but, by themselves, incapable of "self reliance," and whose "sponsors" aspire to supplant,by stratagems of their own, the legal framework in which these weak minorities live. In these situations, as Frederick Hertz remarked,[15] no true self-determination is intended or even possible, because true self-determination "presupposes" conditions which enable a people to form a judgement free from pressure, terror, suggestion, prejudices and ignorance." Moreover, "issues of national self-determination always arouse passions to a high degree, the calculation of consequences is often extremely difficult, and errors in judgement can seldom be made good in a peaceful way." For that reason many so-called "peace proposals" based on the "right of self-determination" are pure and simple war-mongering[16] or the worst examples of appeasement.

For instance E.H. Carr's description[17] of the Munich Agreement of September 29, 1938 and "the negotiations which led up to" it, asserts that these were "the nearest approach in recent years to the settlement of a major international issue by a procedure of peaceful change. The element of power was present. The element of morality was also present in the form of the common recognition by the powers, who effectively decided the issue, of a criterion applicable to the dispute: the principle of self-determination."

That text is typical for a mood of appeasement and credulous faith in deceptive slogans such as "peace in our days." Duff Cooper and Winston Churchill stood almost alone in their disapproval of the sacrifice of Czechoslovakia on the false altar of self-determination, the former resigned in protest as a minister and the latter protested strongly in Parliament without denying that one could also justify some of the complaints of the Sudeten minority. History proved them right in more than one respect. "Peaceful change" on the basis of "self-determination" was, as the Nurenberg documents would later show, a successful stratagem planned by the Nazis which helped them greatly in their early moves in the Second World War.[18] Chamberlain, the architect of "peace in our days" based on appeasement, had within a year steered his country into its most disadvantageous war.

If one would not "forget" or suppress what actually happened, one would understand at once how ominous the U.N. resolutions really are. A clear thinking author like Rosalyn Higgins might have been a little more reserved in her remark: "It therefore seems inescapable that self-determination has developed into an international legal right, and is not an essentially domestic matter."[19] Nevertheless she is, at least, careful to add: "The extent and scope of the right is still open to some debate."[20] She also admits that self-determination need not be recognized when its rebel-fighters are "mainly supported from outside."[21]

Rosalyn Higgins failed to specify the fact, stressed in the literature before 1970, that all declarations of the U.N. before 1970, and in particular General Assembly Resolution 1514 (XV) dated 14 December 1960, relate to colonialism or trusteeship of Non-Self Governing Territories, but not to national minorities in existing states. The last-mentioned resolution concludes in paragraph 7 with a clear prohibition of "interference in the internal affairs of all states," and commands "respect for the sovereign rights of all peoples and their territorial integrity."

The question has been opened up anew, however, by the General Assembly's Resolution 2625 (XXV) of 24 October 1970, which is contradictory in itself. The lesson of the 1939 Munich appeasement was totally ignored. External interference, forbidden in the preamble, is re-introduced as being under "certain"—unspecified—conditions in accordance with the purposes and principles of the Charter. Subsequently the resolution seems to retract this again and declares that: "Every state shall refrain from any action aimed at the partial or total disruption of the national unity and territorial integrity of any other state or country."

Some authors claim that the Resolution raises the "principle" of self-determination to a positive right, but more careful writers say it does so more in theory than in practical detail. Dr. Daniel Thurer explains in his outstanding Zurich University thesis,[22] why the resolution is relatively effective in the field of colonial liberation, but not to the extent of an economic charter (which could bring self reliance) and certainly not so as to make any secession for the purpose of self realization legitimate.

Secession is not allowed because the principle of territorial integrity and sovereignty has to prevail in any case over that of self-determination. Dekker and Meuffels come to a similar conclusion.[23] They vindicated serious peace research by their thoughtful rejection of the radical "war-mongering"[24] thesis of R. Emerson, a thesis which took "the right of self-determination to be no more and no less than one aspect of the right to revolution."[25] Against this Dekker and Neuffels plead for the "*relative character* of the right to self-determination"[26]: The interests and rights of larger and smaller groups must be seen in their *total* justification. C. Eagleton comes to the same conclusion and refers to the "excesses" of self-determination.[27] Similarly Professor S. Calogeropoulos-Stratis is willing to recognize self-determination as a "right" rather than a principle, provided this right is related to and hedged in by other claims and concludes[28]: "No notion of law can be applied in an absolute sense: the excessive right violates the right of someone else and leads to the negation of law itself."

This wise and relevant remark shows the necessity to weigh any claim for self-determination by any one group against counter-arguments by any other group which is directly threatened by such a claim. We must, therefore, question the purpose of any single claim to self-determination, its social and historical justification, if any, in the total social setting, and, finally, we must always be aware of its logical self-contradiction as a juridical absolute. The latter fact is mostly forgotten in the heat of a debate between nation and nation, where logical thinking can hardly enter. Professor Francis, in his recent sociological analysis of inter-ethnic relations and "national minorities" writes: "This right of national self-determination, however, if carried to its logical conclusion, is bound to create serious disturbances of the international order."[29]

One can carry the right of self-determination in two ways to a "logical conclusion." The easiest, but insufficient way, is to put the whole idea into ridicule by demonstrating, that in the (logical) end each single person might determine himself out of any national or ethnic group. That truism would not be an answer to a possible defence of the right, as extreme even as the right of an individual to elect to which group he wishes to belong. Yet such motivated "right of self-determination," both in the sense of a *legal right* and in the sense of an *ethical principle*, depends on one element which, and which only, can make the exercise of the right lawful or ethical, namely *its reasonableness in the circumstances*.

A clear and short analysis of the totally anarchist results of the right of self-determination "carried to its logical conclusion" was written already over fifty years ago by Leonard Nelson in his major work on Legal and Political Philosophy.[30] After pointing out that neither the fact a people is in physical possession of land nor the fact that it has been so once upon a time (the *status quo* or the *status quo ante*) can be a *sufficient* ground for any division or re-division of territory, Nelson states: "Self-determination of peoples is in no way applicable to the juridical solution of this problem. Such self-determination would produce nothing but a sanctioning of international anarchy; because law is always based on limitation of self-determination. Freedom of self-determination for the one party cannot be reconciled with freedom of self-determination for the other party, if both interests come into conflict, that is to say just in the situation, where a legal adjustment should prevail. To seek such adjustment in the self-determination itself is a contradiction in terms."

The above analysis by Nelson is irrefutable, but it has not curbed the emotional appeal of the term "self-determination." The argument that unlimited self-determination must lead, in logic as well as in practice, to anarchy and chaos[31] has largely fallen on deaf ears. Those who court favour with violence-prone minorities, and do so for dark reasons of their own, have even stimulated further violence by proposing that violence is always justified if committed for the sake of self-determination.

Occasionally, however, this rabble-rousing use of the slogan seems to have brought home the fact that the *war-cry* of self-determination may be more destructive than helpful: in this vein M. Zwerin wrote his "case for the self-Balkanization of practically everyone" and it was also well formulated by Hillebrand-Bos, referring to terrorist activities against innocent third parties[32]: "Self-determination of nations is the greatest stumbling-block to the self-determination of mankind."

Notes

1.   First edition 1933.

2.   1882.

3.   Georges Scelle, *Precis de Droit des Gens* II (1934) Paris, Sirey, p. 262. Scelle refers to Th. Ruyssen's article on self-determination in the (1933) *Revue de Metaphysique et de Morale*.

4.   *Op. cit.* (previous note) section VIII pp. 257–295. A laudable exception in S. Carlogeropoulos-Stralis, *Le Droit des Peuples a disposer d'eux-memes* (1973) Bruxelles, Bruylant and in C. Buchheit; *The Legitimacy of Self Determination* (1978) Yale U.P.

5.   William Safire's *The New Language of Politics* (1968, 1972) New York is overly succinct in this matter.

6.   The most reliable and concentrated source for finding out what Wilson really said or meant for some one who does not check all the records in their original state, is the masterly: *A History of the Peace Conference of Paris* edited by H. W. V. Temperley for the (London) Institute of International Affairs in 1920–1924 (vol I–VI). Extracts from President Wilson's speeches in 1918 are in vol I, appendix III, pp. 431–448. All subsequent quotes are from there.

7.   Temperley (see note 6 *supra*) IV, 429.

8.   *Id.* II, 227.

9.   Scelle, *op. cit.*, note 3, p. 291, warns in particular against incensing flirtations with proposals of plebiscite. An identical warning in the sober discussions of self-determination as "a principle dogma in modern politics," by Frederick Hertz, *Nationality in History and Politics* (1944) London, Kegan Paul, Chapter VI, 8 pp. 240–247. See also Charles Boasson, "Galtung's Version of the Middle East and the Theory of Conflict: Can Peace Research Transcend Prejudice and Dogma?" (1973) Journal of Peace Research 133–144, at p. 135.

10.   Temperley (See note 4 *supra*) IV 429.

11.   Inis L. Claude Jr., *National Minorities*, (1955) Harvard U.P. Much information on literature is given throughout and in the bibliographcal note pp. 215–217. Alfred Cobban, *National Self-Determination*, University of Chicago Press, revised edition, is mentioned as having no date, but the editions in London are dated 1945 and 1969. See hereafter note 14 on Dekker and Meuffels.

12.   Norman J. Padelford and George A. Lincoln, *The Dynamics of International Politics* (2nd edition 1967) New York, Macmillan, p. 328.

13.   Brian Crozier in *The Morning After* (1963) London, Methuen, makes us regretfully wonder why de-colonization should have progressed in such cruel ways.

14.   Cocoyoc Declaration (1974) in 6 (1975) *Bulletin of Peace Proposals* 36, 37. The link between self-determination and self-reliance is well argued by Ige F. Dekker and John Meuffels, in their contribution "Structureel Geweld en Zelfbeschikking" (Structural Violance and Self-Determination) in honour of B. V. A. Roling, in the collection *Vrede en Oorlog* (Peace and War), edited by Fenna Van der Burg (1977) Amsterdam, Arbeiders Pers at pp. 180–205 and (notes) 275–279.

15. Hertz, op. cit. note 9 supra at p. 245.

16. Compare Charles Boasson "International Law, Conflict Resolution and Peace Research: A Concise Orientation" (1975) 10 *Israel Law Review*, pp. 178–191 at p. 184.

17. E. H. Carr, *The Twenty Years' Crisis* (1939) London, Macmillan, at p. 282.

18. Compare Winston S. Churchill, *the Second World War*, vol I, The Gathering Storm (1948) Boston, Houghton Mifflin, pp. 279–358. And, not to forget! Alfred Duff Cooper's moving *Old men Forget* (1954) New York, Dutton.

19. Rosalynn Higgins, The Development of International Law Through the Political Organs of the United Nations (1963) Oxford U.P. at p. 103.

20. *Ibid.*

21. *Ibid.* p. 137.

22. Dr. Daniel Thurer *Das Selbst-Bestmmungs Recht der Völker* (1976) Bern, Stampfli.

23. See *op. cit.* note 14 *supra*, at pp. 190–192 and 199–201.

24. See my debate with Johan Galtung, *op. cit.*, note 9 *supra* and compare note 16 *supra*.

25. 60 *Proceedings of the American Society of International Law* (1966) p. 135.

26. *op. cit.*, notes 23 (and 14) *ibid.*

27. C. Eagleton, "Excesses of Self-Determination, 231 *Foreign Affairs* (1953) p. 592.

28. *op. cit.*, note 4 *supra* p. 268. Aucune notion de droit n'est susceptible d'une application absolue; l'exces du droit viole le droit d'autrui et amene a la négation du droit lui meme." Interestingly, the author in his almost exhaustive mention of peoples entitled to self-determination does not mention the Palestinians.

29. E. K. Francis, Interethnic Relations (1976) New York, Elsevier p. 114.

30. Leonard Nelson, "Selbstbestimmung und Vertrag" (Self-Determination and Treaty) paragraph 229 in *System der Philosophischen Rechtslehre und Politik* (1924, reprinted 1964, now in Collected Works, 1970) vol. VI of Collected Works, Hamburg Felix Meiner paragraph 229. The whole paragraph 229 is less than a page (p. 466) in this learned treatise of well over 500 pages. See also my referral to Nelson in *op. cit.*, note 16 *supra* p. 190.

31. See also notes 27, 28, 29 *supra*, and the authors cited there.

32. M. Zwerin, *A case for the Self-Balkanization of Practically Everyone* (1976) London, Wildwood House. H. Hillerbrand Bos, "Zelfbeschikking" in 53 *Nederlands Juristenblad* (4th March) 1978/9 p. 84. Compare also Istvan Biko, *The Paralysis of International Institutions and the Remedies. A Study of Self-Determination* (1976) Harwich, Harvester Press.

The Role of the Arab World in the Decolonization Process of Black Africa

Dr. Olusola Ojo

The shared anti-colonialism of both the Arabs and Black Africans, demonstrated particularly by their unanimous condemnation of colonialism and apartheid in the United Nations Organization (UN) and in non-aligned conferences has tended to obscure the realities of the Arab commitment and contribution to the decolonization of Black Africa. This tendency has been reinforced by the fact that the Organization of African Unity (The OAU) nine of whose members belong to the Arab League, has made the issue of decolonization its cardinal objective since its inception in 1963. Besides the emotional outburst and ritual incantations of Afro–Arab solidarity and brotherhood and the unprecedented increase in diplomatic activities between the two groups of States, following the massive political support Black Africa gave the Arabs during the October 1973 Middle East War, this reality has tended to be further distorted. The aim of this paper is therefore to put the Arab role in the decolonization process in Black Africa in its proper perspective. This will be done by looking at the process of African decolonization through three broad phases—the decade of non-involvement (1945–1955), the era of gradual involvement (1955–1973) and the period of frustrated expectations (1973–1978).

However, before we go into a substantive discussion of these phases, it is pertinent to say that there is a real case to be made for looking at the Arab role in African decolonization. A number of Arab diplomats have questioned the legitimacy of singling out the Arab role in African development or decolonization for investigation. Most of them even see it as a Zionist inspired attempt to destroy the brotherly relations between them and Black Africa. Some have argued that in any case, the exercise is not worth it because the Arabs and Black Africans have always had different and most of the time not complementary priorities.[1]

73

But it should be stated here that most of the Arab territories and peoples are geographically in Africa. There is therefore nothing basically wrong in examining the role of the Arabs or that of Anglophone or Francophone Africa on particular issues affecting the Continent. Besides, six of the members of the Arab League, including some of the most important and populous Arab countries were amongst the founders of the OAU. Three more "African" states have since joined the Arab League. Even if to some extent the areas of concentrated attention of both groups of states were different, the rhetoric emanating from both since 1973 suggest that they havfe now recognized that they both have a common destiny. There is a sense, too, politically in which one can justifiably talk of the Arab in Africa, as distinct from the rest of the continent. It has been alleged that the OAU Arab States are the only regional group that approach all important issues at the OAU as a bloc. There have been instances to support this allegation, as when a Secretary-General was about to be elected to succeed Mr. Ekangaki in 1974.[2] Besides they co-ordinate their policies on issues affecting the Arab World during the September Session of Arab League. Further co-ordination takes place either before or during OAU meetings. Finally, it is needless to argue that there is nothing inherently mischievious in trying to look at the Arab or any other group of countries' role in African decolonization as an academic exercise, even if the findings of such an exercise will be unpalatable to some people. It may even have a positive functional utility in strengthening "Afro–Arab unity" in the sense that both groups of states may realise where some extra work needs to be done for the much-talked about Afro–Arab solidarity to be seen by all as more than a mere illusion.

1945–1955: The Decade of Non-Involvement

The year 1945 is important for the whole process of decolonization in Africa. It marked the end of the Second World War which had weakened the colonial powers economically and which had a salutary effect on the growth of nationalism in Africa.[3] Besides it saw the founding of the United Nations Organization which has since played a crucial role in the process of decolonization. Moreover, the League of Arab States was founded in that year.

By 1945, Egypt, Iraq, Lebanon, Saudi Arabia and Syria were at least nominally independent and were members of the UN. In Black Africa only Liberia and Ethiopia were independent. Given the shared ideological opposition to colonialism by these States one would have expected some form of co-ordination of their policies on decolonization at least in the UN. However, the interests of the Arabs in the decade following the end of the war centred exclusively on the Middle East. They were primarily concerned with their pan-Arab vocation whose end had been vaguely defined as pan-Arab unity. This pre-occupation with exclusively Arab problems during this period meant that Liberia and Ethiopia were the only States concerned with Africa in the UN.[4]

1955–1973: The Era of Gradual Involvement

The picture changed towards the end of the 1950s. With the growing strength of the Afro–Asian Group in the UN and the gradual acceptance of the principle of decolonization by most of the colonial powers, some Arab States led by Egypt started to play a more active role in the UN, by putting pressure on the colonial powers usually in concert with members of the Afro–Asian Group to accelerate the process of decolonization. This change in Arab attitudes had been foreseen by Gamal Abdel Nasser in his *Philosophy of the Revolution* written shortly after the Egyptian Revolution of 1952. In it he asserted that the Egyptians could not in anyway be unconcerned with the "sanguinary and dreadful struggle" between the Africans and the White colonizers in the heart of Africa.[5]

But this pledge to the African struggle for liberation remained a declaration of intent until the second half of the 1950s when Egypt became more actively involved in African Affairs. The Bandung Conference of 1955, occuring at the time of the Baghdad Pact controversy, played a part in the re-evaluation of Nassar's policy towards Africa in particular, and the development of his anti-Western anti-imperialist views in general. He had a vision of the enormous strength an independent and possibly anti-Western Africa would have in world affairs.

In January 1956, therefore, President Nasser set up a Supreme Committee to supervise African Affairs to draw outlines of Egypt's African policy. In February, an African Section was established within the Egyptian Foreign Ministry. African nationalists were encouraged to open offices in Cairo. In late 1957, an African Association was set up in order to effectively co-ordinate the activities of these offices with Egypt's foreign policy. The association organized demonstrations against imperialism in Africa and also arranged trips by leading African nationalists to Cairo. President Nasser also started organizing African liberation movements within the context at Afro–Asian Solidarity Conferences. Extensive anti-Western, anti-imperialist propaganda was broadcast to Africa by the Egyptian radio.[6]

It should be remarked, however, that despite all these efforts and the seemingly total Egyptian commitment to African liberation, Egyptian support was mainly rhetorical until the formation of the

OAU. Even such rhetorical support was not spontaneously given on some occasions. For example, during the Second Conference of Independent African States in Addis Ababa in 1960, the United Arab Republic (as Egypt was then called) made support for a resolution recommending severance of diplomatic and economic relations with South Africa dependent on the Conference recommending similar action against Israel. In fact, the UAR was the only country represented at the Conference that had diplomatic relations with South Africa. One delegate proposed that the Suez Canal should be closed to South African vessels but this was opposed by the UAR delegate. When the Conference finally agreed that member states close their ports to vessels flying ththe South African flag and boycott South African goods, refuse facilities, including the use of their air space to South African aircraft, the Chief Egyptian delegate, Mr. Zulficar Sabre told correspondents that the Resolution would not be applicable to South African ships passing through Suez. He declared that the Canal was "an Arab waterway with international obligations."[7]

Egypt maintained diplomatic relations with South Africa until 1961. The Conference also called upon Arab States to endeavour to prevent the supply of oil to South Africa. On his return to Cairo, Mr. Sabre stated that such an action would be effective if Black African States adopted a similar attitude towards Israel.

Other Arab States were even less forthcoming than Egypt in their support for African liberation, although "colonialism," "imperialism" and "apartheid" were all condemned at almost all conferences attended by both African and Arab States. However, the divergencies in their ideology and interests of the states concerned often reduced these condemnations to platitudinous statements of principles. The overriding necessity to get agreement among all states attending often resulted in such an agreement heaving little or no content at all.

The League of Arab States occasionally and without difficulty passed condemnatory resolutions on South Africa especially after 1960.[8] Problems arose, however, when the more radical members of the League attempted to "force" the Organization to recommend specific measures against the colonial and apartheid regimes in Africa.[9] In 1961, for example, the League resolved not to recognize the South African regime. But difficulties arose over a recommendation to suspend all consular and commercial contacts with the Republic. Again in 1965, the League had no problem condemning the illegal unilateral declaration of indepdendence for Rhodesia by Ian Smith, but most of its members showed no enthusiasm for an African call for the boycott of Rhodesia and her friends.

In the early 1960s the Congo Crisis became a test case of Arab involvement in Black African decolonization. The Crisis was one of those unresolved problems of decolonization, complicated by differing ideological leanings of Prime Minister Lumumba and President Kasavubu and fueled by Great Power global competition for spheres of influence. It is significant that none of the non-African Arab States participated in the military and civilian operations mounted by the UN (Organisation des Nations Unies Ou Congo— ONUC) to put down the crisis.[10] In August 1960, the Lebanese Government repudiated its pledge made in July to send a team of four doctors and four nurses to serve with ONUC, on the ground that Lebanon could not forgo their services for the three months which the UN Secretary-General said was the minimum the team should serve in the Congo. It said Lebanon could only forgo their services for two or three weeks.[11] Even three of the four North African Arab States, Morocco, Egypt and Sudan, that contributed contigents to UNOC withdrew their personnel early in 1961 on the grounds that they were not pleased with the UN activities in the Congo.[12]

However, the level of Arab involvement in Africa increased with the founding of the OAU in 1963. As indicated earlier, the Organization made decolonization its most important area of activities. It set up a Liberation Committee to co-ordinate aid to African Liberation Movements. Some of the OAU Arab States were members of this Committee and it became inescapable for them to be involved in the activities of the Committee.[13] Besides the Arabs saw in the OAU a great opportunity for them to get the Black Africans deeply involved in the Arab–Israeli Conflict. But they could not attempt to get the Africans involved in their own conflict with Israel without showing some concern for Africa's own pre-occupation with decolonization. It is significant that five of the nine OAU States that broke relations with Britain over the latter's handling of the Rhodesian unilateral declaration of independence were Arab.[14]

Two major events in the Arab World during this period, however, led to more Arab involvement in the decolonization process in Black Africa. The first was the emergence of Algeria as an independent state after a seven-year war of liberation; the second was the overthrow of the Libyan monarchy in 1969.

Shortly after its independece, Algeria started a program of military assistance to Black African nationalists. Mr. Eduardo Mondlane, the late President of FRELIMO, the nationalist movement in Mozambique, claimed that Algeria was one of the first countries his movement approached for military help.[15] And during the 1963 founding conference of the OAU, President Ben Bella of Algeria was reported to have played a decisive role in the creation of the OAU Liberation Committee.[16]

The new Libyan leadership which seized power in 1969 also took a more active interest in African Liberation and gave political and material assistance to the Liberian Movements and to the OAU Liberation Committee. Libya housed many African Liberation Movements' offices. When in November 1970 President Sekou Toure announced an attempted invasion of Guinea by Portuguese soldiers, Egypt, Libya and Algeria were among OAU States which offered Guinea support. The increase in the membership of the OAU Liberation Committee from eleven to seventeen in 1972 brought in three more Arab States, bringing the total Arab membership of the Committee to six; Algeria, Libya, Morocco, Mauritania, Somalia and Egypt. In that year also, King Hassan of Morocco, as host, and the newly-elected chairman of the OAU promised a gift of US $1 million to the Liberation Committee.

Any "positive" involvement of the non-OAU Arab States throughout this period was strictly limited to diplomatic support especially at the UN.

November 1973–December 1978: The Period of Frustrated Expectations

Despite a slow and, from the African point of view, unpromising start, Arab governments seem to have gradually become more sensitive to African pressure for a stronger Arab commitment to African liberation. At the Arab League Summit of November 1973, they responded to an African call to review Arab links with South Africa and Portugal by instituting an oil boycott against the regimes. The summit further asked all member states of the Arab League to discontinue economic and political links with both countries.[17] Secondly, at the Afro–Arab Summit Conference held in Cairo in March 1977, Egypt, Kuwait, Qatar, Saudi Arabia and the United Arab Emirates made a pledge of US $6 million to African Liberation Movements.

At first sight, these developments seem to indicate a more serious Arab commitment to African Liberation after the Middle East War of October 1973. But any "change" in Arab attitudes needs to be assessed cautiously. The Arab League has not been able to persuade all its members to honour this commitment. For instance there are still trade contacts between some Arab States and South Africa. In 1975, there were reports of evidence of growing Arab–South African economic links. A number of Arab trade delegations visited South Africa and a South African tour operator, T.F.C. was apparently engaged in negotiation in Cairo to take package tours to Egypt.[18] Saudi Arabia was reported in April 1975 to be concluding an investment and military aid program, including the attachment of personnel with Pretoria.[19] Lebanon maintained consular relations with South Africa,[20] Jordan maintained close economic links with

Rhodesia, undeterred by African opinion or by the British Government's offical protests, from "bursting" UN sanctions.[21] She went ahead in 1974 to make a deal with South Africa involving the sale of sophisticated military equipment to South Africa and Rhodesia. This provoked a strongly-worded note from the OAU to the Arab League and a flood of criticisms from Africa.[22] President Amin of Uganda, one of the staunchest Arab supporters in Africa, even sent a cable to The Arab League Secretary-General complaining about the growing Arab economic, financial and military links with South Africa.[23] The situation has not changed despite pressures from African States.[24] Moreover, the African hopes regarding the oil sanction against South Africa have been frustrated by the refusal of the Arab oil States to take measures necessary for the implementation of the November 1973 Resolution of the Arab League. Following the success of the Arab oil embargo of 1973 in bringing pressure on Israel's foreign friends, the African States saw an extension of the boycott to South Africa and Portugal an effective way of bringing downb the racist and colonial regimes of these countries. In November 1973, the OAU Secretary-General, Mr. Nzo Ekangaki told the Council of Ministers that between 1964 and 1970, 90% of the oil consumed by South Africa came from the Arabian Gulf and that two-thirds of this oil was supplied by Arab States. He further stated that Iraq and Saudi Arabia supplied two-thirds of the total oil import of Portugal.[25] An OAU report to the Ninth Extraordinary Session of the Council of Ministers held in Dar-es-Salaam in April 1975, showed that Arab States supplied about 72% of South African oil while Iran supplied between 20 and 25%[26].

OAU optimism about the possible effects of an oil boycott of South Africa and Portugal was widely shared by the African press. The Daily News (Tanzania) said it would accelerate African Liberation struggles since a boycott would "completely paralyze the economies of these countries."[27] The Pioneer of Ghana declared that it would bring Portugal and South Africa to their senses in their mad effort to perpetuate colonialism, racism and oppression in Africa. It went on:

> The willingness or otherwise of the Arab countries in this direction can help make or mar the fight for the final liquidation of racist minority regimes in Africa and their continued existence on the continent.[28]

Even the South African authorities agreed that an oil boycott of the country by Arab countries could damage the country's economy.

The OAU set up a Committee, comprising Botswana, Cameroon, Ghana, Mali, Sudan, Tanzania and Zaire,[30] to make contact with the

Arab League on the oil embargo and other related issues. In January 1974, it decided to make the enforcement of the November 1973 Arab oil boycott resolutions one of the major issues to raise with Arab Oil Ministers in Cairo later that month. The Committee recommended that a system of blacklisting embargo busters and taking stern measures against them should be instituted by the Arab League—similar to their boycott policy against Israel. It also suggested that such blacklisting should include any ship or tanker, the owner of the ship, the firm using the vessel for the specific operation and the captain commanding it during its voyage to a South African port.[31]

However, in the event, the Arab Oil Ministers refused to accept responsibility for oil reaching South Africa. They also declined to take the measures the OAU Committee had recommended. Rather they argued that they had already done all they could by taking the decision to institute the embargo and maintained that the oil companies that shipped their oil to South Africa were outside their control. However, they promised to tighten control at their ports to see that their oil was not shipped to South Africa, Rhodesia and Portugal.

The African States were not pleased with Arab equivocation on this issue and during the Mogadishu OAU Summit Conference in June 1974 they passed another resolution appealing to the Arab oil producers to implement the League's decision to impose an oil embargo.[33]

The issue has continued as a major source of disagreement between the two groups of States in the dialogue which started between them after the October 1973 Middle East War. In Africa, it was generally, and probably rightly, interpreted as evidence of a lack of the necessary Arab support for African Liberation. The former Nigerian Commissioner for External Affairs, Brigadier Joseph Garba warned shortly before the Afro–Arab summit held in Cairo in March 1977 that Nigeria could not remain indifferent "to the apparent unconcern which many non-African Arab countries seem to be exhibiting towards the problems of Southern Africa." He said that the liberation struggle in South Africa did not "enjoy as much material and moral support" from the Arab as one would have expected. He contrasted Africa's practical total support for the Arabs on the problem of Palestine with the apparent unconcern of the Arabs on the question of Africa's liberation.[34] A Liberian Government-owned newspaper in an editorial also criticized the Arab indifference. It wrote:

> Except for the Arabs in North Africa who have associated with Black Africa through the OAU, the Arabs have shown nothing but indifference to the Liberation cause of the African continent.[35]

The oil embargo issue was again taken up by the Africans at the Cairo Afro–Arab Summit. Paragraph 6 of the draft Political Declaration of that Conference had sought to isolate Israel, South Africa and Rhodesia politically and economically as long as they continued "their racist, expansionist and aggressive policies." The Ethiopian government attempted to amend the clause by adding:

> To this end, the Summit has decided to impose with immediate effect, an oil embargo on these countries and to abrogate all contracts with companies that may continue to supply these countries.[36]

But the amendment was rejected by Arab delegations and African suspicions were confirmed. Ato Berhanu, the Head of the African Department of the Ethiopian Foreign Ministry, who led the Ethiopian delegation to the conference put it this way:

> They (the Arabs) have been fooling us at the Organization of African Unity meetings saying that they have imposed an embargo against South Africa and that (it) is the oil company that is breaking this embargo.[37]

Conclusion

From the above analysis, one can reasonably draw a number of conclusions. Firstly, Arab involvement in the liberation struggle of Africa started late. Secondly, their commitment was more declaratory in nature than concrete. And thirdly, whereas the general pattern of support as operated by the Arab League can be said to be negative, it is important to note as earlier indicated, that a number of OAU Arab States, particularly Egypt under President Nasser, Algeria and Libya have contributed immensely to African liberation. It is equally important to state that Libya and Algeria have traditionally not sold oil to South Africa. This is not necessarily because of these states' anti-apartheid inclinations. Algerian and Libyan oil have been sold to Europe and America mainly because of communication and transport reasons. It is however, not certain whether the two countries would have stopped shipment of their oil to South Africa as they have not done so before. The only thing one can say here is that both countries did follow the Arab line on the modalities of transferring Arab aid to Black Africa despite intense African distaste for such modalities. Besides, their delegations at the Cairo Summit did not support the Ethiopian Amendment.

It is possible to see the Arab lack of serious commitment to the Liberation of Black Africa as part of the overall Arab attitude towards Black Africa. It is equally possible to explain this away by arguing

It is possible to see the Arab lack of serious commitment to the Liberation of Black Africa as part of the overall Arab attitude towards Black Africa. It is equally possible to explain this away by arguing that the preoccupation of both groups of States have been different, namely that the Arab's main concern has been the Middle East and the question of Arab unity whereas African States have mobilized their collective action towards decolonization of Southern Africa and that of economic development of individual states. Even if this can be said to be true before 1973, it is not easy to defend such a claim now (in January 1979). Since 1973, Black Africa has agreed to share political enemies with the Arabs. The Africans declared that Israeli policies in the Middle East is a direct threat to the security of the African continent. Besides, as Brigadier Joseph Garba pointed out "the problem of Palestine is not an African problem."[38] It is incumbent on the Arab States, particularly since relations among states in the international system are based on the principle of reciprocity, "to be prepared to declare more moral and material support for the liberation struggle in Africa."

It is equally difficult to discount the cultural and racial factors which remain at the centre of any explanation of the active Arab involvement in the decolonization of North Africa (these countries were, after all, themselves Arab) and their relative non-involvement in the actual liberation of Black Africa, at least until fairly recently. Their actual role in the liberation of Algeria, Libya, Morocco and Tunisia[39] was never repeated elsewhere on the continent. Even in 1977 before the independence of the former French territory of Djibouti despite repeated protestations of shared objectives and joint liberation strategies, Namibia, South Africa and Rhodesia together did not command as much interest and attention by the Arab League as the tiny territory of Djibouti.[40]

Notes

1.   This section is based on discussions I had with some Arab diplomats in London and Cairo in 1976 and 1977.

2.   The Arabs sponsored the candidature of Somalia's Foreign Minister, Mr. Omar Ateh. The other candidate was Mr. Vernon Mwaanga, the Foreign Minister of Zambia. For more details on this, see Michael Wolfer's *Politics in the Organization of African Unity*, Methuen Co. Ltd., London, 1976, pp. 78–81.

3.   For a more detailed exposition of this theme, see Michael Crowder, "The 1939–45 War and West Africa" in J. F. Ajayi and Michael Crowder (ed.), *History of West Africa*, Vol. 11, London, 1974.

4.   Thomas Hovet Jr., *Africa in the United Nations*, Faber, London, 1963, p. 25.

5. Gamal Abdel Nasser, *Egypt's Revolution, the Philosophy of the Revolution*, Public Affairs Press, Washington D.C., 1955, p. 74.

6. For a detailed analysis of the motivations and actual policy of Egypt in Africa, see Ismael Y. Tazeq, *The UAR in Africa, Egypt's Policy Under Nasser*, Northwestern University Press, Evanston, 1971.

7. *Johannesburg Star*, June 23, 1060 and *The Times* (London), June 25, 1960.

8. The Arab League began to show a keener interest in Africa in 1960, principally because they saw in the emergent African States potential allies in their struggle against Israel.

9. Discussions in Cairo with Dr. Malik Ouda, the Director of the Arab League's Technical Fund and Mr. Helmi Sharawy of the African Association in Cairo in January 1977.

10. For a detailed study of the Congo crisis see Alan James *The Politics of Peace-Keeping*, London 1968; Catherine Hoskynes, *The Congo: A Chronology of Events, January 1960–December 1961*. Oxford University Press, May 1962 and Thomas Kanza, *Conflict in the Congo*, Penguin Books, Middlesex, 1972.

11. See *Middle East Records, Vol. 1, 1960*. The Shiloah Center for Middle Eastern and African Studies, Tel Aviv University, Israel University Press, Jerusalem, p. 35.

12. Morocco and the UAR immediately after the Casablanca Conference of January 1961 asked the UN Secretary-General to repatriate their forces before January 31 and February 1, 1961 respectively. Although Sudan did not participate in the Cassablanca Conference, it asked the Secretary-General on February 20, 1961 to withdraw its personnel from ONUC. See UN Document S(4640. It is significant to note that Ghana, a member of the Casablanca States, and perhaps the strongest critic of the UN operation never withdrew its forces from ONUC.

13. It has, however, been alleged that the OAU Arabs showed little interest, during the Liberation Committee's meetings, in issues affecting Black Africa. They were said to be primarily interested in Djibouti and Palestine, particularly between 1968 and 1977. Discussions with a Frontline State's diplomat and some officials of African Liberation Movements in London in 1976 and 1977.

14. It is important to note that most of the countries that broke relations with Britain had little or nothing to lose from such an action as their relations with Britain were very insignificant. Moreover Egypt already had her own quarrels with Britain over Yemen.

15. Eduardo Mondlane, *The Struggle for Mozambique*, Harmondsworth, Penguin African Library, 1969, p. 128.

16. See Michael Wolfers, op. cit., p. 164.

17. "The Resolution of Sixth Arab Summit Conference held in Algeria from 26th to 28th November 1973," Arab League, Cairo. In eventually breaking diplomatic relations with South Africa on February 18, 1974, Lebanon said that she was complying with the Arab League Resolution. See *African Research Bulletin (ARB), February 1974*.

18. *The Observer Foreign News Service*, London, March 18, 1975.

19. *African Development*, April 1975, p. 14.

20. OAU Doc. ECM(2 (ix) 1975, p. 4.

21. The British Government protested against Jordan's UN sanction "bursting" to the UN Sanctions Committee on October 26 1972 and April 7, 1973.

22. See *West Africa*, August 30, 1974.

23. *Daily Times* (Lagos), February 5, 1975.

24. See, for instance, *South African Digest*, December 1, 1978, p. 21.

25. *ARB* (Economical and Financial Series), November 15–December 14, 1973, p. 2936.

26. OAU Doc. ECM/2 (ix), Annex. II.

27. *Daily News Service*, November 23, 1973.

28. *BBC Summary of World Broadcast–Part IV*. ME/4459/B/3 November 24, 1973.

29. *Ibid.*, ME/4456/B/5, November 21, 1973.

30. The Committee will subsequently be referred to as "The Committee of Seven."

31. OAU Doc. CM/554. Appendix II, Annex. III.

32. OAU Doc. CM/554, Appendix III, Annex. IV.

33. OAU CM/Res 350 (xxiii), June 1974.

34. "Foreign Policy and Problems of Economic Development," An address at the University of Ibadan on February 19, 1977 by Brigadier J. N. Garba, Federal Commissioner for External Affairs.

35. *Liberian Age*, No. 20, 1975.

36. *Ethioipian Herald*, March 13, 1977.

37. *Ibid.*

38. J. N. Garba, "Foreign Policy and Problems of Economic Development," op. cit.

39. Butros Ghali, "The League of Arab States and North Africa," in Yassin El-Ayouty (ed.), *International Organization and Africa*. Hague, 1974.

40. This judgement is based on discussions I had with some African diplomats and journalists who have been involved in African affairs for a long time.

The USA, USSR, China and the Arab-Israeli Conflict

Aryeh Y. Yodfat

This session is devoted to the USA, the USSR, the People's Republic of China and the Middle East, with particular attention to the Arab-Israeli conflict and proposals of its solution. The USA and the USSR are superpowers but it is doubtful if the PRC can be called in such a way. The Chinese themselves surely don't consider themselves as such. In the Middle East the USA is at present playing a major role, initiating moves with the possibility of bringing about solutions. The USSR has been pushed into the passive role of a power which reacts, which might perhaps be able to prevent others from acting, but one unable to press her own proposals. The PRC plays a marginal role, that of watching from a distance. Her growing international role might, however, change that situation.

The USA–Directions and Priorities

The Middle East is generally seen in the USA from two major aspects:

a.   The aim of containing the Soviet Union and diminishing its role and presence as far as possible.
b.   Economic interests-primarily oil, its production, flow, regular supply, price, the petrodollars and where they go.

Other Middle East problems or subjects that concern the United States are subordinate to the two major issues. The latter have a local character, even if their impact may be felt far beyond the region. Among them we may list:

a.   The Arab-Israeli conflict.
b.   The Palestinian problem. Many in the USA see it as a separate problem and not only in the context of the Arab-Israeli conflict.
c.   The position of pro-American states and their being exposed and endangered by radical forces.
d.   The radicalization coming from both the right and the left in Lebanon and Iran, for example,which might undermine stability and order.

e. The unstable situations in Iran, Turkey, Lebanon, North Yemen, Red Sea, the Horn of Africa (. . .the list can be prolonged) and, in fact, in almost all Middle Eastern countries.

It is generally agreed in Washington that the US Government has to deal with those subjects or at least take them into consideration. There are differences of opinion about their importance and the priorities that should be given to them.

In the past the problems of West-East relations (i.e., USA–USSR) had a priority over anything else. Today increasing attention is given also to North-South problems (i.e., relations between the developed industrial world and the developing countries), problems of economy, supplies of raw materials, including oil. The problem of energy alongside the containment of the USSR has become very important (or one of the main—depending on position) American problems in the Middle East.

It is difficult to speak about an "American position" or about an "American priority" on any particular problem. There are positions and priorities of Secretary of State Cyrus Vance, of National Security Adviser Zbigniew Brzezinski, of the former UN Ambassador Andrew Young and others. The administration would like to satisfy everybody, e.g., those who want reductions in the budget and those who want to spend more. As this is impossible, changes appear in policy from one extreme to another or, at least, in proclaimed positions about it.

Israel—an "Asset" or "Burden" to the USA

The above-mentioned problem directly influences American positions on the Arab-Israeli conflict.[1] Those who stress the problem of energy see a dilemma between commitments to Israel and an interest in developing ties with oil producers. Those, or some of them, who stress the centrality of East-West problems see in Israel a strategic ally, an asset, an element that can contribute to the USA in time of need-because of her military power and political stability.

This brings us to two American positions:

One—US support of Israel comes as a result of political, historical and moral considerations,but not strategic ones. US strategic interests lie with Saudi Arabia or with Egypt more than with Israel. According to some officials or the State Department and National Security Council, Israel is a "burden."

Two—Israel is a reliable, democratic, militarily powerful ally in a basically unstable part of the world. Such a view was expressed in a public call to President Carter at the end of 1978 by 170 retired generals and admirals among others. This position was generally accepted in the US from 1967–1973 and proved itself at the time of the Syrian invasion of Jordan in September 1970, when Israel contributed to the prevention of a Syrian -Palestinian takeover of Jordan.

President Carter's statement in his annual State of the Union address to Congress on January 23, 1979, was a compromise between those two positions. He said: "Our firm commitment to Israel's survival and security is rooted in our deepest convictions and in our knowledge of the strategic importance to our nation of a stable Middle East."[2] It could be interpreted that Israel was strategically important, but it referred most specifically to the importance of "a stable Middle East." How about a non-stable Middle East as it actually is?

The US provides Israel with extensive aid. We may ask if it comes because of recognition of the position that was expressed by the generals and admirals or is it just a result of American internal political considerations and of internal American pressures. Positions about this are divided.

The US provides Israel with extensive aid. We may ask if it comes because of recognition of the position that was expressed by the generals and admirals or is it just a result of American internal political considerations and of internal American pressures.

US Proposals to Solve the Arab-Israeli Conflict

There is an almost unanimous American view that the Arab-Israeli conflict acts against American interests and that its solution will make US relations with the Arab world easier and prevent the USSR from returning to its previous positions in the region. It would eliminate the dilemma of the US that had to support Israel in the Yom Kippur War when they had to sacrifice important interests in the Arab world.

Positions differ as to how much the US should invest to bring and end to the conflict.[3] There are, for example, views that the aid to be provided to Israel and Egypt as a result of the peace treaty is too great. There are different views as to how much the US has to be involved, how much pressure should the US exert on this or the other side, how much they will be able to pressure and succeed at it.[4] Some believe that it is possible to exert pressure on Israel but that it is difficult to pressure the Arabs. President Sadat is considered to be weak and if pressed too hard might be replaced by someone who might turn to the USSR. Israel does not have such an option while any Arab country does. Such a situation gives the Arabs negotiating power that Israel does not have in dealing with the US.

The solution of the Arab-Israeli conflict has to come, according to generally accepted American positions, in three areas:

a. Israel-Egypt. An agreement has already been signed but has yet to be implemented.
b. Palestinians and Jordan. In the past the US preferred a Jordanian solution. Today those who call for a Palestinian solution are in the ascendency.
c. Syria.
    Agreements have to include:
a. Israeli withdrawal to the pre-June 1967 lines, with "minor changes" that will be dealt with in the negotiations.
b. A solution to the Palestinian problem, political and territorial, not only humanitarian; recognition of Palestinian rights to participate in talks and in the political process that will decide their future, without definitively stating how this problem will be solved and who will represent the Palestinians.
c. Security arrangements, demilitarized areas, areas of limited forces, international forces controlling implementation. A separation of the question of sovereignty over territories from the question of security arrangements in those territories.

These guidelines are used by American representatives at the Israeli-Egyptian talks.

The USA and the PLO

While there are no official US-PLO ties, there seems to be an American conclusion, without officially declaring or admitting it in public, that only the PLO is able, in the existing situation, to represent Palestinians. It causes the US Government to look for ways to make the PLO join the political process. It is ready to offer the PLO a role of representing Palestinians in exchange for recognition of Israel and acceptance of UN Security Council resolutions 242 and 338.[5]

It seems to American officials dealing with the Middle East that the PLO is leaning toward acceptance of this formula and that there is a gradual moderation in its leadership. They seem to be looking for an appropriate opportunity situation that will enable them to say that conditions have been established to recognize the PLO and have ties with it. Some believe that President Sadat's claims on behalf of the Palestinians came as a result of US initiatives and that Americans have persuaded Sadat to ask for a solution to this problem.

A "Pax Americana" or a "Soviet-American Peace"

The US has striven for peace in the Middle East without the cooperation of the USSR and in spite of Soviet opposition to it. The question is: Can the USSR prevent such American moves? There are different American positions about it. More tend to say that the US can do it without the Soviets. Those who say that there can be no peace in the Middle East without Soviet cooperation bring us back to the Soviet-American statement on the Middle East of October 1, 1977.[6] The Soviets would like America to act as indicated in this statement, but the US is not ready to do so, nor is Egypt or Israel. One of the reasons for Sadat to go to Jerusalem was his wish to bring to an end the situation that was created by this statement which gave him (and Israel) subordinate roles. Direct Egyptian-Israeli ties forced Americans to try to advance a comprehensive peace through Cairo (and Jerusalem) and not through Damascus, Beirut (PLO head-quarters) and Moscow.

USSR Proposals to Solve the Arab-Israeli Conflict

We will now try to review briefly USSR proposals to solve the Arab-Israeli conflict. They generally call for:

a. An Israeli withdrawal to the pre-June 1967 frontiers.
b. The right of Palestinians to establish their own state and of Arab refugees to return to their former homes.[7]
c. International guarantees for agreements made, to Israel and her neighboring Arab states. The Soviets spoke about the guarantees of the UN Security Council, of the USA, USSR, Britain and France or simply about "international guarantees." For the Soviets it is particularly important to be among the guarantors which would give them a legitimacy to be present in the region and to intervene there.
d. End of the state of war between Arab states and Israel. The Soviets spoke about a "settlement," a "regulation" or end of the state of war and only rarely spoke about peace. On many occasions this fourth condition was not mentioned at all.

A settlement of this kind had to be reached, in the Soviet view, at a Geneva conference in which they and the Americans would be co-chairmen. They issued a call to convene the conference as soon as possible, with the participation of the PLO from the beginning and on equal terms with all the other participants. Soviet insistence on PLO participation did in fact prevent the convening of the conference.

The Soviets stopped their call to convene the Geneva conference after signing of the Israeli-Egyptian peace treaty, because they did not see any chance for it in the existing situation and because their friends in the Arab world opposed it. However, a situation might arise in which they again may issue a call to convene that forum or something similar to it.

Generally, the Soviets do call for an Israeli withdrawal to the pre-June 1967 frontiers and there were Soviet statements that they have to be Israel's "recognized" frontiers. There were other statements which could mean a call for an Israeli withdrawal to the UN Palestine partition proposal of November 1947. It seems that the Soviets haven't really decided their position on this matter. The Soviet position is generally a function of their global and regional policy. As for the USSR as such, it does not matter at all whether the Golan Heights or West Bank will be part of Israel or not. Officially, the USSR does recognize the partition lines as Israel's legal frontiers. It does not mean that they call for a return to those lines. In the meantime a situation was established which they cannot ignore.

The Soviet-American statement of October 1, 1977 was, in fact, American readiness to accept somewhat amended Soviet conditions. The difference did not matter much to the Soviets; what was important was that they returned to a leading role in the political negotiation process from which they were excluded by Dr. Kissinger. President Sadat's initiative to carry on direct negotiations with Israel brought an end to that Soviet achievement. It was therefore no wonder that the Soviets were strongly against it.

The USSR Position after the Signing of the Israeli-Egyptian Peace Treaty.

The Soviet communication media sharply attacked the peace treaty signed by Israel and Egypt at the end of Mrch 1979 and the negotiations between them afterwards. There were many Soviet statements as to what the USSR did not want, but they were very careful not to say what they did want and tried to avoid committimg themselves to something concrete. There was an opportunity to strengthen ties between the Soviet Union and those who opposed the peace treaty which the Soviets tried not to miss, but it was done in a way that left options open for changes in Soviet positions if there were changes in Arab or American thinking.

It seems that in spite of a sharp Soviet criticism of the treaty they see it as a reality. The question that stands before them is what will be after it. The most probable answer is that they don't know. The Soviets don't initiate and don't control Arab moves but observe them. If key Arab states decide to change their policy—the Soviets will have to decide whether to continue to keep their present positions or to adapt them to the changing situation.

The Peoples' Republic of China— Watching From a Distance

The Peoples' Republic of China has no direct interest in the Arab-Israeli conflict and her attitude to it is a function of her global policy and involvement in inter-power struggles.[8] Her past position was influenced by ideological considerations and a wish to play a leading role in the "Third World." Such considerations continue to exist but they do not have the importance and weight that they had in the past.

In the early 1950s she was ready to establish relations with Israel but in the mid-1950s began to support Arab states against Israel.[9] In the 1960s at the time of the "Cultural Revolution," she turned from a policy of cultivating ties with existing Arab states and regimes to supporting groups and organizations acting against such regimes. In the 1970s she gradually abandoned ties with revolutionaries and instead extended her relations with states. It caused a gap between extreme militant and revolutionary slogans and a moderate and careful actual policy.[10]

PRC leaders and media continued with their attacks against Israel while acknowledging the fact that she served the purpose of containing Soviet advances in the Middle East. They chose to condemn Israel in the hope of winning over Arab friendship while at the same time hoping that Israel would continue to stand up against the Soviet presence in the region.

The PRC has close ties with the PLO, with al-Fatah, and lesser ones with other Palestinian organizations. Wide PRC political support is given to Palestinians and addresses of PRC representatives in the UN and other international forums devote much space to supporting "Palestinians and other Arabs." In the past the PRC supplied them arms. Today Palestinian organizations need more than light arms and receive extensive military aid from the USSR, Libya, Iraq, Syria and other Arab countries. China cannot and does not want to compete with them.

The PLO and most Palestinian organizations have ties with the USSR and advance Soviet interests. It is just the opposite of what the PRC would like to happen. This has not caused a break in Chinese-Palestinian relations but the opposite.

The PRC support for Palestinians was an important part of her support of revolutionary movements. Today the Chinese stress different things. The priority that is given by them to act against Soviets leaves them little room to manouevre. It seems that if the present situation will continue there will come a growing loss of Chinese interest in Palestinian organizations and of those organizations in China.

As to the Chinese position on the Israeli-Egyptian peace treaty— it is no exaggeration to say that the PRC welcomed it but preferred for her own reasons not to say so directly nor in public.

The PRC wanted it because it strengthened Egypt which has close ties with her, acts against the Soviets and, also, the PRC has always advocated direct contacts of local countries to diminish great-power intervention. But on the other hand, China did not want to express herself openly on it and weaken her relations with all those in the Arab world that oppose it—the PLO, Iraq, Syria, South Yemen, Algeria and others. The Chinese therefore express support of President Sadat in general, but do not say anything on this particular subject, except to quote others. This by itself can be considered as an indirect support of the peace treaty.

As a rule, Chinese do not express clear positions on matters about which there are differences in the Arab world, but only when their direct interests require them to do so. Up to now they succeeded in expressing themselves in a way that was seen, on the one hand, as support to Sadat but, on the other hand, those who oppose peace can see in the Chinese position an abstention from expressing themselves, or at least not expressing themselves as against them.

The PRC has no relations with Israel. It is convenient for her to attack Israel, assuming that it contributes to her relations with the Arab World. Up to now she had no reason to establish diplomatic relations but may decide to do so after such relations are established between Egypt and Israel. She may then decide to begin with unofficial ties, on the "people-to-people" level—commercial, cultural, scientific, sports. In the meantime they prefer to adopt a watch and wait policy and leave decisions for a later time.

Notes

1. William B. Quandt, *Decade of Decisions: American Policy Toward the Arab-Israeli Conflict, 1967–1976*, Berkeley and Los Angeles, University of California Press, 1977; Bernard Reich, "The Evolution of United States Policy in the Arab-Israeli Zone," *Middle East Review*, vol. IX, Spring 1977, pp. 9–18; Steven Spiegel, "The United States and the Middle East Crisis," *ibid.*, pp. 25–33; Herbert Kampf, "The American Interest in Israel's Security" *Midstream*, vol. 23, June-July 1977, pp. 27–34; Stanley Hoffman, "The United States and the Arab-Israeli Conflict," *New Outlook*, July-August 1978, pp. 12–18; John C. Campbell, "The Middle East: The Burdens of Empire," *Foreign Affairs*, vol. 57, no. 3, 1979, (America and the World, 1978), pp. 613–632.

2. *Weekly Compilation of Presidential Documents*, vol. 15, no. 4, (Washington, GPO January 29, 1979), p. 107.

3. "America's Mideast Role: Bigger, Riskier, Costlier," *US News & World Report*, April 9, 1979, p. 28; Harvey Sicherman, *Broker or Advocate? The U.S. Role in the Arab-Israeli Dispute, 1973–1978*, (Philadelphia, Foreign Policy Research Institute, 1978).

4. According to George W. Ball, Under-Secretary of State from 1961 to 1966, "If America should permit Israel to continue to reject inflexibly any

suggestion of a return to earlier boundaries and the creation of a Palestinian state and to refuse even to negotiate about Jerusalem, we would be acquiescing in a policy hazardous not only for Israel but for America and the rest of the world." (George W. Ball, "How to Save Israel in Spite of Herself," *Foreign Affairs*, April 1977, pp. 453–471). He argues in another article that "unlimited" US support permits Israel to ignore the Palestinian problem. (idem., "America's Interests in the Middle East," *Harper's*, October 1978, pp. 18–21). An opposite view less accepted by the US administration, proposes that the USA should acknowledge that the crux of the Arab-Israeli conflict is really the Arab refusal to accept a Jewish state in Palestine and abandon the view that the West Bank is the crux of the conflict. The USA has to confine itself to the role of a mediator, and inform Damascus, Amman, the Palestinian Arabs and Riyadh, that "if they want an alteration in Jerusalem's policies they had best start negotiating with Jerusalem, as Sadat has done, and quit relying on Washington to 'deliver' the Israelis." (Douglas J. Feith, "The Settlements and Peace: Playing the Links with Begin, Carter and Sadat," *Policy Review*, (Washington, D.C., no. 9, Spring 1979, pp. 25–39).

5.   President Carter said on September 29, 1977, that it was obvious to him that there can be no Middle Eastern peace settlement without adequate Palestinian representation." The PLO "Don't represent a nation. It is a group that represents a substantial part of Palestinians." He said: "We will begin to meet with them and to search for some accomodation or some reasonable approach to the Palestinian question if they adopt 242 and recognize publicly the right of Israel to exist." *(Department of State Bulletin*, October 31, 1977, pp. 584–586). An address by President Carter in Aswan, Egypt on January 4, 1978, included a recognition of the importance of the Palestinian problem and of the need of its solution. He said: "...there must be a resolution of the Palestinian problem in all its aspects. The problem must recognize the legitimate rights of the Palestinian people and enable the Palestinians to participate in the determination of their own future." *(ibid.,* February 1978, pp. 11–12).

6.   *Pravda,* (Moscow), October 2, 1977; Raymond Cohen, "Israel and the Soviet-American Statement of October 1, 1977: The Limits of Patron-Client Influence," *Orbis*, vol. 22, no. 3, Fall 1978, pp. 613–634.

7.   The Soviets spoke about "the right" to establish a Palestinian state but did not call for its establishemnt. It means that Palestinians might decide to use that right in another way, e.g., by joining Syria. They did generally not say clearly where will the refugees return—to Israel, after her withdrawal, or to the proposed by them Palestinian state.

8.   Aryeh Y. Yodfat, "China and the Middle East," *New Outlook*, vol. 22, no. 4 (191), May–June 1979, pp. 33–38.

9.   Michael Brecher, *Israel, the Korean War and China*, (Jerusalem Academic Press, 1974).

10.   Aryeh Y. Yodfat, *Between Revolutionary Slogans and Pragmatism: The PRC and the Middle East*, (Bruxelles, Centre d'Etude du Sud-Est Asiatique et de l'Extreme Orient, 1979); idem., "The PRC and the Middle East," *Asia Quarterly*, (Bruxelles), 1977/3, pp. 223–236, 1978/1, pp. 67–78, 1978/4, pp. 295–308.

International Communications—
Soviet Union and The Middle East Conflict

Alan Zaremba

Introduction

The international community has long been involved with the Middle East Conflict. It is a conflict that has serious global implications and is not one that can be viewed solely from a Middle or Near East perspective. The problemn has had international dimensions and repercussions since Israel became a state in 1948 (Warburg, 1968: V). The facilitation of normalized interaction between the belligerent nations therefore, is a function to an extent of international attitudes and perspectives. It would be less than reasonable to assume that a remedy for the Middle East problem could result without certain international agencies' actions and the concomitant input of member nations.

    Consistent with this recognition, an analysis of nations' perspectives regarding the Middle East conflict is essential. Of particular import are the perspectives held and conveyed by the Super Powers. This monograph is a quantitative analysis of the attitudes and perspectives of the Soviet Union regarding the key issues in the Middle East conflict.

Method

Perspectives regarding the Middle East will be assessed by examining newspaper editorials which appeared in the *Moscow News* — a major newspaper in the USSR—for a sixty-day period after the outbteak of the Yom Kippur War on October 6, 1973. This time sequence is chosen as it represents the last major outbreak between the belligerents and provides a time in which international attention was focused on Mid-East issues. Editorials are used because they provide a good sample for investigating and analyzing international perceptions and attitudes (Pool, 1952: 12). They have been used extensively in previous studies with similar designs. The RADIR studies under the direction of Harold Lasswell in 1941 (RADIR—Revolution and the Development of International Relations), employed editorials to facilitate research (Holsti, 1967: 44). Pool's study of prestige newspapers in 1951 is also a notable example of research which utilized editorials for its sample (Pool, 1953:9). Editorials in general are reflective of a national perspective. "Both in totalitarian and liberal states the elite has accepted the obligation and desirability of stating its policy through this medium [editorials]" (Pool, 1952:10).

The *Moscow News* is a weekly publication which is published mainly for tourists (Merrill, 1973:153). It does, however, convey a national perspective of the USSR. All of Russia's papers are conceived as a branch of the government with the purpose of promulgating government philosophy (Merrill, 1971:147). Content Analysis is a methodology which has been used in international studies before and is appropriate for analyzing characteristics of content. It denotes an objective, systematic and quantitative method for the analysis of communication content. It is intended to provide precise and concise descriptions of what the communication says in terms appropriate to the purpose or problem at issue (Holstii, 1967:3).

The categories in the analysis are constructed to answer the following questions:

(1) Whom does the *Moscow News* perceive as:
  (a) the aggressor?
  (b) legitimately owning the land?
  (c) imperialistic?
  (d) intransigent?
  (e) utilizing terrorist tactics?
  (f) genuinely seeking peace?
  (g) having overall culpability?
  (h) having justification for their actions?

(2) Does the *Moscow News* feel Zionism is practical?

An explanation of the key words and/or phrases in these questions is necessary.

Aggressor: Aggression is generally defined as an unprovoked or warlike act; specifically, the use of armed forces by a state in violation of its international obligations. The aggressor nation in this study refers to the country that exhibited aggression.

Land Legitimacy: The land in question is (1) the land that Israel was granted by the UN partition resolution *as well as* (2) the "occupied territory." Legitimacy refers to who rightfully deserves to own the land.

Imperialism: Imperialism is defined as the policy and practice of forming and maintaining an empire by the conquest of other countries and the establishment of colonies or some type of sphere or influence. Imperialism refers here to either Arab or Israeli policy of land annexation for the purpose of state expansion.

Intransigence: Intransigence refers to either Arab or Israeli stubborn resistance to meet and discuss possibilities for peace.

Genuinely seeking peace: This is the opposite of intransigence. This refers to either Arab or Israeli willingness to negotiate for peace.

Terrorism: Terrorism refers to acts similar to the Deir Yassin incident.

Culpability: Culpability in this work refers to the country who is generally deserving of blame for the conflict.

Action justification: Action justification simply refers to the legitimacy of the actions taken in the conflict.

Zionism practical/impractical: This refers to the practicality of the fundamental tenet of Zionism. It is a belief that Israel is a sovereign state, which serves as a homeland for its inhabitants and for Jewish people anywhere who choose to emigrate and become its citizens (Aunery, 1971:178).

The quantitative procedure that will be implemented will consist of the tabulation of the frequency of the sentences that contain the phrases conveying the meaning:

Israeli Aggression	Israeli Terrorism
Arab Aggression	Arab Terrorism
Israeli Imperialism	Israeli Peace Seeking
Arab Imperialism	Arab Peace Seeking
Israeli Land Legitimacy	Israeli Illegitimacy of Holdings
Arab Land Legitimacy	Arab Illegitimacy of Desire for Land
Israeli Intransigence	Israeli Action Justification
Arab Intransigence	Arab Action Justification
Zionism is practical	Israeli Culpability
Zionism is impractical	Arab Arab Culpability

The units will be the sentences in which the phrase is found. Each descriptor within the unit will be accorded a value of one. If two phrase meanings are found in one sentence, each is accorded a value of one.

Results

The purpose of the Soviet Press is to promulgate the philosophy of the government of the USSR (Merrill, 1971:147). The *Moscow News*, consistent with that philosophy, reports and editorializes in the same columns. The *News* does not have an editorial page or an editorial section as such. Each article gives the opinions of the editors or publisher which are essentially the views of the government (Merrill, 1971:147). Editorials in the *Moscow News*, therefore, are defined as any article within the *News* with content that deals at least peripherally with the Middle East conflict. There were nineteen such articles found in the *Moscow News* in the period being examined. From this point, the word editorials refers to those nineteen articles.

There were ten editions of the *News* during the examination period. As explained earlier, the *Moscow News* is a weekly, not a daily, publication. As is the case with many other weekly publications, the *News* postdates its editions. An issue dated October 13–20, for example, was written previous to that date. The determination of the date of the writing of the article was ascertained by subtracting seven days from the date that the *News* was stamped as having been received by the Buffalo and Erie County Public Library. According to the US Post Office, it takes an average of one week to receive such issues from Moscow. The October 13–20 issue, therefore, stamped October 11, 1973, was not examined for this study. The war began on October 6, 1973, therefore, examining a copy probably written, at the latest, on October 4, 1973, would be pointless for the purposes of this research. The first editorial which appears in the *Moscow News* regarding the Arab–Israeli conflict is in the October 20–27 issue stamped October 14. This supports the date determination procedure. The last issue examined is dated December 22–29 and stamped December 17.

All of the issues of the *Moscow News* contained at least one editorial. One issue contained five editorials and another four. There was an average of 1.9 editorials per issue. The *News* averaged 617.9 words per editorial with a total of approximately 11,740 words in articles dealing with the Middle East conflict. In the nineteen articles, there were 333 tabulations. There was an average of 17.5 per article.

Aggression

Aggression had the greatest frequency of tabulations of all the categories. Ninety-seven of the 333 tabulations or 29.1 percent of all tabulations were in the area of Aggression. Table 1 presents the frequency and percentage of the total tabulations for each category in the study. As Table 1 indicates, the Aggression category had more than twice the tabulation frequency than any one of the other categories.

It is clear from the data that the *Moscow News* considered the Israelis the aggressor in the conflict. They unequivocally state, "A battle is raging between the aggressor Israel and the victims of aggression, Egypt and Syria." "Tel Aviv's Recklessness," Oct. 20,

Table 1
**Frequency and Percentage of the Total Tabulations
For Each Category**

	Israel		Arab		Total	
Category	Number of Tabulations	Percentage of Total Tabulations	Number of Tabulations	Percentage of Total Tabulations	Number of Tabulations	Percentage of Total Tabulations
Aggression	97	29.1	0	0.0	97	29.1
Imperialism	28	8.4	0	0.0	28	8.4
Land Legitimacy	0	0.0	27	8.1	27	8.1
Terrorism	46	13.8	0	0.0	46	13.8
Peace Seeking	2	.6	9	2.7	11	3.3
Illegitimacs	21	6.3	0	0.0	21	6.3
Intransigence	44	13.2	0	0.0	44	13.2
Zionism	0	0.0	4	1.2	4	1.2
Action Justification	0	0.0	18	5.4	18	5.4
Culpability	18	5.4	0	0.0	18	5.4
Super Power/ International Culpability	—	—	—	—	19	5.7

* Total Tabulations Equal 333.

1973). All ninety-seven of the tabulations were Israeli Aggression tabulations. The *Moscow News* repeatedly admonished the Israelis for their purported Aggressive behavior. In three editorials ("Statement by the Soviet Government," Oct. 20, "Tel Aviv's Recklessness," Oct. 14, and "Tel Aviv's Recklessness," Oct. 27), more than ten tabulations for Israeli Aggression were chartered. There was an average of 5.1 Israeli Aggression tabulations per article. The following typical examples of statements tabulated in this category reveal the unequivocal nature of the newspaper's philosophy.

> In recent days, Israel had established considerable armed forces on the cease fire lines with Syria and Egypt had called up reservists and, having thereby heated up the situation to the limit, unleashed military operations ("Statement by the Soviet Government," Oct. 20, 1973).

> As a result of Israel's stubborn continuation of aggression against the Arab countries, military operations have again flared up in the Middle East ("Firm Support," Oct. 20, 1973).

> Israel has been for several years now constantly firing up the situation in the Middle East by its reckless aggressive action ("Statement by the Soviet Government," Oct. 20, 1973).

> Tel Aviv has committed a new grave act of Aggression ("Tel Aviv's Recklessness," Oct. 27, 1973).

In all nineteen articles, there was at least one tabulation for Israeli Aggression. Table 2 presents for each category, the frequency and percentage of the total articles in which there was at least one tabulation. As Table 2 indicates, there were no other categories with tabulations in each article. It is apparent that the *News* considered aggression an important focus of contention in the conflict.

Table 2
Frequency and Percentage of Editorials Containing
At Least One Tabulation For Each Respective Category*

Category	Israel N†	Percentage‡	Arab N	Percentage	Total N	Percentage
Aggression	19	100.0	0	0.0	19	100.0
Imperialism	12	63.1	0	0.0	12	63.1
Land Legitimacy	0	0.0	17	89.5	17	89.5
Terrorism	9	47.3	0	0.0	9	47.3
Peace Seeking	2	10.5	5	26.3	5	26.3
Illegitimacy	13	68.4	0	0.0	13	68.4
Intransigence	17	89.5	0	0.0	17	89.5
Zionism	0	0.0	3	15.0	3	15.0
Action Justification	0	0.0	11	57.8	11	57.8
Culpability	11	57.8	0	0.0	11	57.8
Super Power/ International Culpability	—	—	—	—	10	52.6

* This chart would read, for example, re Israeli Aggression: nineteen editorials or 100 percent of all the editorials contained at least one tabulation for Israeli Aggression.
† Number of editorials with at least one tabulation.
‡ Percentage of total editorials with at least one tabulation.

Imperialism

The category of Imperialism contained 8.4 percent of the total tabulations. This category ranked fourth in tabulation frequency. All twenty-eight tabulations were in the area of Israeli Imperialism. The *News* felt that Israel was imperialistic and that this tendency towards political expansion was the root cause for the war. They write:

> It is no secret to any one that the cause of this situation is the expansionist policy of Israel ("Statement by the Soviet Government," Oct. 20, 1973).

> ...the cause of the present situation in the Middle East is the expansionist policies of Israel's ruling circles ("Firm Support," Oct. 20, 1973).

The Israeli aggressors . . .seek to keep the Middle East in an explosive state which they need to effect their far reaching expansionist designs ("Firm Support," Oct. 20, 1973).

The statements are typically "condemning the expansionist policy of Israel" ("Statement by the Soviet Government, Oct. 20, 1973), or characterizing the Israeli government as "fascinated by its expansionist ambition." ("Statement by the Soviet Government," Oct. 14, 1973). There were 1.47 tabulations for Israeli Imperialism per article. Statements which were tabulated as Israeli Imperialism appeared in twelve of the nineteen or 63.2 percent of the articles.

Land Legitimacy

There were twenty-seven tabulations representing 8.1 percent of the total tabulations in the area of Land Legitimacy. All twenty-seven of the tabulations were in the area of Arab Land Legitimacy. The News was adamant regarding the Palestinian rights to the "occupied territories." An article in the December 8th issue, for example, reads:

> . . .All Israel-occupied territories must be returned to the Arab States and the lawful rights of the Arab population of Palestine must be restored ("Arab Unity Strengthening," Dec. 8, 1973).

Again, on October 27, they write:

> . . .Israeli troops must be withdrawn from all Arab territories occupied since 1967 and all parties must recognize the legitimate rights of the Arab people of Palestine ("Denouncement and Support," Oct. 27, 1973).

The News however, did not take a clear stand regarding the legitimacy of Israel's statehood. The closest comment to such a sanctioning appeared in an editorial of the November 10 issue of the News. In an article entitled, "The Road to Peace in the Middle East" the paper reads:

> . . .the view recently expressed in the Washington Post is worth noting. It wrote that although Israel had the right to existence, the recent developments again posed the question of whether Israel had the right to continuously occupy alien territories, provoke the vengeance of the Arabs and a dragged-out local conflict, [sic] and maintain the constant threat of a third world war.
> To this reasonable question, the nations of the whole world answer firmly and unequivocally: No! [italics mine] ("The Road to Peace in the Middle East," Nov., 10, 1973).

The closest reference to the sanctioning of Israeli statehood is the inclusion and non-refutation of the italicized clause. Had the

News chosen, it could easily have begun the excerpted passage with the words, "the recent developments." The clause regarding Israel's right to exist was included, was not refuted and thus constitutes some type of tacit approval or, more likely, in light of its overall philosophy, acknowledgment of the existence of the State of Israel. No explicit statement was made, however, and therefore, a definite philosophy cannot be determined. There were 1.42 tabulations per article in this category. Seventeen of the nineteen or 89.5 percent of the articles had at least one tabulation for Arab .and Legitimacy. The *News* apparently considered the land legitimacy of the Arabs an important area of contention.

Terrorism

There were forty-six tabulations in the category of Terrorism. This represented 13.8 percent of the total tabulations, a percentage which ranked second among the categories. As in the previous categories discussed, the results of the analysis in this category were mono-dimensional. All forty-six of the tabulations were in the area of Israeli Terrorism. The *News* vehemently condemned the purported Israeli terrorist acts. The newspaper writes:

> . . .the Israeli military are turning lethal weapons against peaceful citizens, against civilian targets and even carry out attacks on the ships and purely civilian institutions of states that take no part in the war ("Tass Statement," Oct. 27, 1973).

> This month's hostilities reached unparalleled intensities with heavy casualties on both sides including the loss of life among the civilian population as a result of the barbaric bombing of peaceful towns and villages in Egypt and Syria ("The War in the Middle East Must End," Nov. 17, 1973).

> Recent events have ripped away the masks from the Israeli chieftains. They are using deadly weapons against civilian and nonmilitary targets. Many towns in Syria and Egypt have been barbariously bombed and many civilians have been killed ("Tel Aviv's Reckless-ness," Oct. 27, 1973).

> On October 9, Israeli aircraft dropped bombs on the Soviet cultural center situated in one of the districts of Damascus, where there are no military targets, but only missions of foreign states. There are victims among Soviet and Syrian citizens who were in this building ("Tass Statement," Oct. 27, 1973).

The *News* is consistently vitriolic in their condemnation of the alleged acts of terrorism. There were 2.42 tabulations per article. It should be noted, however, that one of the articles, "Tass Statement," had twenty-two tabulations. Nine of the nineteen, or 47.3 percent, of the editorials had at least one tabulation.

Peace Seeking

There were eleven tabulations in the area of Peace Seeking. This represented 3.3 percent of the total tabulations. The only category which had fewer tabulations was the category concerning the practicality of Zionism. This category was the only one among the ten bipolar categories which was two dimensional. Of the tabulations, 81.8 percent were in the category of Arab Peace Seeking and 18.2 percent were in the Israeli Peace Seeking category. Despite the dual polarities, it was clear that the News felt that the Arabs were the party which ingenuously and continually sought peace.

> It is well known that the Arab states have shown quite a lot of restraint and readiness to seek a political settlement of the conflict on a just basis ("Statement by the Soviet Government," Oct. 20, 1973).

> Everyone is well aware that the Arab states have displayed utmost restraint and a preparedness to accept a political settlement on a just basis ("Tel Aviv's Recklessness," Oct. 27, 1973).

> The Arab people are alien to warmongering ("Just Settlement for the Middle East," Dec. 1, 1973).

Israeli Peace Seeking was mentioned only twice:

> Representatives of the ARE and Israel signed a document concerning the observance of the cease fire agreement ("Undelayed Task," Nov. 24, 1973).

> Recently, Egypt and Israel began exchanging prisoners in accordance with the bilateral protocol of November 11. The fact in itself is positive ("Just Settlement for the Middle East," Dec. 1, 1973.

As the above two quotations indicate, the Israeli Peace Seeking efforts were not unilateral. There were no statements regarding any individual initiatives taken by Israel to secure peace. In fact, the last statement quoted above which ends with, "The fact in itself is positive," is immediately followed with:

> However, Israel is stubbornly refusing to observe other provisions of the protocol on a ceasefire and the withdrawal of troops to the positions of October 22 ("Just Settlement for the Middle East," Dec. 1, 1973).

There were .57 tabulations per article. Five of the nineteen articles or 26.3 percent had Arab Peace Seeking tabulations. Two of the nineteen, or 10.5 percent, had Israeli Peace Seeking tabulations.

Illegitimacy

There were twenty-one tabulations in this category representing 6.3 percent of the total tabulations. This ranked sixth in frequency among the categories. All twenty-one of the tabulations were in the area of Israeli Illegitimacy. As would be expected from examining the data in the related area of Land Legitimacy, the *News* felt that Israeli illegitimately possessed land. The articles call for the Israeli's withdrawal from territory which, according to the *News*, does not belong to Israel. There were 1.1 tabulations per article. Thirteen of the nineteen articles had tabulations in the area of Land Legitimacy. This represents a frequency of 68.4 percent.

Intransigence

There were forty-four tabulations in the area of Intransigence. This represented 13.2 percent of the total tabulations. The category had the third highest frequency. All forty-four of the tabulations were in the area of Israeli Intransigence. Moscow perceived the Israelis as sabotaging peace efforts intended to resolve the conflict. The following are typical of the repeated statements to this effect in the *News*:

> The efforts of the Arab countries have invariably come up against Tel Aviv's obstructionist position ("Statement by the Soviet Government," Oct. 20, 1973).

> Israel has obstructed the efforts to bring about a fair settlement of the Middle East conflict. ("Firm Support," Oct. 20, 1973).

> Tel Aviv has sabotaged all attempts at a just political settlement in the Middle East ("Tel Aviv's Recklessness," Oct. 27, 1973).

> The Israeli aggressors having engineered a new eruption of hostlities in the Middle East crisis, are going out of their way to sabotage the October 22nd and 23rd Security Council Resolutions . . .("The Road to Peace in the Middle East," Nov. 10, 1973).

> Tel Aviv has in every way obstructed the operation of the UN task force ("Undelayed Task," Nov. 24, 1973).

Israel was characterized as "frustrating all the efforts aimed at establishing a just peace." ("Statement by the Soviet Government," Oct. 20, 1973). There were 2.3 tabulations per article in this category. Seventeen of the nineteen articles or 89.5 percent contained tabulations in the category of Israeli Intransigence. This intransigence as indicated by its frequency, was considered by the *News* to be a major area of contention.

Zionism

Zionism tabulations were the most infrequent compared to the other categories. Only four tabulations in the Zionism category appeared in the entire period. These tabulations represented 1.2 percent of all the tabulations. All four tabulations were in the area of "Zionism is impractical." The *News* considered international Zionism impractical as it was considered by them to be one of the forces behind the Israeli aggression.

> The Israeli aggressors, supported by the imperialist forces and international Zionism, seek to overthrow the progressive regimes in the Arab countries and to keep the Middle East in an explosive state which they need to effect their far reaching expansionist designs ("Firm Support," Oct. 20, 1973).

> The government of Israel supported by external imperialist forces and International Zionist circles, heeded not the voice of the broad international public and aspired once again by military might to impose upon this region of the world the kind of order it desires ("Resolute Protest," Oct. 20, 1973).

> Israeli Zionists, who get broad military support from outside, [desire] to seize more Arab territory ("For Lasting Peace," Nov. 10, 1973).

The fourth tabulation corresponded to a statement that criticized Zionist propaganda. There were .21 tabulations per article. Three out of the nineteen articles, or 15.8 percent, contained at least one tabulation for the category, "Zionism is impractical." The frequency of Zionism tabulations indicate that this was a relatively insignificant area of contention as perceived by the *Moscow News*.

Action Justification

There were eighteen tabulations in the area of Arab Action Justification. This represents 5.4 percent of the total tabulation. Only Peace Seeking, Culpability, and Zionism had as few or fewer tabulations. All eighteen of the tabulations were in the area of Arab Action Justification. The *News* perceived that it was apparent not only to themselves but to "all sober minded people" (a phrase often employed by the *Moscown News*) that the actions of the Arab peoples are justified:

> The justness of the Arab states' demands for the withdrawal of the aggressors troops from all Arab territories occupied in 1967 is recognized by all ("Statement by the Soviet Government," Oct. 20, 1973).

> The Arab states, victims of the aggression, are exercising their right to self defense and [are] waging a legitimate battle ("Tel Aviv's Recklessness," Oct. 27, 1973).

Phrases such as "just struggle" or "just cause" are typical of those which were tabulated as Arab Action Justification. There were .95 tabulations per article in this category. Eleven of the nineteen or 57.9 percent of the articles had at least one tabulation in the area of Arab Action Justification.

Culpability

There were eighteen tabulations in the area of Culpability. This represented 5.4 percent of the tabulations and had the same tabulation frequency as the Action Justification category. All eighteen of the tabulations were in the area of Israeli Culpability. The remarks in the *News* were unequivocal and often very similar. The *Moscow News* plainly considered Israel the guilty party:

> The responsibility for the present development of events in the Middle East and their consequences falls wholly on Israel and those external reactionary cricles which constantly encourage Israel in its aggressive ambitions ("Statement by the Soviet Government," Oct. 20, 1973).

> The responsibility for the present development rests wholly and completely on Israel and those foreign reactionary circles which regularly encourage Israel's aggressive aspirations ("Tel Aviv's Recklessness," Oct. 27, 1973).

> They [Israel] bear full responsibility for the blood again being spilt [sic] in the Middle East . . .("Firm Support," Oct. 20, 1973).

There were .94 tabulations per article. Eleven out of the nineteen or 57.8 percent of the articles had at least one tabulation in the area of Culpability.

Super Power/International Culpability

Nineteen of the 333 tabulations were in the area of Super Power/ International Culpability. This represented 5.7 percent of the total tabulations. This category ranked seventh among the categories. Although only 5.7 percent of the tabulations were in this category, it was apparent that the *News* perceived the United States, the other super power, as a guilty power. Actually, there were six different, sometimes nebulous, groupings to which guilt was attributed for some part of the conflict. They were the United States, oil monopolies, imperialist forces, reactionary circles, reactionary and imperialist forces, and outside forces. Guilt was attributed to the United States 42.1 percent of the time. It is highly probable that additional targets of admonition nebulously labeled "imperialist forces," "reactionary circles," "reactionary and imperialist forces" and "outside forces" are all intended to suggest the United States. If this is so, then 94.8 percent of the Super Power/International Culpability tabulations are attributable to the United States. The first quotation cited below is indicative of a statement admonishing reactionary and imperialist forces which suggests the identity of the force. [Israel is] "enjoying the support of the same reactionary and imperialist forces which in Chile, as in Indochina, brutally oppose the forces of peace and progress." ("Denouncement and Support," Oct. 27, 1973). There are many statements which explicitly depict the United States as a culpable party:

> The United States [should] immediately cease its supplies to the government of Israel and also end all support enabling Israel to pursue its aggressive, expansionist policies ("Denouncement and Support," Oct. 27, 1973).

In contrast to the role played by the United States, the News perceives the Soviet Union as endeavoring to seek peace.

> The Soviet Union, which maintained close contact with the friendly Arab countries, took every political measure within its power to facilitate an early end to the war and the creation of conditions under which a new outbreak would be excluded so that peace in the Middle East might become permanent and durable ("A Period of Hope and Concern," Nov. 17, 1973).

> The Soviet Union is prepared to and will make its constructive contribution to this cause [peace] ("The Road to Peace in the Middle East," Nov. 10, 1973).

It is important to note, however, that the News threatened Israel with statements that implied possible Soviet military participation:

> If Israel's ruling circles presume that their actions against peaceful cities and civilian targets in Syria and Egypt will remain unpunished, they are profoundly deluded. Aggression cannot remain unpunished and the aggressor must bear harsh responsibility for his action ("Tass Statement," Oct. 27, 1973).

> The continuation of criminal acts by Israel will lead to grave consequences for Israel itself ("Tass Statement," Oct. 27, 1973).

> ...we have been also considering other possible measures whose adoption the situation may require ("The War in the Middle East Must End," Nov. 3, 1973).(Quote from Brezhnev supported by paper)

Additionally, it is important to note that the *News* perceives world opinion as supporting the Arab cause. It would seem that with the exception of the United States, the *Moscow News* applauds the attitudes and efforts of others in the world arena:

> ...Thanks to the collective effort of several countries additional opportunities have opened up for a political settlement in the Middle East ("Undelayed Task," Nov. 24, 1973).

> World Public opinion resolutely condemns the new aggressive act by Israel ("Tel Aviv's Recklessness," Oct. 20, 1973).

> Israel is now seen by the international public as an imprudent aggressor ("For Lasting Peace," Nov. 10, 1973).

> The numerous comments in the press abroad describe the Statement [Statement] by the Soviet Government as fresh evidence of the support by the USSR of the just cause of the Arab nations. This is particularly true of the press of the Arab countries ("Tel Aviv's Recklessness," Oct. 20, 1973).

There were .95 tabulations for Super Power/International Culpability per article. Ten of the nineteen, or 52.6 percent of the articles, had at least one tabulation.

Summary

The *Moscow News* was pro-Arab in philosophy as Table 3 indicates. Of all tabulations, 99.4 percent were pro-Arab and only 0.6 percent were pro-Israeli. Of the 312 tabulations in the bipolar categories, 310 were pro-Arab and only two were pro-Israeli.

The analysis of the *Moscow News* editorials reveals the following perceptions:

1. The Israelis were the aggressors.
2. The Palestinians have the right to the occupied territories.
3. (a) The Arabs made the significant intiatives to secure peace.
   (b) The only peace initiatives taken by the Israelis were those that were made concurrently with the Arab countries.
   (c) The Soviet Union sought peace.
   (d) World opinion supports the Arab nations.
4. The Israelis frustrated and sabotaged peace efforts.
5. (a) The United States exacerbated the conflict by urging Israel to pursue its aggressive ambitions

Table 3
Overall Tabulations

Category	Pro-Israel	Pro-Arab
Aggression	0	97
Imperialism	0	28
Land Legitimacy	0	27
Terrorism	0	46
Peace Seeking	2	9
Illegitimacy	0	21
Intransigence	0	44
Zionism	0	4
Action Justification	0	18
Culpability	0	18
Total	2	312
Percentage of Total Tabulations	0.6	99.4

(b) The United States supplied military weapons which escalated the war.

(c) The Soviet Union sought peace.

(d) World opinion supports the Arab nations.

6. The oil policy compelled objectivism.

7. The cause of the war was Israel's expansionist political philosophy.

8. Israel used terrorist tactics.

9. International Zionism served as a catalyst for Israeli aggression.

References

Holsti, O. (1969). *Content Analysis for the Humanities and Social Sciences*, Reading: Addison Wesley.

Merrill, J. (1970). *The Foreign Press*. Baton Rouge: L.S.U.

Pool, I. (1952). *Prestige Papers*. USA: Stanford University Press.

Warburg, J. (1968). *Crosscurrents in the Middle East*. New York: Atheneum.

Wilcox, Dennis L. (1967). *English Language Newspapers Abroad*. Detroit: Gale Research.

Africa in World Politics:
The Case of the Organisation of African Unity and the Middle Eastern Conflict
S.K.B. Asante

The Arab-Israeli conflict has intruded into the African political arena since 1955, when at the Afro-Asian conference at Bandung, Israel was criticised in a resolution adopted by twenty-eight nations who supported the rights of the Arab people of Palestine.[1]

The Arab-Israeli issue was raised again at the very first conference of Independent African States held in Accra in April 1958. However, in spite of the pressure on the part of the African Arab countries to gain the support of the sub-Saharan states, the trend, by and large, was to exclude the Middle East from the deliberations of African councils. Consequently, at the 1960 Conference of Independent African States held in Cairo, Egypt was unable to obtain African support for a resolution calling for sanctions against Israel.[2] In contrast, at the Casablanca Conference held in 1961 three African states (Ghana, Guinea and Mali) joined Egypt and Morocco in "linking the problem of Palestine with the general theme of the defence of independence and security on the African continent." They also considered Israel as an "instrument of imperialism and neo-colonialism, not only in the Middle East but also in Africa and Asia."[3]

By 1962, Gamal Abdel Nasser, the Egyptian leader, had realized that he must play down the Israeli question in order to avoid alienating certain African governments; and in 1963, the North African states decided to exclude the question of Israel from the agenda of the Addis Ababa Conference, a move which was interpreted as a desire to place the objective of the conference — African Unity — above all others. While Nasser acquiesced in this resolution.[4]

The decision not to discuss the Israeli question at the inaugural meeting of the OAU should not be explained only in terms of the Arabs' interest in the creation of the Organization of African Unity. For Egypt's new, low-key policy was predicated on Nasser's desire to normalize relations with conservative French-speaking African states with whom Egypt had no diplomatic relations prior to 1963. For this same reason the Egyptian leader did not press the OAU

Summit Conferenceheld in Cairo in July 1964 to adopt a resolution on the Middle East. He only made "a general call to understanding that important key to African unity."[5] It should be noted, however, that Algeria proposed a boycott against Israel on the ground that the Arab minority in Israel was subjected to "a most deplorable form of racial discrimination." In anticipation of the Arab states' resolution at the United Nations General Assembly of 1975 in which Zionism was equated with racism, President Ahmed Ben Bella in 1964 compared the policy of racial discrimination followed by Israel with that of South Africa[6]: African governments, however, were not ready to endorse Algeria's call for the boycott of Israeli economic and technical assistance.In response to the argument that the assistance Israel was able to give was not her own but indirect assistance from the United States and other Western countries, Tom Mboya of Kenya declared that the actions of African states "should not be influenced by such an argument, for we receive direct aid from the United States already." In the same way," he continued, "some Arab countries receive aid from the Soviet Union now, and we will not refuse to accept aid from them on this account." Mboya concluded that "all countries today either co-exist or are inter-dependent, relying on each other's generosity, assistance, or co-operation."[7]

Meanwhile, the two major contenders in the Middle East crisis — Egypt and Israel—had begun to concentrate on wooing African support for their own positions. Israeli's diplomatic offensive in Africa was swift and spectacular. Up to 1956, Israel had practically no presence in Africa—only an embassy in South Africa and a consulate general in Kenya. This situation changed radically and dramatically in the next few years. Shortly after Ghana's attainment of independence, formal diplomatic relations with Israel, at embassy level, were established in 1957. The friendly and cordial relations between Ghana and Israel were characterised by mutually beneficial co-operation in many fields, principally, economic, commercial and cultural. To cite a few examples, Israel had, since 1957, been offering scholarships for training Ghanaians in medicine, agriculture, farm management,communications, rural and community development and business promotion.[8] Also, Israel provided Ghana with experts to advise on methods of improving her agriculture and horticulture, marketing, banking and economic planning. The Black Star Line, Ghana's National Shipping Line, was first established as a joint venture between the Government of Ghana and the Israeli Zim Shipping Line. In addition, cultural ties developed into the conclusion of cultural agreements between the two countries. It was the desire of both countries to increase their store of knowledge and understanding of the peoples and potentials of the two countries as a means of promoting international peace. The last cultural agreement between Israel and Ghana was signed on March 1, 1973.[9]

Israel decided to concentrate on Ghana for two main reasons. First, Israel hoped that this newly independent state would be looked upon as an example of what Israel could do for Africa in the fields of economic, technical, medical and cultural developments. Secondly, Israel recognized Kwame Nkrumah's potential for becoming the spokesman for Africa. It was thought that support for Nkrumah might lead to a weakening of Nasser's role in Africa. The striking success of Israel's aid to Ghana aroused the interest of other countries, and Israel found that the Ghana model served as a valuable pattern for Israel's economic activities in other parts of Africa. The other African states welcomed Israel's economic aid. This was because the Israeli model for economic development was attractive to many African leaders who did not accept either capitalism or communism as proper vehicles for development. In addition, Israel's small size helped allay any fear that Israeli aid might be linked to colonial ambitions.[10]

Thus the Israeli aid programme grew rapidly to encompass several sub-Saharan countries. By 1961, therefore, Israel was represented in 16 independent African countries. By 1970, more than one-half of the member states of the OAU, 21 in all, had cooperation treaties with Israel. Israeli experts and personnel of various sorts in Africa numbered 21,483 in 1971, as opposed to only 530 in Latin America. Thus, Israel's isolation in the Middle East led her to be an important practitioner of Realpolitik. But what were the main objectives of Israel's African policy? first, containment of Arab influence, through military assistance, if necessary; secondly, extension of economic relations with the non-Arab African states since Israel's logical economic partners, the Middle Eastern Arab states, were unwilling to engage in any transactions with her; and thirdly, gaining diplomatic support among non-Arab African states for use against the Arabs within the OAU and the United Nations. Trade ties as well as strategic political considerations were also important as long as the Arab-Israeli conflict continued. It was also argued that the building up of friendship on the African continent might at least prevent the Arab states from building boycott walls around Israel in Africa.[11] On the whole it can be said that Israel's policy towards Africa was a mixture of enlightened self-interest and what might be called altruism. Apart from developing fruitful economic ties with Africa countries, Arnold Rivkin has argued that Israel also hoped to develop investment opportunities which "afford employment opportunities for her technicians, provide a return on capital invested and, in sterling areas, achieve savings in foreign exchange."[12] While giving free play to the material benefit they hoped to derive from

Africa, the Israelis couched their projected contribution to Africa in almost spiritual terms, as evidenced in various statements by Prime Minister David Ben-Gurion.[13]

Israel's bilateral agreements with a significant number of African states, and her consequent involvement in Africa's economic, cultural, technical and social developments, aroused Egyptian leaders who quickly detected the danger to Arab interests inherent in such Israeli activities. Egypt therefore decided to initiate a counter offensive with a view to tipping the balance in Africa in her favour.[14] Consequently, in 1960 the Arab League began to intensify its political activities in Africa. The Arab Information Committee drew up a complete plan to check and oppose the infiltration of Israel in Africa. This new campaign was aimed at "the enlightenment of African leaders on the real nature of Israel."[15]

On the economic level, Egypt indulged in massive efforts to compete with Israel for providing goods and services in Africa. To stimulate trade with Africa, Egyptian economic missions were despatched in large numbers to various African capitals, and two new shipping lines were established linking Suez and Alexandria to East and West African ports. The El-Nasr Company opened branches in several African capitals: Accra, Bamako, and Conakry (1961); Dakar, Douala, and Lagos (1962); Miamey (1963); Nuakchott (1964); and Brazzaville (1965). Trade exhibits were opened in various African cities to publicize Egyptian products. Trade figures for Egypt and several African countries in the 1960s show, for the most part, a steady rise in import and exports.

Besides, Egypt extended loans and credits to African governments to assist in financing industrial development programmes. Somalia, for example, was granted a five million pounds sterling loan in 1960. In the following year, Chad, Guinea and Mali each received long-term loans in the amount of six million pounds for funding construction and other development projects. In 1962, Nigeria was given a three million pounds loan. In addition, hundreds of Egyptian technicians and teachers were sent to various parts of Africa.[16] This was accompanied by student exchange programmes for Africa, and scholarships were granted to African students to study in Egyptian educational institutions. In the year 1960 alone, 2,840 scholarships were given to African students—primarily from Chad, Guinea, Nigeria, Senegal, Somalia and Zanzibar—to study in Egypt.[17]

As a result of these activities, African states found themselves thrust into a cross-current between Israel and the Arab States. On the one hand, the Arab nations had supported both morally and materially the liberation struggle in Africa. On the other, the African states valued the economic and technical assistance they were being offered by Israel. Consequently, the independent African states were determined to keep the long-standing quarrel between the Arabs and Israel out of African politics. Their approach was a pragmatic one; they were eager to receive aid from whatever country it was available, and Israel was willing to provide them with moderate but valuable amounts of assistance in agriculture, industry and defence. It was not surprising, therefore, that African states attempted to maintain cordial relations with both Israel and the Arab states.

However, by the mid-1960s relations between the African states and Israel had started to change. In a recent scholarly work, Elliott P. Skinner has noted a number of factors which appear to have accounted for the change in relations between Israel and Africa even before the "June War" of 1967. Among them was the general attitude of Israel's Western friends in Africa towards the Israeli ventures in the continent. The British, for example, were most unhappy about their gradual eclipse in Africa by Israel in providing military aid to Ghana, Serra Leone, Tanzania, Uganda and Zambia. Fear among European expatriates led to their opposition of Israeli ventures in Africa, and the attempt to "sabotage or frustrate their relations with the Africans."[18] British expatriate officials refused co-operation with Israeli fishing instructors where their help was essential.[19] Besides, the experts of the United Nations Development occasionally accused Israeli technicians of attempting to turn U.N. Development Programme "projects into purely Israeli ones, thereby ignoring the contributions of other states."[20]

Perhaps the most important factor which seriously threatened to jeopardize Israel's relations with the Africans was the conflicting national interests between Africa and Israel as expressed in their voting behaviour in the United Nations. In the primary interest of her survival and the "protection of Jews in the diaspora, especially those in Soviet Russia," Israel allied herself closely with the United States on most major issues. On the other hand, the major political interest of the African nations since the Conference of Independent African States held in Accra in April, 1958 was to give all possible assistance to the dependent people in Africa in their struggle to achieve self-determination and independence.[21] It was the common stand on colonialism and racial expression that brought the representatives of 31 African States to the Summit Conference at Addis Ababa in May 1963 where the Organization of African Unity was born. At this conference some African leaders saw the liberation of the rest of Africa as a matter of duty; others like Ben Bella saw it as a prerequisite for peace, unity and prosperity, and as a matter of national interest closely related to their own country's security and economic stability.[22] Both in speeches and resolutions, the issue of the liberation of the rest of Africa was emphasized.

This major interest of Africans ran counter to that of some America's allies, especially Portugal and South Africa. As a result, the African states were often in sharp conflict with the United States and by extension with her allies. This posed a problem for Israel who initially attempted to balance its interests in the West with those in Africa. The tactic she adopted was to abstain in those U.N. ballots "which pitted the Africans against the West and even voted with the Africans."[23] Hence her support in 1961 of the imposition of economic sanctions upon South Africa when the anti-apartheid resolution was presented at the United Nations, for in the view of Mrs. Golda Meir, Israeli's Foreign Minister, "Israel cannot allow itself to miss any opportunity to contribute to the removal of racialism."[24] Israel was, however, unable to maintain this position for long. By the mid-1960s, her voting behavior changed. Not only did Israel abstain from voting on the anti-colonial declarations in the United Nations, she also refused to vote against South Africa on the racial question. Significantly, too, "Israeli submachine guns sold in Europe were alleged to have armed Portuguese troops in Angola."[25] This development led to initiation of diplomatic counter-offensive or adoption of an anti-Israel line by some African states. For example, Israel's attempt to establish a consul-generalship in Zanzibar in 1965 was refused by the Tanzanians. Many African capitals began to open their doors to the representatives of the Palestine Liberation Organisation (P.L.O.). The May 1965 Afro-Asian People's Solidarity Organisation which was held in Winneba, Ghana, supported "resolutions which endorsed the Palestinian struggle against Israel."[26] In spite of all the pressure, diplomatic relations between Israel and the African states continued undisturbed until the outbreak of full-scale hostilities between Israel and her Arab neighbours on 5 June, 1967.

The Six-Day War marked the first turning-point in Israeli-African relations. It was the beginnin of the O.A.U.'s confrontation with Israel. The June War of 1967 had political and diplomatic repercussions among the African states. While Guinea was the only tropical African country which broke relations with Israel when the war broke out, almost all the African states were forced to formulate a policy on the Middle East problem or review existing policy.[27] However, the conflict on the whole produced a stand-off between the Arab states and Israel in their relations with black Africa. Many observers considered this development a victory for Israel, since Egypt hoped and Israel feared that the crisis might win friends in Africa for Cairo and lose some for Jerusalem. On the contrary, the few political gains and losses by each side seemed small and roughly balanced.[28] Somalia's call in 1967 for an emergency OAU summit to enable the organisation to take a stand on the "June War" was rejected by the majority of the OAU members. It was argued that the United Nations alone was the appropriate authority to deal with the conflict. The African states did not have a united position when the emergency session of the UN General Assembly met in July 1967. Fourteen of a total of thirty-two African states voted with Egypt in favour of the Yugoslav resolution which called for the immediate withdrawal of Israeli forces to the positions held before the outbreak of the Six-Day war. Eight states joined Israel in voting against the resolution. Ten nations abstained from voting in an attempt to avoid any entanglement in the Arab-Israeli conflict.[29] A Latin-American resolution backed by the United States found a relatively higher degree of support among African delegates. Seventeen African representatives voted in favour of the resolution that linked withdrawal to the end of the state of belligerency and made it conditional upon discussion. Only ten states joined Egypt in casting negative votes. Another five nations joined Israel in abstaining.[30]

The African states again took a position on the Middle East when the Assembly of Heads of State and Government met in Kinshasa in September 1967. The meeting chose to adopt a "Declaration" rather than "resolution" on the Middle East crisis. The African leaders carefully abstained from calling Israel "agressor" and merely expressed concern at "the grave situation that prevails in the United Arab Republic, an African country whose territory is partially occupied by a foreign power." All that they offered to Egypt was "sympathy" and a promise to work within the United Nations in order to secure the evacuation of the United Arab Republic's territory.[31] It was a carefully worded resolution.

The "June War" showed the Israeli leaders that seven years of effort in Africa was proving largely fruitless. For the years following the war saw an intensification of Arab states' diplomatic counter-offensive in Africa. Libya's oil royalties and Saudi Arabia's, Kuwait's and Bahrein's gold reserves gave the Arabs a financial footing in some African countries. Not only did the Arab states multiply heir diplomatic missions south of the Sahara between 1967 and 1973, but also many African capitals began to open their doors to the representatives of the Palestine Liberation Organization (P.L.O.). The Arab states particularly stressed the need to demonstrate Islamic solidarity and expressed willingness to provide African governments with capital needed for economic development. In 1972 alone, King Faisal of Suadi Arabia paid visits to Chad, Mauritania, Niger, Senegal and Uganda.[32]

As a result of these activities, Israeli-African relations, which were euphoric until the Six-Day War, began steadily to be marked since then by progressive mutual disenchantment. Between March and December 1972, five African states—Uganda (March), and Chad (November), and Niger, Mali and Congo (December—followed

Guinea's 1967 example by breaking diplomatic ties with Israel. African political leaders no longer hesitated to make violent attacks on their former allies, the Israelis. For example, President Nguouabi of Congo turned his back on the Israelis, whom he called "the spearhead of imperialism in central Africa." Although countries like Nigeria and Senegal managed to maintain good relations with Israel despite mounting Arab diplomatic pressures,[33] the majority of African states came out gradually in support of Security Council Resolution 242 (November 1967),[34] and the OAU promised to work within the UN to bring about the withdrawal of foreign troops from Egyptian territory occupied in 1967. Such support was based on the concern of the African states over the question of territorial integrity, as well as the fear that they might one day find themselves in a similar situation if South Africa were to decide to follow the Israeli precedent of preemptive strike against neighbouring African countries. Thus the defeat of the Arabs in the "June War" of 1967 added a new dimension to the situation. Whereas in the period preceding the war "the conflict had been presented to sub-Saharan Africa in terms of the plight of the Palestinians," after it the issue at stake "became that of the territories which Israel had occupied, particularly those which formed part of Egypt,"[35] a founder member of the OAU.

Arab pressure and counter-diplomatic offensive finally began to pay off. At the Seventh OAU Summit meeting of September 1970 at Addis Ababa a specific item was included on the agenda for the first time, under the title "The Continuing Occupation of Part of the Territories of the UAR by Foreign Forces."[36] Although a precedent had been achieved, the resolution did maintain a certain impartiality. Concern was expressed over "The occupation of a sister state," yet at the same time the resolution stipulated that the UN Security Council's Resolution 242 of 22 November 1967 should be applied in its totality—without making withdrawal an essential precondition to settlement.[37]

The OAU actually began to take a more active role, however, in the June 1971 Summit meeting at Addis Ababa. It was at this meeting that the organization abandoned its objectivity. The agenda title was this time quite explicit, "The Continued Aggression against the UAR." The resolution's title makes manifest the political intent of that document.Under the title "Resolution on the Continued Aggression Against the United Arab Republic,"[38] the OAU proceeded to issue a forceful call for action for "strict implementation" of UN Security Council Resolution 242 of 22 November 1967. Its basic thrust was "full support" for the Jarring Mission, especially for Jarring's initiative of 8 February 1971, "as a practical step for establishing a just and lasting peace in the Middle East." The operative principle is "immediate withdrawal of Israeli armed forces from all Arab Territories to the lines of 5 June 1967," and the impasse of the Jarring Mission is blamed on "Israeli defiance" in refusing to withdraw to Egypt's international frontier.[39]

This was the most forceful OAU resolution on the Middle East crisis since the 1967 war, especially since it called for a specific African initiative directed towards implementation of Security Council Resolution 242 and renewal of Egyptian-Israeli indirect talks under Jarring's auspices. That initiative is expressed in the resolution's request to President Ould Daddah of Mauritania, the then chairman of the OAU, to "consult with the Heads of State and Government so that they use their influence to ensure the full implementation of this resolution." Under such general terms, the African continental organization ventured for the first time out of its traditional politico-diplomatic bailiwick, which has been governed by the OAU's "unwritten principle of dealing closely with 'African' affairs."[40] Following the African diplomatic tradition developed under the OAU umbrella for peaceful settlement of disputes in Africa, a ten-man committee was formed to contact the leaders of Israel and Egypt in an attempt to resume the UN mission, which had been grounded because of Israel's refusal to accept Jarring's proposals. This accorded with the interests of Egypt. It could expect to continue its advantageous internal position within the OAU and the UN. Israel, on the other hand, apparently did not object to the mision because there was no insistence that the Committee would have to carry out the June 1971 resolution and because it did not want to endanger its good bilateral relations with many African states.

The OAU was careful in the selection of heads of state to serve on the Middle East Peace Committee. Chaired by an Arab sympathizer, President Moktar Ould Dabbah of Mauritania, the Committee included heads of state representing countries known to have good relations with either the Arab states or Israel, or considered neutral. They were Cameroon, Ethiopia, the Ivory Coast, Kenya, Liberia, Mauritania, Nigeria, Senegal, Tanzania and Zaire. Out of this a sub-committee of four headed by President Leopold Senghor of Senegal was set up in August 1971 at a meeting in Zaire, Kinshasha, to represent the OAU on a fact-finding mission. The African leaders hoped that this OAU decision to mediate the Arab–Israeli conflict would serve the following objectives: First, to restore peace and tranquility in the northeastern section of the African continent since Egypt is an African state whose territory is partially occupied by a foreign power. Second, to show appreciation for the support the Arabs had rendered the liberation struggle in Africa in international conferences—African, Afro-Asian and non-alignment—as well as in the UN. Third, as an indirect benefit, the mission would help African states to avoid making a choice between Israel and the Arab states since it had become increasingly difficult to maintain diplomatic relations with both sides. Further, the mission was to show that small and distinterested nations could and should play a role in any Middle East settlement to reduce the influence and involvement of the super-powers. This would be a way for African leaders to prove their independence from the Great Powers, since all of them subscribed to a non-aligned policy even though they are generally closer to the West than to the Communist countries. The four leaders—Presidents Senghor of Senegal, Ahamadu Ahidjo of Cameroon, Mobutu Sese Seko of Zaire, and Yakubu Gowon of Nigeria—tended to be moderate in African terms. They undoubtedly saw this as an opportunity to increase the active participation of the African states in the international system. At the same time, they shared an awareness of the effect an important international role and the attendant publicity can have in enhancing their domestic political positions.[41]

The conclusions of the "Four Wise Men," as indicated by reports of their deliberations, showed somewhat more sympathy to the Israeli position and greater objectivity than was contained in the OAU resolution of June 1971. The mission was unable to find a compromise between the Egyptian demand for immediate withdrawal and the Israeli insistence upon negotiating first. The interpretation of the African memorandum, and the Egyptian and Israeli responses, caused a division of African opinion in the General Assembly, or allowed that division to come to the surface to a greater degree. Such a division in African ranks was caused by conflicting interpretations of the meaning of the African initiatives, the African memorandum, and the responses to it. The mission, however, did obtain from both sides expressions of a desire to resume the Jarring mission, but could not overcome the impasse on the terms for its continuation.

The lack of agreement among the Committee of Ten about the report of the "Four Wise Men" made them reluctant to support it at the United Nations in December 1971. Thus the Middle East debate at the Twenty-Sixth UN General Assembly witnessed a display of disunity by the OAU states over their own committee's memorandum. When members held meetings in the corridors of the UN before the Assembly debate they failed to reach a consensus.[42] Against the fifteen African states which insisted that the recommendations of the "Four Wise Men" form the "basis of the UN resolution there was a majority of eighteen states which wished to pledge their support for Egypt's position."[43] Thus the bulk of African votes went to the 21-power Afro-Asian resolution which called for the "withdrawal of Israeli armed forces from territories occupied in the recent conflict" and the "termination of all claims or states of belligerency and respect for the acknowledgement of the sovereignty, territorial integrity and political independence of every state in the area and its right to live in peace within secure and recognised boundaries free from threats or acts of force." It also expressed "full support for all the efforts of the Special Representative to implement Security Council Resolution 242 (1967)." The resolution passed with a vote of 79 for, 7 against, and 36 abstentions.[44]

The general shift of views among the African delegations from the Committee report may be explained in terms of the change in political environment. In the United Nations, Egypt could use leverage unavailable within the Middle East regional system itself.[45] It could call upon the solidarity of the African states with a fellow member of the OAU and the "Third World," who tend to vote together on North–South issues such as decolonisation and economic development.[46] The approximately 14:1 ratio of Arab to Israel votes in the UN could also be important on votes of particular concern to Africans, such as the liberation of Southern Africa. More particularly, the Arab votes could be important in elections for major positions and committees within the UN system.

The real decisive turning point in the OAU–Israeli relations came at the Rabat OAU Summit meeting in June 1972. Here, the OAU for the first time "took an emphatically non-conciliatory stand on the Middle East issue."[47] A strongly worded pro-Egyptian resolution was passed which denounced Israel's negative and obstructive attitude which had prevented the resumption of the Jarring mission. It called upon Israel "to declare openly its adherence to the principle of no annexing (of) land by force" and "to withdraw immediately from all occupied Arab territories to the lines existing before June 1967." The conference also called upon all United Nations members to refrain from supplying Israel with weapons, military equipment or moral support."[48]

The Rabat resolutions represented a hardening of the African position. The change in the African attitude was a direct consequence of Africa's deep disillusionment with the Western powers.

It is against this background of OAU's disappointment in the Western powers that Africa began to reappraise the whole Middle East conflict. Scholars like Zdenek Cervenka have argued that the growing disillusion with the Western nations led Africa to search for new allies—the Arab states.[49] This, however, appears to be too much of an oversimplification of the realities of the situation. For it is quite obvious that the position of Israel in Africa was in fact not compatible with the geo-political situation in this continent where there are some eight Arab countries and where there are strong Moslem communities. Besides, throughout the African leaders tried to indicate as solemnly as possible why they disapproved of the Israeli attitude in the Middle East conflict. They could not forgive the Israelis for having deliberately separated themselves from Egypt, a member state of the OAU, a part of its national territory. The disillusionment with the Western powers led Africans not so much as to search for new allies as to vigorously reassert themselves in the politics of the time in the light of their own long range interests and the principles contained in the OAU Charter.

The African states which met in Addis Ababa in May 1973 to commemorate the tenth anniversary of the founding of the OAU could not ignore the Middle East as they did in 1963. They posed a tough resolution warning that "the attitude of Israel might lead OAU member states to take, at the African level, individually or collectively, political and economic measures against it, in conformity with the principles contained in the OAU and UN Charters.[50] It should be noted that the Addis Abab resolution represented a significant move in the direction of the Egyptian position; it reflected the growing opposition among African nations to continued Israeli occupation of Arab lands. When Israel blatantly refused to show any consideration for what seemed to be the "legitimate concerns" of Africa, African states felt compelled to squarely meet the Israeli challenge. By November 9, after the Yom Kippur War, all of the black African states, with the exception of South Africa's satellites, Botswana, Lesotho, Swaziland and Malawi, had ruptured relations with Israel.[51]

Following the October War of 1973, the OAU Council of Ministers met in November to consider the Algerian proposal for "consideration of the current Middle East situation with particular references to its effects in Africa."

The OAU's failure in its attempted mediation of the Egypt/Israeli sector of the Middle Eastern conflict precipitated a series of transformations in the international relationships between Africa and Israel. These transformations isolated Israel, and brought to a dramatic end Africa's long period of romance with Israel. Regardless of what happens in the relations between the Arabs and the Israelis or between these two groups and the great powers, it is clear that relations between the African states and Israel have entered a new phase. However, Israel's activities in Black Africa since the 1973 Middle East crisis would seem to suggest that this new phase is neither spectacular nor significantly different from the pre-1973 Israeli African relations. For according to official sources, Israeli exports to independent African countries have almost doubled despite the almost complete break in relations. Almost all these exports were bound for those countries with which Israel had no official relations.[52]

It is worth noting, too, that friendly embassies in at least ten African states have provided facilities for Israel, whilst commercial activities by Israeli private companies are said to be booming. These included construction projects by the Histadrut's Solel Boneh in Nigeria, industrial activities by the giant Koor syndicate, building projects in Kenya, hotels in the Ivory Coast and tourist trade development. Besides, a corps of about 100 Israeli technical experts, seconded by Western enterprises in Africa, continue to work in rural and labor projects; and African administrators and students continue to study in Israel. The Histadrut's Afro-Asian Institute, which in the past has trained over 6000 Africans from 30 countries in labor and cooperative organisations, has received as estimated 900 African students since 1973.[53] Thus, despite what many people might have thought, Israel's activities in Black Africa had not ended with the 1973 Middle East War.

The second major transformation which the OAU's intrusion into the Middle East crisis precipitated was the emergence of new kind of Arab-African solidarity. Its essence was that the Arab countries managed for the first time to convince Black Africa that Israel was a real threat to the peace and security of the continent. As a result, Egypt's struggle for the recovery of its territory occupied by Israel was put on the same level with the liberation of southern Africa from the white supremacy which tops the list of the OAU priorities. Thus the Arab states and the OAU have been brought together in the process of harmonization of policies regarding both the Middle East conflict and the southern African conflict. This has created more ideological interaction between the Palestine Liberation Organization and the African Liberation Movements.

It cannot be denied, however, that since the forging of the Afro-Asian alliance at the emergency session of the OAU Ministerial Council at Addis Ababa in November 1973, the relations between the independent African states and the Arabs have been one of change and continuity. On many occasions the Arab's professions of brotherhood and solidarity appeared to the majority of Africans to be nothing more than empty rhetoric. This was particularly evidenced by the Arabs' persistent rejection of OAU plea for preferential oil prices for African states, when the soaring oil prices were dealing a devastating blow to the development plans of these countries.[54] By 1974 the cost of oil imports to thirty African states which did not have enough oil of their own had risen from $500m in 1973 to $1300m.[55]

The extent of African disillusionment with the Afro–Arab cooperation was reflected in their confrontation with the Arabs at the 1976 OAU Kampala summit. The summit significantly failed to reach agreement on a proposed charter which would have institutionalised Afro-Arab cooperation.

Furthermore, the Arabs' call for the expulsion of Israel from the United Nations was opposed by five African states: Ghana, Sierra Leone, Senegal, Liberia and Zaire. Subsequently at the "Group of 77" conference in Lima, Peru, and at the United Nations in November 1975 when voting on Resolution 3379, identifying Zionism as a form of racism, the Africans and the Arabs were not noticeably attached to one another. Four African states voted against the resolution while twelve abstained. Even the election of a new President for the African Development Bank was to lead to rupture.

By 1976, however, the increase in the economic and military cooperation between Israel and Africa's inveterate enemy number one, South Africa, had brought many "disillusioned" African States back to firm support of the Arab cause. This was reinforced by the visit of the South African Premier John Vorster to Israel in April 1976 and the attendant suspicion about Israel's involvement in the South African nuclear programme. Besides, the Entebbe raid by the Israeli commandos on 28 June 1976 which was described as "the rape of Africa" caused a great deal of resentment among many African states who saw this as a threat to international peace and security. There were the underlying fears that Israel's dangerous precedent could be imitated by South Africa. All this led to a search for new forms of Afro–Arab cooperation which was inaugurated at the joint meeting of the Council of Foreign Ministers of the Arab League and the OAU held in Dakar in April 1976.[56] The March 1977 Afro–Arab summit in Cairo confirmed the cooperation between the Arabs and the independent African states.

The Arab-African alliance, if fully developed, could play a decisive role in attaining both political and economic objectives of the OAU. Economic cooperation would bring together those who possess raw materials, energy sources and capital. Food supplies from unexploited agricultural land in Africa to arid countries in the Middle East would reduce the Arab's dependence on the West. For it is ridiculous, as President Kaunda rightly noted at the recent Afro–Arab summit in Cairo that "Zambia still buys Saudi Arabian oil from New York and Arab states still buy African tobacco, tea and copper products from European markets."[57] No doubt Afro–Arab cooperation could become mutually beneficial. The total result of close cooperation would likely result in the emergence of a formidable power in international politics.

The OAU's active involvement in the Middle East conflict is also significant in some other respects. In the first place, despite its temporary importance, the OAU 1971 mission to Cairo and Jerusalem did little to enhance the long range goal of facilitating a peaceful settlement in the Middle East. The mission shows how difficult it is for small states in the periphery of the international system to help to resolve major conflicts in whch the Great Powers have palpable interests.[58] However, in relation to its immediate stated aim of bringing about the resumption of the Jarring mission, the OAU could claim partial success since Dr. Jarring's mission was officially resumed in August 1972, although little credit was given to the OAU for this.[59] Secondly, it would appear that the United Nations was strengthened by the OAU's involvement in the Middle East conflict, since a regional organization with about one-third of the UN members supported the continuation of an important mediatory role for the UN. For the OAU itself, the attempt at being a quasi-intermediary among parties with whom it would like to remain on good terms provided experience in international transactions, particularly on an issue with global ramifications. The episode indicated that such a task, even though it was supposed to relate to other small states, could be overwhelmingly complex. As stated above, many African leaders came to realize the problems involved in trying to act in conflict situations with diametrically opposed parties which "touch upon the primary interests of actors in the international system."[60] The future will indicate if the African leaders will make finer distinctions among types of conflicts and their protagonists before undertaking such active role again. In any case, they have been able to gain a greater awareness of the costs and gains for active intermediaries. Then, too, each of the African participants in the OAU Middle East mission was undoubtedly able to improve his image domestically as having played an important international role.

Notes

1.   See George McTurnan Kahin, *The Asian-African Conference, Bandung, Indonesia, April 1955* (Ithaca, New York: Cornell University Press, 1956), p. 82.

2.   *New York Times*, 25 June 1960.

3.   Doudou Thiam, *The Foreign Policy of African States* (London, 1965), pp. 65–66.

4.   Tareq Y. Ismael, "Religion and UAR African Policy," *The Journal of Modern African Studies*, Vol. 6, No. 1, May 1968, p. 68.

5.   *Africa —Political, Social and Cultural*, Vol. 1, No. 7, July 1–31, 1964, p. 126.

6.   *Ibid.*, p. 122.

7.   Tom Mboya, *Freedom and After* (London, 1964), p. 232.

8.   J. H. Sackey, "Should Ghana Have Broken Relations with Israel?", a paper presented at a symposium organised by the Political Science Association of the University of Ghana, 28 November 1973.

9. *Ibid.* Also, see Z. Y. Hershlag, ed., *Israel–Africa Cooperation* (Research Project on Israel–Africa Cooperation, Tel Aviv University, Israel, 1973) and see also M. Mushkat, *Israel —A Model of Economic Development?* Intereconomics, Hamburg, No. 8, 1970.

10. Israel's relations with Ghana were not wholeheartedly welcomed by Ghanaians .Fears were expressed as to the eventual Israeli domination of Ghana's economy. These were made evidence in Parliamentary Debates, 29 October, 1959.

11. *The New York Times*, 16 October, 1960.

12. A. Rivkin, "Israel and the Afro-Asian World," *Foreign Affairs*, Vol. 37, No. 3, 1959, p. 495 and see also M. Mushkat, *Die Israelisch–Afrikanische Zusammenarbeit*, International African Forum, Muenchen, No. 7–8, 1971.

13. Ben-Gurion, "Israel's Security and Her International Position," *Israel Government Year Book*, 5720 (1959–1960), p. 69. Cited in Elliott P. Skinner, "African States and Israel: Uneasy Relations in a World of Crises," *Journal of African Studies*, Vol. 2, No. 1, Spring 1975, p. 5.

14. Doudou Thiam, *op. cit.*, p. 62.

15. Jacques Baulin, *The Arab Role in Africa* (Baltimore, 1962), pp. 46–49.

16. "UAR Technical and Cultural Aid to African Countries," *Remarques Africaines*, 19 October 1967, pp. 517–20, in Ismael, Appendix III.

17. Baulin, *op. cit.*, pp. 77–78.

18. Elliott, P. Skinner, *op. cit.*, p. 13.

19. Mordechai E. Kreinin, *Israel and Africa* (New York, 1964), p. 166, and see also M. Mushkat, "Gibt es Besonderheiten in der Israelischen Entwicklugshilfepolitik? *Deutsche Geselschaft fuer Auswaertige Politik*, Bonn, 1969.

20. Skinner, p. 14.

21. Conference of Independent African States' resolution on "The Future of the Dependent Territories in Africa." Cited in Zdenek Cervenka, "Major Policy Shifts in the Organisation of African Unity, 1963–1973," in K. Ingham, ed., *Foreign Relations of African States* (London, 1974), p. 326.

22. Proceedings of the Summit Conference of Independent African States, Addis Ababa, OAU Secretariat, 1963, Vol. 1, p. 27.

23. Skinner, p. 14.

24. Samuel Decalo, "African and the Mid-Eastern War," *Africa Report*, vol. 12, No. 7, October 1967, p. 10.

25. Kreinin, *Israel and Africa*, p. 179.

26. Skinner, p. 15.

27. Sackey, *op. cit.*

28. *Ibid.*

29. *The New York Times*, 5 July, 1967.

30. *Ibid.*

31. *African Research Bulletin*, vol. 14, no. 9, 15 October 1967, p. 856.

32. "Islam: African Advance," *African Confidential*, vol. 15, no. 7, 5 April, 1974, p. 2.

33. For a detailed discussion of Nigeria's relations with Israel, see O. Aluko, "Israel and Nigeria: Continuity and Change in their Relationship," *African Review*, vol. 4, no. 1, 1974, pp. 43–59.

34. The operative paragraphs of Resolution 242 include the following:

(a) Withdrawal of Israeli armed forces from territories occupied in the 1967 conflict;

(b) termination of all claims or states of belligerency and respect for sovereignty, territorial integrity, and political independence of every state in the area and its right to live in peace within secure and recognised boundaries, free from threats or acts of force. Further paragraphs refer to freedom of navigation through international waterways in the area, a just solution of the refugee problem, territorial inviolability, and establishment of demilitarized zones.

35. Ran Kochan, "An African Peace Mission in the Middle East: The One Man Initiative of President Senghor," *African Affairs*, vol. 72, no. 287, April 1973, p. 187.

36. For text see AHG/Res. 62 (vii) Addis Ababa, 4 September 1970.

37. See Ran Kochan, p. 188.

38. For text see AHG/Res. 66 of 22 June 1971, Addis Ababa.

39. For details see Yassin El-Ayouty, "The OAU and the Arab–Israeli Conflict: A Case of Mediation that Failed," in Yassin El-Ayouty, ed., *The Organization of African Unity After Ten Years: Comparative Perspective* (New York, 1975), pp. 189–212.

40. Jan Woronoff, "OAU/Middle East," *Africa Report*, January 1972.

41. Susan A. Gitelson, "The OAU Mission and the Middle East Conflict," *International Organization*, vol. 27, no. 3, Summer 1973, p. 415.

42. Ran Kochan, *op. cit.*, p. 191.

43. *Ibid.*

44. General Assembly Resolution 2709 (xxvi) on 13 December 1971.

45. Susan Gitelson, *op. cit.*, p. 417.

46. See David A. Kay, "The Impact of African States on the United Nations," *International Organization*, vol. 23, no. 1, Winter 1967, pp. 20–47.

47. Ran Kochan, *op. cit.*, p. 195.

48. A. H. Res. 67 (ix). See also *African Research Bulletin*, vol. 9, no. 6, 15 July 1972, p. 2498; *New York Times*, 15 June 1972.

49. Zdenek Cervenka, "The Organization of African Unity and the African–Arab Solidarity," an unpublished paper sent to the author in December 1973.

50. OAU Resolution, AHG/Res. 70 (x).

51. *New York Times*, 17 February 1974.

52. *Africa*, no. 68, April 1977, pp. 41–2.

53. *Ibid.*

54. For details see Z. Cervenka, *The Unfinished Quest for African Unity: Africa and the OAU* (London, 1977), pp. 167–8.

55. *Ibid.*

56. *Ibid.*

57. *Africa*, no. 68, April 1977, pp. 41–2. Adeoyo Akinsanya has in a recent article made some interesting speculations on the future relations between Africa and the Arab world. See "The Afro–Arab Alliance: Dream or Reality," *African Affairs*, vol. 75, no. 301, October 1976, pp. 525–529.

58. See Jorge I. Dominiques, "Mice that Do Not Roar. Some Aspects of International Politics in the World's Peripheries," *International Organization*, vol. 25, no. 2, Spring 1971, pp. 175–208.

59. Dr. Jarring's official resumption of his mission appears to have been more directly related to the desire of Secretary-General Waldheim to reactivate the UN role. See Gitelson, p. 418.

60.*Ibid.*, p. 419.

One More Peace Scenario
for the Middle East

Mario'n Mushkat

Extreme nationalistic trends are still growing in our times in many parts of the world. The simultaneous deepening of the inter-dependence of all nations does not reduce them. The large and small, the rich and poor, the industrialized and underdeveloped nations, those called socialist and capitalist, nations that possess deadly weapons and nations that are almost unarmed, all of them increasingly interact and to a certain extent frequently become uniformised in their ways of life and culture. But at the same time they are divided by political systems and ideologies, religious and racial differences, standards of living and, above all, by socio-economic and strategic designs, and real and imaginery needs and interests.

Nationalism, therefore, has not yet been restricted by continually expanding powers and scopes of activities of various international organizations, like ecological, developmental and others. Nor has it been contained by the almost universal awareness that without limiting sovereign-oriented tendencies and the ensuing arms race the survival of our race becomes increasingly less certain in the nuclear era.

That is why one might safely assume that the national states, including those in the Middle East, will continue to exist, at least in the next decades. Yet, in 1964 the "Palestinian Liberation Organi-zation" (PLO) adopted the extreme line of liquidating a national State—the State of Israel (a member of the United Nations and legitimately recognized by more than 100 other states) and of reducing the Jewish residents of the planned in its place "Palestinian Democratic State" to five percent of the population (only those who lived there before 1917 and their offspring would be allowed to remain).

To use the wording of the known Austrian communist leader, B. Frei, this proposal, supported by different Arab states, is actually a new version of Hitler's "final solution."[1]

This genocidal plan has remained formally unchanged till today, in spite of various nebulous PLO declarations, permitting one to conclude that in the first stage it will acquiesce to the creation of a Palestinian state only in the territories occupied by Israel in the 1967 war.

There are no signs of the PLO's willingness to recognize Israel, even in the borders in which it existed before the Six Days War, or to meet even with those Israelis who accept the plans for the formation of a Palestinian state alongside Israel (as, *inter alia*, has been proved by the failure of the "New Outlook" and other symposia called for this purpose) or to consider seriously modes of common peaceful coexistence in a federal or other similar frameworks.

This is one reason more why even some Israeli friends of the Palestinian cause regard the latter PLO declarations with a high degree of suspicion, especially since they are proposed by an organization which still has not abandoned yet its terrorist tactics. Moreover, in the past, it entered into friendly relations with the former Idi Amin regime, and recently with Khomeini's government, as well as with other similar movements and systems that, like the new Iranian leaders, are inspired by the Nazi and similar anti-Israeli and militaristic sources and fanatical ideologies.

It is therefore difficult to expect that the Israelis will accept the "Palestinian Democratic State's" designs, recognize its speaker, the PLO, and negotiate what actually are the terms of their surrender, the more so since the memory of the Holocaust is still fresh as well as the memory of the Arab refusal to agree (a) to the decision of the League of Nations after World War One on the creation of a "National Home" for Jews in the Palestinian mandate territory which was, after all, their historical homeland; (b) to the formation of a bi-national state as postulated by the Jewish National Liberation Movement, the Zionist Organization, in the period between two world wars and before 1948 by the United Worker's Party, an important part of the latter movement; (c) to the United Nations' partition plan which postulated after World War Two the creation of a Palestinian State alongside the Jewish state; (d) the recognition of Israel after its establishment, a refusal which led to five bloody wars; and (e) to abandonment of aggressive plans after the first breakthrough in the Arab–Israeli relations, created by the Egyptian–Israeli Peace Treaty.

We also have to keep in mind that unlike the French expelled from Algeria, 95% of Israelis, if ordered or forced to leave the realm of the "Democratic Palestinian State" will not have a similar option. It is not merely a metaphor when some of them talk about the threat of being thrown into the sea or, at best, of accepting a life of discrimination and repression as they live in the present ghettos in Syria and Iraq.

Pierre Vermeylen, one-time member of the Belgian government, probably took all this into consideration when he stated as follows:

> On reproche à Israël de ne pas reconnaître les representants du peuple palestinien, l'O.P.P.
> Comment Israel pourrait-il le faire?
> L'O.L.P. s'est érigé en ennemi irréductible d' Israël et, sans pouvoir se prévaloir de l'accord de ses prétendus mandants, proclame ouvertement ne pas reconnaitre l'Etat d'Israël et vouloir sa destruction complète. Pour elle seuls les Juifs fixés en Israël avant 1948 pourraient y rester, sous la domination arabe.
> L'erreur commise par nous, lorsque nous avons toujours reculé devant les exigences d'Hitler, sans nous préserver du choc final, les Israëliens ne veulent pas la commetre.
> Il faut reconnaître qu'ils ont raison..
> N'oublions pas qu'Israel est dans la position de la Tchécoslovaquie de 1937 et de la Pologne de 1939.
> Les Israëliens, après deux millenairs de persécutions, ont le droit à notre soutien' nous devons, avant tout, les preserver de la destruction qui les menace.[2]

No similar explanation can be given for the Arab non-recognition of Israel. This is one reason more for the asymmetry of the belligerents' position. The consequence of asymmetry is the continuation of the Middle East Conflict and the growing threat to peace in the region and to world security. After all, we have to take into account the stakes of the superpowers in this oil-rich area. We should consider the Soviet presence in Ethiopia and South Yemen, as well as the USSR's ties with Syria, Iraq and still with Libya. And we should also consider the Israeli's determination to fight at all costs the PLO's plans to destroy their independence. It might also be worthwhile to recall in this context that the PLO's program seems to be utterly unrealistic, among other things also because of the lack of Arab consensus in this matter, which is reflected in the reluctance of many Arab states to support the PLO formally and effectively. They hesitate to do this for fear of the possibility that a Palestinian state might become a Soviet base, hostile to Muslim traditions and creed or a center used for undermining their governments.

They seem to prefer a solution for the Palestinian issue based on Jordanian and/or Syrian rule or condominium.

Not less dangerous, because it is certainly fraught with frictions and inter-Arab and Arab–Jewish conflicts, is the proposal to replace Israel and Jordan in their pre-1967 frontiers by Jewish and Arab cantons under presumably joint, but actually Palestinian rule. Not only Israel, but Jordan, too, will certainly oppose this plan. Besides, Jordan considers its own entity as the proper homeland for the Palestinians, if necessary, in a form of a federation or confederation.

On top of everything, the "cantonal" plan is extremely unjust. It denies the right of self-determination to Jews and to Jews only and this is at a time when the international community recognizes this right with regard even to tiny Pacific islands and other mini-communities. Even J. Galtung, who had renewed this plan a few years ago (in fact, this plan is already some generations old) had to admit that the desire of many Jews to resettle in Palestine has been irresistible and their nation-building there irreversible.[3]

This assessment of the problem contradicts Galtung's groundless supposition that Israel is a product of colonialism or neo-colonialist policies. In a sense, it is true that Israel coming into being was accelerated by the consequences of Hitler's extermination policies, the unwillingness of other European and not only European powers to save their Jewish victims from crematories, and earlier, of the British manoeuvers in the Palestinian mandate territory to set Jews and Arabs against each other in order to assure the continuation of their imperial reign in this area. All this paved the way for the establishment of the Jewish state, no one can doubt this.

Almost all former colonial metropolises, but especially the Tsarist, Ottoman, Nazi and Arab pogroms, as well as Soviet anti-Semitism added stimulus to Zionist dreams and to the efforts for their realization. Taking these facts into consideration, one can maintain that colonialism, too, contributed to the rebirth of the Jewish State, although one can claim with even greater certainty that it was mostly Arab inflexibility which contributed more strongly than anything else to the realization of Zionist dreams. Today, this inflexibility is one of the main causes of the continuation of the conflict. It is one of the main causes of the rise of fanaticism and rigidity among Israelis and of the growing superpower involvement in the area. However, while a large majority of Israelis still support the Shemtov–Yariv formula[4] (this formula states that it is in Israel's interests to recognize and negotiate with any Palestinian movement which will recognize Israel, including, therefore, the PLO supporters, provided they put an end to their rejectionist stand and terrorist policies), no parallel tendency, formally announced, can be found among Arabs. Movements similar to the Israeli "Peace Now" movement do not exist in the Arab countries. Nor are there "dove" groupings in these countries that would exert pressure on their governments, as has been done by Israeli doves from Labor and Liberal parties.

However, it will be wrong to conclude from all this that steps towards Palestinian–Israeli reconciliation should be given up as hopeless, that there is no chance of achieving coexistence between Jews and Arabs and that there is no point in continuing the search for the solution of their conflict. The previous analysis leads us to the conclusion that a workable compromise between the Jews of Israel and the Palestinian Arabs can only be achieved on a basis of reciprocity. The right to self-determination of both parties must be respected and all attempts to subjugate, destroy or undermine the legitimacy of one of the parties must cease.

There are no widely accepted scenarios for peace, and there are no visions of "what it will be like," since there is no official or even symbolic behavior by which the parties may show one another how they are likely to act in the transitional period towards a more certain future. Still, the promise of change is inherent not only in the Israeli–Egyptian Peace Treaty, or in the prolongation of the cease-fire by the still adversary parties in the region and in the outside pressure on them to enter into peace negotiations. What can also bring change is the growing awareness among Arabs that they are unable to defeat Israel and among Israelis that the prolongation of the *status quo*, of "no-war—no peace" situation is fraught with many complex and even threatening problems. As regards the Arabs, many of them are beginning to realize that the Israeli–Egyptian autonomy scheme for the Palestinians may lead to a successful realization of the Palestinian goal in a situation of peace.

Today, an increasing number of Israelis believe that without giving up the greater part of the territories occupied in 1967, the democratic foundations of their political system might be endangered, while a satisfactory solution of the Palestinian claim for independence is the only way to achieve peace in the region, to avoid a status of a minority and to keep the Jewish character of their state.

The decision to bring the conflict to an end in all its aspects and in this way, too, to clear the area of all forms of foreign intervention will have to be taken by the parties themselves. The parties must achieve a reasonable compromise as a basis for reconciliation. Probably, this goal will not be achieved in the near future because of Soviet opposition. The USSR has excluded itself from the peace-making process by breaking off its relations with Israel, and by relying on the aggressive elements in the Arab world. Thus it has paved the way for American superiority in the areas of former Soviet influence, and not only in Egypt. The attainment of real peace may be determined by a change in the Soviet position, but, above all, by a kind of a formal agreement between all actors in the region. The Arabs would have to renounce their aim to reverse the situation completely back to 1967 or even to 1947. The Israeli hawks, too, must stop dreaming about the permanence of the *status quo* on the eastern and northern fronts and must realize that the arrangement with Egypt and the American guarantees are not enough to bring about a true peace to the area. They will have to give priority to security issues over historical and emotional considerations, to acquiesce to the Palestinian claim for independence and accept the notion that only peace can bring security, reconciliation and co-operation.

All this is not easy, but possible. It will be necessary for the Palestinians to accept the existence of the State of Israel, and not only in the first stage of arrangement, but for ever. They will also have to accept the Egyptian–Israeli Peace Treaty and to realize that it also promises the beginning of a better future for them. If they continue to fight the Israeli–Egyptian autonomy scheme, they may lose everything, whereas its acceptance will, with time, bring the realization of the core of their national aspirations.

Strengthening this kind of tendency in both camps corresponds to the directives of the Security Council Resolution 242 of November 22, 1967, and to other documents, including the commitments of all parties to act in favor of peace which is necessary for furthering their enlightened interests.

In order to begin acting in this direction, it is important to avoid the perception of a legally dubious term "self-determination" in a dogmatic or an abstract way. "Self-determination" should not mean that the realization of the right of one party must abolish the right of another party. This watch-word conceived in absolute terms has frequently produced calamities for both the claimants and the opponents, while the compromise has almost always led to the fulfillment of all parties' national aspirations.

Needless to stress that for the sake of a proper settlement it is also necessary to avoid envisioning peace as a merely static process of implementing an international or other legal brief. On the contrary, it must be viewed as a dynamic process which only starts with the signing of the relevant documents.

It is clear that the way to a comprehensive peace in the Middle East, that is, peace between the Israelis and all the Arabs, and especially between Israeli Jews and Palestinian Arabs, must be one which will liberate the Jews from the nightmarish trauma of pogroms and persuade the Arabs to give up their hopes of becoming an exclusive and dominant factor in the area, through de-Zionization, that is, through the liquidation of the State of Israel. The Israeli–Egyptian Peace Treaty or its corrolaries or, if necessary, transitory arrangements between other parties, should be conceived as the starting point for a cultural, economic and even a political progress which must encompass the peoples who have deeply influenced one another's destiny.

It is, of course, impossible to deny completely the Jewish history of the last 2000 years and its impact on the history of the Middle East in the former centuries and on its present situation; but it is also impossible to deny the hundred years of Arab presence in the region, just as it is necessary to take into account all the irrevocable facts of the last three decades. These facts, the consequences of the four wars in 1948, 1956, 1967 and 1973 and the Soviet–Arab opposition to the still isolated Israeli–Egyptian Peace Treaty overshadow the problems which have to be finally solved in the interests of all participants in the conflict and of the security of the world as a whole.

The premise constituted the starting point of the Israeli Peace Association's project published in 1970 under the title *The Middle East in the Year 2000*.[5] The document postulates that all present Arab states will continue to exist in the next century and that the Palestinian problem will be resolved either in the context of an existing Arab state or through a newly constituted Palestinian entity which will be federated, confederated or will otherwise cooperate with one of the existing states in the region. Another premise is that the present frontiers in the Middle East will in time lose their importance and become as those in Western Europe—open borders based on a functional framework of cooperation among all the countries in the area.

The project asserts that the civilization of the Middle East in the year 2000 will join in the universal Moslem–Christian–Jewish heritage, into which 21st century modern technology can be integrated. Before the end of the present century, improved medical services and a rising standard of living will contribute not only to the doubling of the population but also to a higher life expectancy. The former will be achieved due to a reduction in military expenditure and from devoting the income from oil to constructive investment dedicated to desert development, improved educational institutions, increased scientific research and the institution of a free and rapid communication system.

As we have already mentioned, the main feature of the civilization in the area will be based on the common principles of the Jewish–Christian–Moslem heritage combined with modern technology. This will allow, on the one hand, the continued existence of the diversity of nations, each with its own unique national culture, and, on the other hand, their multilateral economic cooperation in the form of a common market. The headquarters of the Middle East common market will be established in the reconstructed Lebanese capital Beirut. This not only will reflect this area's relations with the rest of the world, but will also allow the development of each member country according to its unique capabilities, with the aim of becoming more or less complementary to each other.

In this framework, Egypt, the first Arab peacemaker in the area, will most probably become a center of engineering industries: steel, cars and other motor vehicles. Iraq and the Gulf will be the center of petrochemical industries, Syria and Jordan of food industries and textiles and Israel of electronics, computers and chemistry. Reconstructed Lebanon will again become a center of banking, trade, transport and communication services.

That is why as early as in 1970 it was possible to assume that, once it achieved peace, the Middle East would become, in addition to being an important supplier of fruits and other agricultural products to Europe and a center for European tourism, also a source of knowledge. Through the exchange of expertise in the area, it will provide scientific guidance and planning services, of value to developing as well as to many industrialized countries.

Considering the general developments in the world arena, all of the above is quite feasible, but, of course, can be achieved only on condition that all nations involved find enough courage to follow Egypt and Israel's example. The countries must talk, negotiate and crown their negotiations with action, and inaugurate an era of cooperation. It is clear that if they do not find the courage to do so, then, the prospects of having the region partake in a renewed effective process of détente directed towards real disarmament and non-intervention and in peace-building development will be minimal. Progress then will only be determined by outside pressures. In such a situation neither the above-mentioned outline nor any other peace scenarios, in spite of the Peace Treaty between Egypt and Israel, will be of any great value, nor will any other model of relationships be helpful in eliminating the cold—and even hot war atmosphere, tensions and bloodshed in the region. However, the possibility of finding the proper breakthrough towards a comprehensive peace lies neither in the imagination of forecasters nor in the wisdom of experts in the law of nations, future research or peace research. It only depends on the behavior of the nations involved. Unfortunately, elements which would justify optimism with respect to this and other regions are still lacking. After all, we live in times when military expenditures are growing, although, paradoxically, their growth has made possible the first step towards peace in a one part of the Middle East. However, its other parts and many regions in Asia and Africa continue to be a theatre of foreign armed interventions and bloody internal conflicts. Let us recall in this context that world military expenditures have increased by about 40 percent since 1963 and reached the figure of more than 500 thousand million dollars a year in 1979. The Third World's share in the total has increased from about four percent in 1963 to about 15 percent today.

It is true that 80 percent of military money is spent on conventional armament and forces, but the greatest single threat to mankind is that of nuclear war. In 1963, the nuclear arsenals contained about 4000 relatively primitive warheads. These were enough to destroy civilization. Today, nuclear arsenals contain tens of thousands of sophisticated nuclear weapons, with a total nuclear power equivalent to about one million of Hiroshima bombs.[6] While these awesome figures illustrate the danger to human survival, the conventional arms race in general and in the Third World (including the Middle East), in particular, points to a no lesser danger. Any local confrontation is fraught with this danger, especially in such a "neuralgic" area as the Middle East.

That is why all models which stress the prevalence of peaceful orientations in the nuclear era are so fragile. We must not disregard the fact that military might still guarantee political influence in the realm of the Soviet bloc. Not only does it assure the cohesion of the Communist multinational empire, but it also determines the status of the Soviet Union as a superpower in spite of its economic backwardness and the repressive traits of its socio-political system. Its military might makes it possible for it to maintain and enlarge spheres of rule and influence in large parts of Europe and of other continents, including the Cuban and Afghan territories, which are in not too distant neighbourhood of the United States and of the oil sources of Western Europe.[7]

This and other aspects of our realities do not dismiss the contention that international law, peace and future research might contribute to the prospects of reconciliation of former foes and of strengthening regional and world security already in our generation. They indicate the difficulties of this task and show how hard it is even to sketch a reliable peace-assuring world model. They indicate the importance of doing all that is possible for the realization of the centuries-old vision of global security, economic progress and social justice.

Notes

* This paper is a revised and enlarged version of the final paragraphs of the author's study "Future Research—Its Models of a Peaceful World and Its Contribution to Their Implementation," published in the book *Science and Technology*, ed. by H. Bucholz and W. Gmelin of the WFSA, K.G. Saur, Muenchen, New York, London and Paris, 1979, pp. 1080–1096.

1.   See *The Wiener Library Bulletin*, vol. XXIX, no. 2/1970, p. 73.

2.   Reprinted in the *Tribune Libre* of *Le Journal d'Indépendance*, 22–23, Sept. 1979.

3.   J. Galtung, "Middle East and the Theory of Conflict," *JPR*, no. 3–4/1971, pp. 173 and ff.

4.   V. Shemtov, former member of the Israeli Government, is a leading figure in the Labor Alliance. General Yariv also was a minister. Today he belongs to the leadership of the Democratic Party. A similar view was voiced by the Chief Sepharadi Rabbi of Israel, Ovadia Jossef, and by the Chief Rabbi of England, Dr. I. Jacobowitz. See *New Outlook*, vol. 22, no. 7 (144), October 1979, pp. 2 and 15.

5.   See *Beyond the Frontiers of Time: The Middle East in the Year 2000*, A Project, The Association of Peace, Tel Aviv, 1970.

6.   *Statement on World Armaments and Disarmament*, SIPRI, Stockholm, 1978, p. 5ff., and SIPRI *Yearbooks* of 1979 and 1980.

7.   R. Aron, "The 1978 Alastair Buchan Memorial Lecture," *Survival*, vol. XXI, no. 1(1979, p. 6.

Pax Hierosolymitana

Raffel Barkan (Benkler)

Jerusalem lies at the core of the Middle East conflict. It's problems, not unnaturally are many-faceted; emotional and ideological, religious and national, legal and political, municipal and diplomatic, principled and pragmatic. All these aspects must be considered when a solution is proposed. Every suggestion must meet the requirements of these factors.

But before discussing any suggestion, both its basic assumptions and the causes of its motivation must be considered.

Basic Assumptions

The basic assumption I have adopted was already set nearly 50 years ago and has so far stood the test of reality; it is daily more and more self-evident: "Eretz Yisrael/Palestine is the common homeland of two peoples—the Jewish people returning to it and the Arab people inhabiting it.

This assumption stands up to a number of tests. (1) The ideological: We combine the national liberation movement with the social liberation movement; human liberation is impossible without human equality—a nation's liberation cannot come while it rules over another nation. (2) The normative-legal: A basic norm of international law, independent recognition or international treaties, is the "right of nations to self-determination." This right is inalienable, though it can be applied in various ways, selected by the nation itself: Absolute separation and self-realization, or joint sovereignty, along with another nation. (3) The political-pragmatic: If two peoples claim the same piece of land, and both desire peaceful co-existence, each must concede part of ts claims (without thus conceding its right) and reach a permanent arrangement together. This basic assumption does not stand up, however, to the purist religious test, one in which religion consists of monolithic-exclusivist belief.

139

Two Nations, One Land

Out of this basic assumption, *Hashomer Hatzair* once came to
its idea of bi-nationalism: To establish in the whole of Eretz Yisrael
one state, in which the two peoples would be equal partners. In
Europe today there is a similar tendency towards integration across
ethnic divisions. But it seems that an idea good for latter-day
national states, is not so easily accepted by younger peoples which
are still in the process of their nation-building (note also the African
orthodoxy on this subject). Therefore, the political solution must be
determined by allowing both peoples in Eretz Yisrael independent
sovereignty through partition, while aspiring for many common
meeting points.

There is one disadvantage to the idea of partition: It is a *dis-
associative* way for solving a crisis. It is good, perhaps, for a short
time, or for separating Israel from Egypt, while the Sinai desert
stands between them. It is not good for two peoples living in the
same country itself. I do not know whether the UNSCOP (U.N.
Special Committee on Palestine, 1947) members gave special thought
to this aspect of the problem, but the solution they suggested came
as close as possible to the ideal. While proposing partition of
sovereignty, they also proposed economic union between the two
states. That was a constructive path, an *associative* solution, bringing
the two sides to the conflict together in a joint framework. Only this
path, the associative, leads to a real solution.

If the dis-associative path is not good for the whole country, it is
even less relevant to the Jerusalem problem. How is it possible to
separate neighbours intertwined with each other in a single city,
each demanding its right to it and unable to live with a barrier
between them? Here, too, the UNSCOP solution was well-founded. It
suggested turning Jerusalem into a *corpus separatum*, to be run
by an international mandate for ten years; only then would the
inhabitants decide, by referendum, on their future. The solution was
good—a united city and associate processes, but it failed for two
reasons: neither side was able to give up the city (even for only ten
years); it could not be agreed that the city should be separated from
other parts of the country, and administered by foreigners (even
international ones).

The "solution" was found on the battlefield, within a sort of
gentlemen's agreement (unwritten, and non-premeditated, it seems)
between David Ben-Gurion and King Abdullah: the city was divided
for 19 years. It was a dis-associative solution, good enough, perhaps,
for a cease-fire, maybe even for an armistice, but not real peace. Ben-
Gurion saw this error: in his later days, when Jerusalem was
reunited, he raised an audacious proposal-to destroy the Jerusalem

walls, symbol of the city's partition, to make it impossible to re-divide.

Here we must come to the first basic assumption: no peaceful solution can consider a re-partition of Jerusalem. Any solution must be associative, must lead to cooperation. This basic assumption meets the tests listed above. The question is only practical—but we shall come to this later.

A cardinal question is: how many states will exist between the desert and the sea; what political entities will exist in Eretz Yisrael?

The "Third State" Bogey

It is quite possible, though by no means conclusively proven, that it would be much better for Israel if the Palestinians were to desire a joint expression of their sovereign rights with trans-Jordanian residents: that is—there would be two states between the desert and the sea. In such case, we say that it is of no interest to Israel whether the Palestinians rule Jordan, accept the supremacy of King Hussein, or choose one of the three options of federation, confederation or personal union under the crown of trans-Jordan. But just the same, we cannot determine for the Palestinians—if they want to apply to themselves their right to self-determination and to establish another state on this side of the Jordan.

If two states are to exist between the Jordan and the sea, the question of their capitals will be complicated. The Hashemites of the desert say that Amman is their capital, that they want Jerusalem only as a city within their borders. But if there will be a federal structure, or political union, it will be demanded that Jerusalem be the capital of the western district. Israel can demand that its neighbour's capital be Amman, as in the past, but will it have sufficient backing for this claim? I doubt that. If there will be three separate states—the Palestinians will undoubtedly demand Jerusalem for their capital.

Furthermore, it seems to me that the main reason guiding those who insist on only two states in Eretz Yisrael is that they want to by-pass the problem of Jerusalem, to leave it whole and united within Israel, as its capital. All who think they can get their way like this err, as they erred in thinking it possible to ignore the Palestinians' aspirations for self-determination by posing the question: "I don't know who the Palestinians are . . ."

About 2975 years ago (the estimated date when Jerusalem became David's city), Jewish presence was established in Jerusalem. But the Jewish people have experienced many changes since.

Today it expresses itself through a national revolution, which like all national revolutions, is a product of the modern age. Parallel to those of the Jewish people, the national aspirations of the Arab arose and grew. Parallel to the establishment of Israel, the separate aspirations of the country's Arabs also developed, aspirations of a separate people within the Arab nation. Thus, it is impossible to ignore their demand for national sovereignty, with Jerusalem as its capital.

The second basic assumption: just as the Jews will not give up Jerusalem as Israel's capital, neither will the Palestinian Arabs give up Jerusalem as their capital.

If we accept these two basic assumptions, we understand that solving the Jerusalem problem must involve a political formula satisfying the demands of the two peoples dwelling in Eretz Yisrael, a solution consistent with the basic ideological principles and with norms of international law. At first glance, it looks like a matter of squaring a circle: *one united city—but common to two sovereign nations and serving as the capital for both of them.* But, with a little intellectual effort and a great deal of will-power, it is possible to find a solution which can meet these requirements and be quite practicable.

Solution vs. Solution

To solve the problems implicit in these basic assumptions and to "square" the circle, I proposed, a number of years ago, my own solution to the problem, which I called "Jerusalem Peace."

A surprising sequence of events followed the plan's circulation. It was originally an interim conclusion of a study of Jerusalem's status according to public international law, finished in March 1971. One month later there was a noisy explosion among the Israeli public following release of the Foreign Ministry's "master plan," known by the name of its author Dr. Benvenisti. To my great surprise, I found upon reading the Benvenisti plan that it almost corresponded to my plan. In July of that year I presented it as a "working paper" at the Helsinki Conference of the Intrernational Peace Academy (based in New York), and it was included in the published conference proceedings. It would be less than truthful not to mention that the original copyright for anything touching on solutions to Jerusalem's municipal problems should belongto the mandatory Chief Justice Sir William Fitzgerald, who came to similar conclusions in 1945, while serving on a special investigatory committee for solving the problems of relations between the two peoples and three religions in the city.

The Plan

The City's Status. Jerusalem will be the capital of two states—Israel and the Arab state—and the two states' supreme institutions (such as presidential seat, legislative houses, high courts, government offices, etc.) will be located in appropriate quarters of the city.

Jerusalem will be a demilitarized city, in which neither one of the two states will be allowed to station military forces (unless otherwise agreed, for special events), except for special guard units (like the Knesset guard, etc.). Public order will be maintained by local police of the various quarters.

The City's Structure

The metropolis of Greater Jerusalem will be administered by a number of sub-municipalities, within a single overall structure, like the Greater London Council, as suggested by Sir. W. Fitzgerald, or like Paris's twenty arrondissements. Some of them will be under Israeli sovereignty, others under Arab sovereignty

The Residents' Status

Every inhabitant of Greater Jerusalem will be a citizen of his/her state (city residents will not be allowed to hold citizenship in both states, even if one or both of them allow dual citizenship of any kind). Every inhabitant will be bound by the obligations of the state of which he/she is a citizen (loyalty, military service, taxes, etc.), subject to its laws and enjoying all rights of citizenship conferred by it.

Judicial authority of the appropriate state will apply in Jerusalem, too. Crimes committed in a borough of the city will be tried by the state which has jurisdiction over the borough. A citizen of state "A" who committed a crime in a borough of state "B" would be brought to trial according to the laws of state "B," but have the right to additional counsel, from state "A," in an advisory capacity.

Territorial Question

The exact borders are unimportant, and must be determined in a peace agreement. But, it seems to me, the best possible framework would be that of Greater Jerusalem, as envisaged in the Jerusalem master plan drawn up in 1968. It covered a metropolitan area including, besides the present area of jurisdiction, another 18 quarters. I divided this area into eight sub-municipalities (Meron Benvenisti's plan spoke only of five—but in a smaller area).

Composition of the Population

We should not shy away from facing the question "Who will be a majority in Jerusalem?" And certainly, our counterparts should also be concerned with the same query. But it is a fact that since 1840, Jerusalem has had a Jewish majority, and Israel need never concede this situation. In 1967, Jews constituted a majority in this greater Jerusalem—211,900 to 168,200 non-Jews. According to estimates taken from the master plan,this ratio will be 330,000 to 257,000 in 1985, and 497,000 to 393,000 in 2010.

Municipal Structure

The eight sub-municipalities will take care of many areas, as determined by the central overall administration.

The Greater Jerusalem Council will include representatives of all eight sub-municipalities, proportionately according to their populations. According to 1968 population figures (and according to the area included in his plan) Benvenisti suggested a council of 51—31 Jews and 20 Arabs. According to my plan, this would become (1967 figures) 28 Jewish representatives and 23 non-Jews.

The Greater Jerusalem Council would deal with matters of central concern, or made more simple and efficient by central concern:

Preparing a masterplan (this must, of course, be coordinated with the separate planning authorities); coordinating activities of the sub-municipalities, including a certain amount of supervision; regional and local development, stemming from the central plan; along with this, economy and tourism; a number of central serices, such as regional sewage, a coordination of fire-fighting, water and electricity, drainage and garbage removal, municipal airport, industrial areas; transportation; housing; parks and historic structures and, of course, supervision of holy places (though their care will be entrusted to other bodies, as seen below).

Inducing Cooperation

Coordination of dual Sovereignty: Since Jerusalem is seen here (despite its unification) as a city under political sovereignty of two separate states, a means of coordination between the two states must be found to ensure operation of the city bureaucracy. Therefore, a rigid basic law must be passed in both states, whose details will be determined in an addendum to the peace agreement. It must include a means for approving the city's budget, and allocations for the central municipality; it must include methods for approving the city planning scheme and coordination of the different laws concerning municipal administration and emigration from one borough of the city to another. Of course, it must grant the city the power to levy taxes and legislate municipal regulations.

Achievement and strengthening of peace will in any case give Jerusalem a special status, something like Washington D.C., with the essential difference that it will be the capital of two states, not one. This added international factor on Jerusalem's map, and the confederative factor (in the beginnings of economic relationships) will further the special status, and it will find expression in the basic "Jerusalem Law."

Holy Places

Freedom of worship and access to holy places must be ensured to members of both nationalities and citizens of both states. The holy places themselves wil be administered by their appropriate religious authorities, as stipulated by the Ottoman *Firman* of 1757, and as has come to be accepted over hundreds of years of historical development. It should be noted, of course, that the Jerusalem Law will legally sanction this situation and enable the sub-municipalities (and the umbrella-municipality) to supervise conduct in and around the holy places, to judge whether the spirit of the law and of the peace agreement is being maintained.

The city's economy: It was stated above that the city will be open and free. But this would not be the sole consequence of such dual-sovereignty in the city. In fact, it would require a common economic policy of Israel and the Arab state as well, for development of the joint capital. For this, too, parallel ways and means must be included in the Jerusalem Law. There must be, of course, a common currency, or at least coordinated exchange rates, with both currencies accepted as legal tender in the city. It would be superfluous to point out that this would require creation of something like an "Israel/ Palestine Common Market" between the two sovereign states. In other words, we return to the proposed partition of Israel/Palestine (UN General Assembly Resolution 181(II), Nov. 29, 1947), in which economic union between the two nation-states supposed to arise in the country was suggested.

UN headquarters: For a number of years now, in fact since the international political pendulum returned to the "old world," due to the Third World's awakening, there has been talk of moving the UN headquarters to the eastern hemisphere. Jerusalem's special standing in the whole world's consciousness, its special status as the capital of two states (according to this suggestion) and as a meeting place between east and west could all provide an excellent framework for UN headquarters.

A declatory proposal by Israel to move the UN seat to Jerusalem, and an announcement that it would agree to a special arrangement with it, reserving land for such purpose, granting immunity and

autonomous administration to its bodies (like the present arrangement with the US) would advance a plan such as this one, and could
even create a partial buffer zone in the city (not a buffer zone as in
Sinai, but a UN headquarters area, perhaps in the Gilo-Bet Jala
region, and diplomatic residences). A place where the UN is located
would be an excellent guardian of the peace; what state would
want to endanger its representatives or give up the existence
of a "marketplace" for espionage (like Switzerland, for example)?
Naturally, too, location of such a centre would bring economic
prosperity to the city and to the two states whose capital it would be.

To all appearances, the programme seems difficult and complicated, indeed utopian. Its complexity, in particular, may impede
its implementation. But—"If you will it, it is no dream."

Back To Basics in Peacemaking in the Middle East

Elias H. Tuma

The Problem

It may be idealistic to visualize a state of peace as normal between the nations of the Middle East, given the long period of conflict in the region. However, coexistence is the norm by which nation states have abided in recent history and according to which a United Nations can exist. A state of war, therefore, must be the result of intervening forces that disturb the peace and lead to war; the removal of these forces would remove the causes of war and restore peace.

The real world is a little more complex, as may be seen in the Middle East conflict. First, the basic assumption of peace as the norm may be challenged; a truce between nations may be more like it. Second, the disturbing forces may be more apparent than real and therefore may be hard to identify or specify, in which case they may be elusive and not subject to easy removal. Third, and most important of all, the original causes of war or conflict may have been transformed or overshadowed by the new conditions that have developed since the beginning of the conflict: the parties to the conflict in the Middle East have changed; new leaders are now in charge; the environment has been altered and new alliances and power centers have emerged. Nevertheless, we may agree on certain basics to identify the problem and prescribe a solution.

(a) The conflict in the Middle East, as presently constituted, is mainly between the Palestinian Arabs and the Israelis. The Arab states have been drawn into the conflict by empathy, by historical and national identification with the Palestinians, and by miscalculation regarding their ability to resolve the issue by force. Had the conflict between the Palestinian Arabs and Jews been resolved by the British Mandate government or by the United Nations, it is unlikely that the Arab states would now be at war with Israel. And had the Arab states correctly calculated their strength relative to the power of Israel and its supporters, it is unlikely that they would have allowed themselves to be drawn into the conflict by way of war.

It might have been true sometime in the past, as Golda Meir has suggested, that "the root of the issue is the Arab attitude to Israel's very existence and security. Once the Arab countries accept the legitimacy of Israel as we have always accepted theirs, there is no reason for their intransigence against negotiating the differences between us."[1] If so, why "now that the leading Arab states are ready to recognize Israel on condition that it return to the 1967 borders, with certain ameliorations, Israel refuses . . .?" as Nahum Goldman has put it.[2] Actually the Arab states also demanded the recognition of the rights of the Palestinians to self-determination as a condition, but this barely affects Goldman's query. Rather, it lends support to the premise that the root of the issue is the Palestinian Israeli conflict.

(b) It is possible that the conflict in Palestine and the establishment of the State of Israel have interfered with certain aspirations and designs for unity and the creation of Arab states larger than has been possible. Such aspirations, however, could not have been more than lofty dreams. The tendency toward unification was still relatively weak as late as the end of the Second World War.[3] Nevertheless, the shock suffered by the aspirants to Arab unity because of the creation of the State of Israel and their own defeat in the war must be seen as ushering the era of chronic distrust between the Arabs and the Israelis.

(c) The wars between Israel and the Arabs have caused suffering and dislocation which have strengthened the feelings of distrust and have led to deep-seated fears and insecurity on the part of both the Arabs and the Israelis. The Arabs worry about Israel's power as they remember their own humiliation in the war, while Israel worries about the enemy that is bound to grow stronger and more bitter as time passes. The problem, therefore, has evolved into a psychological block woven out of distrust and fear.

(d) While the dimensions of the conflict may have changed, war between Israel and the Arab states is still a function of the Palestinian–Israeli conflict, and solving that conflict would to a large extent remove the causes of war between Israel and the Arab states. Of course, conflict between them may continue, but it would take a different character; it would become subject to resolution by non-violent means, as common among other nations. For example, they may have a conflict because of ideological inclinations, power alliances, and economic or political competition. These differences, however, would no doubt be in the tradition of a cold war, rather than the hot violent war that has prevailed. This generalization applies to differences in the religious beliefs, political sympathies, and in the economic systems that exist in these countries.

Given these observations, peacemaking in the Middle East depends on three major steps: Removal of the causes of war between the Palestinian Arabs and Israel; restoration of justice to the parties that have suffered injustice in this war situation; the creation of an atmosphere congenial to development of security and mutual trust between the warring parties. These steps will be treated in that order, after which I shall explore the prospects for peace in the near future.

Removing the Causes of War

If we look at the history of the conflict, we find its origin to be in the fight for the territory of Palestine and the right to establish hegemony over it. Though some Israeli leaders have suggested variable boundaries for the disputed territory, that issue was settled by the British government as far back as 1922, and all national and international documents since then have treated Palestine as the territory under the British Mandate and which was specified in the 1947 Partition Plan passed by the United Nations.[4] The Palestinian Arabs and the Jews claimed the right to consider Palestine their home and neither party was about to surrender that claim. After almost thirty years of conflict and a stalemate, the United Nations advocated partition in 1947, thus allowing both parties to realize their claims to a part of Palestine. Therefore, if the war solution—which has failed so far— were to be replaced by a peace solution, it would be necessary to abide by the idea of partition, which has not been revoked by the United Nations, nor strictly speaking, has it been rejected by the State of Israel. Now we have a new situation: for the first time the Palestinians and other Arabs who had rejected partition are now ready to accept the idea of partition and coexistence with a State of Israel.[5] This change is significant because it makes the idea of partition acceptable to all the parties to the conflict.

Acceptance of the idea of partition, however, leaves unresolved the issue of boundaries: how to divide Palestine between the two peoples, without infringing on the rights of other countries in the region and in a way that would render the solution feasible, realistic, and consistent with the aspirations of both parties. In the meantime, the 1947 Partition Plan has been implicitly superseded by the United Nations' Resolutions 242 and 338 which have called on Israel to withdraw from the territories occupied in the 1967 war; those prewar boundaries may therefore serve as the solution boundaries.

Interestingly enough, Israel has agreed to withdraw from the territories belonging to Egypt and Syria, in return for peace, according to the Camp David agreements. Thus, once more the conflict is focused on the Palestinian territory and on the relationship between the Palestinians and Israelis.

While both the Palestinians and the Israelis have agreed on partition, they will publicly claim historical and/or occupancy rights to the whole of Palestine. The Israelis base their claims on historical rights, redefinition of the geography of Palestine, and on their military capability to sustain their occupation of the extra territory. However, it is unlikely that Israel would want unification with the Arabs lest they become the majority.[6]

The Palestinians, on the other hand, insist on unification and the creation of a democratic secular state in which Arabs and Jews live in harmony. Presumably their insistence on unification is a defense mechanism and a tool of bargaining in order to secure their just share of Palestine. It is not likely, however, that either the Israeli or the Palestinian claim is going to be fulfilled. Should Israel succeed in retaining the territory occupied in the 1967 war in defiance of the United Nations' resolutions and without regard to the claims of the Palestinians, a dangerous precedent will have been established which gives logic to the argument that lands lost in war can be restored only by war, as some of the Arabs believe. In contrast, withdrawal from these territories and abidance by the UN resolutions would give credence to the basic formula of coexistence between nations. It would also enhance the prospects for mutual recognition of sovereignty, preclude expansionism by means of war, and render peaceful coexistence a real possibility. On the other hand, it is unlikely that a secular, democratic, unified state will be established since that would change the character of the State of Israel and contradict the aspirations of the Jews. The Palestinians can do little at this point to give credence to the formula of coexistence since they are not in occupation of any of the disputed territory. However, they can show receptivity to the initiatives that could lead to withdrawal, as a fundamental step toward peace. Israel has the key to this solution: it must take the initiative, express its readiness to withdraw, and show its acceptance of peaceful co-existence with its neighbors.[7] The expression of receptivity by the Palestinians and the initiative by Israel would also serve to confine the conflict and the solution to the area of Palestine. Furthermore, these steps would represent a commitment by both parties to the idea that war gains cannot be retained and hence expansionism by war cannot be tolerated. The failure to take such steps would imply the lack of interest or sincerity in calling for peace; war would continue.

Receptivity by the Palestinians and initiatives by Israel do not imply that the 1967 boundaries must remain the same. They imply only that modification of these boundaries must be based on mutual agreement. They would legitimize the boundaries, create harmony where there is conflict, and pave the road to a peaceful settlement.

Restoration of Justice

To restore justice in any situation can at best be an approximation of what might have been ideal. A hurt that has been inflicted can rarely be undone and therefore the restoration of justice depends to a large extent on the perception that justice has been restored. The perception will be reflected in a change of attitude by the injured party toward the other. When one party agrees to restore justice and the other party is receptive, the act of restoration becomes negotiable with respect to the form, degree, and rate of implementation.

The Palestinian Israeli conflict has left behind a displaced people who have have lost property, home and the freedom to determine their own fate, as other people do.[8] Therefore, to be able to change their attitude toward the Israelis, they must be able to perceive that an attempt to approximate justice is being made.[9] Probably the first and foremost step in that direction is for Israel to recognize the right of the Palestinians to self determination within the framework of a negotiated settlement.[10] Recognition of the right of self determination can only be a first step, but most other steps hinge on it. Once the right of self determination has been recognized, the Palestinians will be able to negotiate the restoration of justice, its form, degree, and rate of implementation. As long as the Palestinians are not able to negotiate on equal footing with the other party, they will continue to feel unjustly treated, that the solutions are imposed on them, and that their rights are being compromised. Hence, no amount of compensation for lost property or modification of boundaries will suffice as long as such measures are not based on negotiated agreements by equals. It is indeed peculiar that the Israeli leaders hesitate on this issue. As far back as 1931, Ben Gurion stated clearly that:

> the right of self determination is a universal principle. We have always and everywhere been among the most fervent defenders of this principle. We are entirely for the right of self determination of all peoples, of all individuals, of all groups, and it follows that the Arab in Palestine has the right to self determination. This right is not limited, and cannot be qualified by our own interest . . .It is possible that the realization of the aspirations (of the Palestinian Arabs) will create serious difficulties for us but this is not a reason to deny their rights . . .[11]

The right to self determination, however, carries obligations, namely acceptance of the responsibility to abide by the agreements concluded. Acceptance of the responsibility itself is a measure of the restoration of justice. In other words, the rights and obligations of enjoying a just position go together. If the Palestinians make a bad decision, let them take the responsibility, rather than blame it on others as they do so long as they are not able to negotiate freely and equally.[12] Similarly, acceptance of the obligations and responsibilities of self determination implies recognition of the status of the other parties in the conflict.

In the case of the Palestinians, the right of self determination has still another function: it shifts to them the responsibility to resolve the issue of the Palestinian refugees. Given the context in which self determination can be exercised, the Palestinians will become responsible to solve the problem of the refugees within a framework which by definition, must be consistent with the sovereignty of the other states in the region, including Israel. That would remove another of the causes for the perception of injustice by the Palestinians.

A negotiated settlement within this framework must lead to the conclusion that not all lost property can be restored to its owners and must be compensated for by other means. However, regardless of how much compensation they are offered, it can be sufficient only if it is perceived as just by the people themselves. That perception is tied to their ability to negotiate as people with equal rights. Some might suggest that the Jews who migrated from the Arab countries left behind land and property and therefore, they deserve compensation. That may be true, but there is no reason to tie the two situations to each other. The Palestinians were not responsible for the migration of the Jews to Palestine, but the creation of the State of Israel can be regarded as a direct cause for the loss of land and property by the Palestinians and for their inability to assert their right of self determination. Furthermore, the Jewish migrants have in the meantime been rehabilitated and settled, while the Palestinians have continued to be displaced. Finally, the restoration of justice to the Palestinians can be done only through negotiation between Israel and the Palestinians, while compensation of the Jewish migrants from the Arab countries must be negotiated with those countries.

It is important to note that there too the Palestinians can only express appreciation of a changed Israeli attitude. But the initiative must come from Israel by expressing readiness to negotiate compensation and/or repatriation with the Palestinians. Receptivity and readiness to accept by the Palestinians will mean that justice is on the way to being restored. Only then can the practitioners of peacebuilding embark on the difficult task of erecting the structure of peaceful coexistence.

Building Mutual Trust

Once the above conditions have been satisfied, the building of trust becomes relatively easy or at least feasible. Some might argue that the building of trust must precede the above steps, but that would create the chicken and egg riddle. Each individual measure by either party will be considered suspect unless it is based on a commitment by both parties to a fundamental change in their philosophy, goals, and attitudes toward the other party. The building of trust by the Palestinians and the Israelis involves taking certain actions and refraining from others.

Measures to Take: The Palestinians, first and foremost, must find it possible to acknowledge the existence of the State of Israel and the right to exist as an independent state in the region. They must, furthermore, find it possible to reflect the change of their attitude in their Covenant and in the official declarations of their leaders. They must redefine their goals and methods in consistency with their new attitude. In other words, they must redefine their goals in harmony with Israel's sovereignty, security and independence. Statements to that effect by PLO representatives have been coming out recently but not in official capacity or as a direct indication of this changed attitude.[13]

The Palestinians, in order to gain trust of the Israelis, should proceed to formalize the process of selecting the leadership and of decision-making in consistency with recognized international procedures. It is true that the Palestinians can hardly be expected to hold elections in the true sense of the term as long as they have no territorial unity or freedom. But they can approximate the process to a certain degree. They can also open the channels of communication and debate among the Palestinians so that decisions can be the result of extensive participation by the people, far more than has been the case. The importance of this transformation lies in the effect more than in the procedures. Once debate and popular participation have become widespread, it becomes possible to negotiate with the leaders with confidence and security that the agreements reached with them will be respected and protected.

It may be difficult for the Palestinians to proceed on these fronts while forced to act as guerilla fighters with no definite political base to act from; yet, the benefits of such steps can be far-reaching. It may be appropriate at this time to declare a government-in-exile in order to facilitate the implementation of these changes. A government-in-exile would be the vehicle to channel the ideas and support of the Palestinians, as well as it would stimulate trust and confidence in the prospective negotiations. Such a government would also settle the issue of who shall speak for the Palestinians. And it would be a major step toward full acceptance by the international community. Israel would then have little reason not to deal with the Palestinians directly, or to pretend that they do not exist.[14]

Finally, the Palestinians must come up with a plan or a solution proposal as an alternative to what has been offered but rejected. Israelis as well as many Palestinian intellectuals feel at a loss as to what the Palestinian leaders have in mind short of the unified, democratic, secular state they have called for. There is need for guidance with respect to the future, both in terms of goals and in terms of policies and strategies. A vacuum does exist because of this lack of a feasible alternative. It should be stressed that any new plan by the Palestinians and any guidelines suggested ought to be based on a positive optimistic outlook toward the future. It is high time for the Palestinians to capitalize on what may be positive in the approaches they are presented with, and to replace the rejectionist negative attitude they have displayed with a receptive positive attitude toward current and prospective peace initiatives.

The Israelis, on their part, in addition to taking initiatives as discussed above, must proceed to redefine their philosophy of Zionism and statehood, or to restore the original definition as understood by their progressive leaders. Even Zionist and Jewish leaders regard the Israeli government's interpretation of Zionism as a "distortion of the Zionist ideal."[15] They have called for a return to the "Other Zionism" which regards peace, coexistence, humaneness, and creativity as essential ingredients.[16] The return to that "other Zionism" or the redefinition of Zionism are necessary to alleviate the fears of the Palestinians and other Arabs who regard Zionism as exclusivist and expansionist and thus racist and imperialist.

They consider Zionism, as expressed in the policies of the State of Israel, as exclusive because it makes immigration and settlement in Israel an exclusive right of the Jews wherever they happen to be. At the same times, Zionism is interpreted as expansionist because of the continued occupation of territory far beyond the internationally recognized boundaries of Israel and of Palestine. Hence the Arabs feel insecure because of this potential expansionism. Israel must, therefore, proceed to redefine Zionism to remove this possibly faulty interpretation.

The Israelis have been living in a state of war for a long time. Probably half of the people of Israel have never lived in a state of peace and may be afraid to face a peace situation.[17] The Israeli economy is a war economy and the budget for defense is more than a third of the national income of the country. It is not possible for the Palestinians to believe that Israel wants peace as long as such a high percentage of the budget is devoted to the building of an arsenal. Therefore, it is of major significance in gaining trust that the economy be reshaped as a peace economy. In place of arms purchase and manufacturing, productive peace commodities can be supplied. Instead of spending that high percentage of the income on defense, it may be possible to rechannel some funds to the establishment of peace industries. In other words, the planning of a peace economy may be quite strategic in gaining trust of the Palestinians and other Arabs. Obviously, this cannot be implemented before peace is achieved, but planning for that day and the elimination of the unnecessary expenditure on arms would go a long way to dispel the current view that Israel needs war to sustain its economy, keep its labor force employed, and secure aid from the outside.

The Israelis must known by now that they cannot ignore the Palestinians forever. It would, therefore, be a step in the right direction for them to begin to show political consideration toward the Palestinians and deal with their leaders directly, whoever these leaders may be. They must respect the right of these people to choose their own leaders rather than stipulate who the leaders may or may not be. Such a stipulation would itself be in violation of the right of self determination. Accordingly, it is of major significance to the peace efforts at this time that Israel should negotiate with the PLO or their designates. As long as the PLO are recognized by the United Nations and by the Arab League as well as by the Palestinian people, Israel must respect that judgment and proceed to negotiate with them. To continue to ignore the PLO is an obstacle to peace and a symbol of what has been described as "Israeli rejectionism," which is "neither accidental nor tactical. Rather it is very profound and deeply rooted to the point where it may be regarded as strategic. This rejectionism leaves little room for imagining that Israel really seeks peace with the Arabs or desires it."[18] Obviously, Israel can put conditions on recognition of the PLO such as cessation of violence, modification of the Covenant, etc., and thus remove its rejectionism and make negotiation with the Palestinians possible.

Israel would gain trust among the Arabs if it would recognize and support the aspirations of the people of the Middle East against foreign imperial interests. Israel has been seen as a spearhead of imperialism which exploits and suppresses the developing countries, including those of the Middle East. This view is shared by Jews and other non-Arabs who sympathize with Israel. As George Wald has put it, "In the late sixties I spoke at several universities and in Israel to repudiate the New Left accusation that Israel had become "the outpost of American imperialism in the Near East. I am deeply embarrassed to realize that I could not do so now." After detailing indicators of this imperial policy, he adds: "Yet I would do all that I could to defend America from from attack, even with my life. It is my country. In a real sense, Israel is my other country. I would like to be proud of both. My recent experience has frequently made me ashamed of both."[19]

To alleviate the thrust of this attitude toward Israel, it would be useful for Israel to back the people of the region against outsiders in international parleys, as long as the claims of these people are for freedom, independence, and peaceful coexistence. A variation of this step is for Israel to recognize the rights of the Middle East people, including the Palestinians, to choose their own alliances, including alliance with the Soviet Union. Once Israel has recognized this right, it should be advantageous to include, rather than exclude, the Soviet Union from peace negotiations. As a matter of fact, the sooner Israel acknowledges the usefulness of Soviet participation the better will be chances of success, if only because the Soviet Union may be a moderating factor in these negotiations.

Measures and Policies to Terminate: Distrust and insecurity can result from action as well as from inaction. The measures recommended above will fill gaps created by inaction. However, it may be equally important to terminate certain actions by both parties in order to build up trust and pave the way for peaceful coexistence. Both the Palestinians and the Israelis can afford to adopt new policies and attitudes, and scale down or cease practices that are antagonistic, provocative, and hurtful to the other party. Some of these practices are simply acts and policies that are not essential parts of the war activity, and these are provocative and hurtful especially because they are known to be as such. Let me illustrate, again starting with the Palestinians.

The Palestinians were virtually ignored until they resorted to acts of violence indiscriminately on an international scale, especially against civilians. Then they were noticed. They won recognition by the United Nations and were able to establish offices in various countries around the world. In many ways this was a victory. Now, however, they gain little by such acts. On the contrary, they tend to lose sympathy around the world because of them. It is true that their struggle must continue until their aspirations have been realized. But the military action need not be directed against non-military targets. It is true that guerilla war strategy aims at the weakest link and hits to hurt as much as possible, but such ceases to be the case once a certain threshold has been reached and political maneuvering has become proficient. I suggest that the Palestinian struggle has reached that threshold; world opinion has begun to swing in their favor; and they have the mechanism to pursue their objectives politically. Even within Israel there are sympathizers with the Palestinian cause, but these sympathizers are estranged by the attacks on civilians and non-military targets in acts of cruel violence. My point is that the Palestinians can afford to dispense with these tactics in order to builde trust and invite confidence in their call for peace with justice.

Similarly, the Palestinians, despairing of their misfortune over the last few decades, seem to have followed Churchill's motto that he would ally himself with the devil to achieve victory. Thus, the Palestinians have found themselves allied with non-secular, non-democratic, and artificially unified states, contrary to their own call for the creation of a democratic, secular, unified state in Palestine. Allying themselves with Idi Amin and celebrating the victory of Ayatollah Khomeini are anything but endearing to people who truly believe in secularism, democracy, and unity. It is obvious that none of these alliances can in a serious way help them achieve their goals. Therefore, the alliance with these forces can only be counter-productive. It can even antagonize dedicated Palestinians who lean toward human rights and democratic and secular principles. The Palestinians will be better off without these alliances.

Finally, having been forced into a stateless position, the Palestinians have struggled to stay viable. To face Israel militarily, they needed a launching station for their armed activities. Jordan served the purpose until the Black September of 1970 when they were brutally silenced by the Jordanian army. Syria was virtually closed to them as a launching station, given the Israeli occupation of the Golan Heights and the creation of a demilitarized zone. Lebanon was the only place left. However, given the internal factionalism of Lebanon and the meddling of Israel in Lebanese affairs, the behavior of the Palestinians has resulted in disasters to the Palestinians themselves and more so to Lebanon. Foreign soldiers now occupy the land; armies of faction leaders, Zu'ama', exercise feudal fascistic powers. The people suffer. Obviously, the Palestinians cannot be blamed for all these disasters, but they must not allow themselves to sacrifice the unity or sovereignty of a host country for their own sake. They must be creative enough to conduct their struggle without infringing on the stability or viability of the host country, especially when they know that their opponent would use any excuse to infiltrate new territory, encourage instability, and weaken the unity of the Arabs.

There are no saints in war. Israel has proven itself even more capable than the Palestinians of provoking distrust and antagonism and of inflicting hurt by actions that are not necessary to the conduct of war with the Palestinians. The Israelis have managed to ally themselves with colonial powers; they have ignored the sovereignty of their neighbors; and they have demonstrated that they can be cruel, arbitrary, and indiscriminate in hitting the Palestinians. Their alliance with Britain and France in 1956 against Egypt, their alleged cooperation with King Hussein against the Palestinians in 1970, and their continued intervention in Lebanon have convinced most Palestinians and other Arabs of the colonialist-imperialist character of the State of Israel. Israeli leaders have for years been debating the fate of King Hussein and how Jordan may be used in solving the Palestinian problem, regardless of Jordanian sovereignty.[20]

Israel has gone further in that direction by allying itself with racist countries like South Africa and Rhodesia, and with corrupt regimes like that of the deposed Shah of Iran. To argue that Israel needed these alliances is neither obvious nor convincing even to Israelis. Israel does not need South Africa or Rhodesia, nor did it need Iran. The moral support of these countries has been counterproductive. Their military aid, as far as can be ascertained, is virtually nil; and their economic support is rather modest. Nor can Israel make a case that the alliance with these countries is needed to protect Jews living there, because in none of them have the Jews been in danger of persecution by the authorities. The opposite may turn out to be the case. By allying itself with racist and anti-human-rights governments, Israel has managed to antagonize the black majority in South Africa and Rhodesia and the revivalist Muslims in Iran, and thus may have endangered the Jews still living in these countries. Israel has, by this behavior, created suspicion among the Arabs of its intent toward the Palestinians. Many believe that Israel wants to keep the Arabs in the occupied territories under Israeli rule as hostages, and to provide cheap labor as has been characteristic of colonial countries. To rebuild a peaceful relationship with the Arabs and create mutual trust with the Palestinians, Israel would do well to radically revise its policies in these areas. Israel should also try to explain or eliminate the inconsistencies between preaching democracy and human rights values and the alliance with regimes that are anything but democratic. One can hardly fail to observe the similarities between Israel's raids into Lebanon and Rhodesia's raids into Zambia, in total disregard of the sovereignty of these neighboring countries, and the cruel effects of these raids on innocent civilians.

This points to another Israeli policy which needs to be modified in order to build trust, namely the retaliatory air attacks, against targets inside Lebanon. These attacks have not always been against military targets, nor have they been defensive. It is also clear that these raids have not been effective in achieving security in Israel. On the contrary, they have been costly materially and morally and have caused pain and possibly hatred. To build peace would definitely require revision of this approach which can hardly be different from terrorist activities anywhere else, the fact that they are carried out by the national armed forces notwithstanding. If Israel wants to penalize the guerilla fighters for their attacks, it should make sure it penalizes the responsible individuals.

However, the most important policy revision relates to the Israeli government's policy toward the Arabs within Israel and the occupied territories. Homes have been demolished and individuals have been deported by summary military action without conviction or trial.[21] The Arabs within Israel have been subjected to acts of discrimination, scare tactics, and brutality. Some question the validity of these charges or their extent. But it is the Arab perception of the treatment suffered at the hands of Israel that counts. That perception paints a dismal picture and generates distrust regardless of the truth or falseness of the charges.

Israel's reform of its oppressive policies must include the cessation of land grabbing within Israel and the occupied territories. Confiscation of Arab land in the name of security and/or to establish new settlements represents the most serious source of distrust of Israeli intentions toward the Arabs and Arab land. It is useless to suggest that these policies are necessary for security or survival. They are perceived as expressions of domination, expansionism, and the lack of respect for the rights of others. Those others can hardly be expected to believe the statements of Israeli leaders about peace when those same leaders condone and encourage land grabbing and forced settlement in the occupied territories.[22]

Can Israel afford to scale down its repressive and expansionist policies and still maintain security? Most probably yes. The question may be whether it can afford not to. One may argue that by applying a system of law and due process, the government may be much more successful in building trust and inviting the cooperation of its Arab citizens and even of the Palestinians in the West Bank and Gaza to combat guerilla attacks on non-military targets. The present Israeli measures and policies tend to alienate the Israeli Arabs, harden the negative attitudes of the Arabs of the West Bank and Gaza and invite more attacks by the Palestinians.

Obviously neither the Palestinians nor the Israelis are going to cease these activities overnight, nor will one party change its attitudes without the promise and expectation of a reciprocal change by the other. Here also Israel can afford to take the initiative, while the Palestinians can afford to show receptivity toward such initiatives. The Palestinians say, and justly so, that they have little left to compromise on; they have been on the losing side throughout. Israel has been on the winning side. Hence, it is easier and less risky for Israel to take the initiative and scale down or cease the hurtful activities and begin a chain reaction in building trust and laying the foundation for a peaceful settlement.

The Prospects

Forecasting in the Middle East is dangerous, especially after President Sadat has shattered the traditional diplomatic procedures by his unprecedented visit to Jerusalem. In this case, forecasting is even more difficult because I have left out important variables such as the East-West relations and the continuing cold war between them. I have left out internal Arab problems which can hardly be ignored and I have left out the role of oil in the conflict. These are important omissions, but I am not sure they need to be analyzed in this context. Problems can be complicated or simplified by the way people view them. I have tried to view the Palestinian–Israeli conflict on its own merits. Neither Israel nor a state of Palestine can be a superpower; neither can afford to be involved in the cold war between the superpowers; and neither has an overwhelming relation to oil as a major producer or consumer. It is, therefore, conceivable that the Palestinians and the Israelis can minimize the impact of external forces in trying to reach a settlement, if such is their intention. Accordingly, I have based the above analysis on these assumptions: the Palestinians and the Israelis want peace; they have the main say in the matter; and they are fully capable of approaching peace by direct negotiation.[23]

The main outlines of a peaceful settlement are fairly well-known: mutual recognition by the Palestinians and the Israelis of each other's right to exist as sovereign and independent within a state of their own, side by side in Palestine. Self-determination by the Palestinians, security of Israel, and direct negotiation of all other issues form a sound basis for a peaceful settlement. Direct negotiation between the two parties is the shortest cut toward a solution. The best policy for the Palestinians right now is to challenge the Israelis publicly to step forward, accept recognition and proceed to negotiate peace within a framework of coexistence and security. The Israelis can equally well put the Palestinians on the spot by offering to recognize their right to self determination within internationally recognized boundaries if they commit themselves to respect the right of Israel to exist as a sovereign state in the Middle East and proceed to negotiate a peaceful settlement. If either party refuses the challenge, it is bound to suffer the consequences while the other party reaps all the benefits of such a positive political encounter. If neither refuses, both will reap the benefits and peaceful coexistence becomes a potential reality. President Sadat has shown this approach to be workable. The Palestinians and the Israelis need only to try it for themselves.

Notes

1. "Israel in Seach of Lasting Peace," *Foreign Affairs*, vol. 51, no. 3, April 1973, p. 451.

2. "Zionist Ideology and the Reality of Israel," *Foreign Affairs*, vol. 57, no. 1, Fall 1978, p. 76.

3. The attitude toward Israel began to change toward moderation in the mid-1950s under President Nasser.

4. Re the geographical reintegration, see Sidney Zion and Uri Dan, "Israel's Peace Strategy," *New York Times Magazine*, April 8, 1979.

5. For illustration, Sabri Jiryis, "Political Settlement in the Middle East: The Palestinian Dimension," *Journal of Palestine Studies*, vol. VII, no. 1, Autumn 1977, pp. 3–35; Walid Khalidi, "Thinking the Unthinkable: A Sovereign Palestinian State," *Foreign Affairs*, vol. 56, no. 4, July 1978, pp. 695–713; "An Opening for US–PLO Talks." Meeting between Yasser Arafat and Congressman Paul Findley, November 25, 1978, reported in *Journal of Palestine Studies*, vol. VIII, no 2, Winter 1978, pp. 173–175; M. M., "Falling on Deaf Ears?" *New Outlook*, January/February 1979, pp. 5–7.

6. Mr. Begin's autonomy plan for the occupied territories is a way out of the dilemma for Israel: it leaves the territories under control but does not integrate the people within the State of Israel as citizens.

7. Both parties claim that their expressions in favor of coexistence have been ignored by the other party.

8. Some argue that the Palestinians had never had that right and therefore could not have lost it.

9. The issue of justice and injustice from a legal standpoint is not being debated here: it is sufficient that the Palestinians perceive their treatment by others as unjust and therefore a change of attitude on their part is basic to a viable solution.

10. Some argue that recognition of the Palestinian right to self determination by the United States may be equally effective in changing the Palestinian perception.

11. Quoted in Eric Rouleau, "The Palestinian Quest," *Foreign Affairs*, vol. 53, no. 2, January 1975, p. 266.

12. It is common among the Palestinians to argue that only when the PLO became strong did they have a say in their own affairs.

13. See reference in footnote 5.

14. A structure akin to a government in exile already exists: see "Terrorism — Weapon of the Weak," *1979 Britannica Book of the Year*, Encyclopedia Britannica, Inc., p. 132.

15. Nahum Goldman, "Zionist Ideology and the Reality of Israel," *Foreign Affairs*, vol. 57, no. 1, Fall 1978, p. 72.

16. L. F. Stone, "The Other Zionism," *Harper's*, September 197?, pp. 65–72. A more extreme critique is Alfred M. Lilienthal, *The Zionist Connection: What Price Peace?* New York: Dodd, Mead, 1979. Lilienthal recommends de-Zionization of Israel and establishing a secular, binational Palestine.

17. For a good statement of these fears, see Lesley Hazelton, "Israel: Learning to Live with Peace," *New York Times Magazine*, April 29, p. 29 ff.

18. Sabri Jiryis, "Israeli Rejectionism," *Journal of Palestine Studies*, vol. VIII, no. 1, Autumn 1978, pp. 61–84.

19. "A Statement on Israel," New Outlook, 20th Anniversary International Symposium, 1977, pp. 1 and 4.

20. It is still current to think of a Palestinian state that would absorb Jordan and divide the West West Bank with Israel, thus liquidating Jordan as a national entity. Sidney Zion and Uri Dan, "Israel's Peace Strategy," *New York Times Magazine*, April 8, 1979, p. 21 ff.

21. For details see Ann Lesch, "Israeli Deportation of Palestinians from the West Bank and the Gaza Strip, 1967–1978," *Journal of Palestine Studies*, vol. VIII, no. 2, Winter 1979, pp. 101–131; this list includes names and places, dates and even ages of the deportees.

22. For updated data on these settlements, see Ann Lesch, "Israeli Settlements in the Occupied Territories," *Journal of Palestine Studies*, vol. VIII, no. 1, Autumn 1978, pp. 100–119.

23. Direct negotiation does not preclude other parties.

Co-Existence of Jews and Arabs
In One Country

Franz Ansprenger

Concepts of peace making are always highly complex propositions. The concept of peace means much more than simple "non belligerency." We must differentiate between the legal and the historical aspects of peacemaking and the economic and the psychological ones.

We want to look specifically at the process of peacemaking in the Middle East that are aimed at a solution of what is called usually (and superficially) the "Israeli–Arab Conflict." In this instance, my proposition is to differentiate mainly between the *international* (or foreign-policy) aspects of peacemaking, and the *domestic* (or internal-policy) aspects.

International Peace means, under normal circumstances, the conclusion of a peace treaty between two or several states which had previously been at war. The most important issue of any peace treaty is the agreement on borders. Many wars began as border conflicts. Many peace treaties have dealt with border changes (annexation of land by the victor from the vanquished), or the recognition of boundaries. The basic assumption is that as soon as every government is able to enjoy unfettered sovereignty over a clearly delimited piece of land, and over a clearly defined group of human beings, without interference from its neighbour, peace will be established.

Domestic Peace means something rather different. If we speak of a peaceful situation within a country, we are not looking for clearly delineated borders. On the contrary, we want to see the construction of many networks of co-operation, for spiritual and material exchanges. Domestic peace needs, among many things, the existence of efficient political forums to debate various group options and balance different interests. These forums must be open to all people living in the country, and the rule of law (of a legal system common for all) must be firmly established. The prerequisites for efficient domestic law are much stricter than for international law: Domestic Peace, however, cannot be maintained without effective sanctions against law-breakers. The prerequisite of domestic peace is co-operation or (as a minimum proposition) co-existence of human beings in a common area. "Domus" is the latin word for "house."

We must concede that in our modern world domestic and international peace are interrelated. There is no clearcut international conflict without domestic involvement; certainly not in western democratic societies where domestic support is needed for all major steps of foreign policy. On the other hand, there is no domestic situation that exists without international impact: in other words, absolute sovereignty of governments over land and over people no longer exists. Even the superpowers realize that they are not alone in the world. The borders of the Soviet Union, of the USA or of China may be very clearly delineated and well protected: Yet Moscow is still not fully sovereign in the matter of dissidents, Washington in the matter of fuel prices, and not even China in the matter of modernization.

Again reflection is requested, so that we can proceed to concede that domestic and international politics are interrelated and interdependent, does not mean that we are allowed to ignore one of the two aspects. Even in situations where it looks at first glance, as if one of the two aspects were preponderant, closer scrutiny shows that the other one also must be taken into account.

As I am going to apply these ideas to the Middle East, to "Two Peoples living in One Country," I want to draw attention to the same problem in another situation: One People in Two Countries—in Germany. Obviously, peace in Central Europe since 1945 has been maintained by means of international politics. Both superpowers involved agreed even to recognize the borders they had drawn at Yalta, without a formal treaty. In Berlin, it is the Wall which means Peace, and the mutual acceptance of seperate sovereignty on both sides of the Wall; the degree of co-existence and co-operation that does exist (visa regulations, transit agreements, diplomatic missions etc.) is dependant on international policies. But why are the two Superpowers so extremely careful to assume direct sovereign control in Berlin, and to respect it vice versa (in the case of the Soviet Union this is done by tightly controlling the East German government)? Because they are both aware of strong domestic undercurrents among the German people, of the continued existence of many family relations cutting across the border, common language, common customs, watching of Western TV programs in the East etc. I think that the peaceful situation in Germany, is effective only because the different actors (governments, including the two German governments) do not ignore the domestic factors involved.

Now what is the central issue of the conflict in the Middle East? Centrally and originally, I think that this is not an "Arab–Israeli"-conflict: it is not a conflict between the sovereign state of Israel (including *all* its citizens) and the sovereign states of Egypt, Jordan, Syria, etc.—such a conflict indeed exists (or did exist before the conclusion of the Peace Treaty beteeen Israel and Egypt), but it is dependant on a different conflict: the struggle between the *Jewish* people of Israel and the Arab people of *Palestine* for the one country that the Jews call Eretz Israel and the Arabs call Palestine.

It is not necessary to make this semantic problem clear, for an Israeli audience, but it is quite necessary to do so wherever you talk about the conflict elsewhere: Eretz Israel and Palestine, for Jews and Arabs, are not names of different countries. There is no concept in their political tradition of that, no room in the minds for a country called Palestine existing "alongside" a country called Israel, or vice versa. What they both mean is the *same* country—and a rather small piece of real estate indeed (even if car drivers would respect the maximum speed regulations, which they do not).

The Jews (not all Jews in the world, but the Jews of Israel) live in this country, have been struggling for it, call it their country and claim self-determination on this piece of land; that is not only their "legitimate right," but they have a legal title under international law, certainly since the United Nations has enacted the two Human Rights Conventions.

The Arabs (not all the Arabs in the world, but those who live in Palestine or are convinced that their fathers did live there) have been defeated in struggling for this country, but stick to their "legitimate rights," and they have the same legal title under international law as the Israeli Jews have.

For this situation we can blame the international lawyers. They have never clearly defined, what a "people" must be in order to determine itself, and they have not included any geographical definitions in the Human Rights Conventions. There is no other way out of the first difficulty, than to admit that any group of human beings who effectively determine that they are a "people" can claim national self-determination. The two groups of human beings have done this: the Israeli Jews by creating their own political (democratic) system within the Zionist movement, during the 1920s and by fighting wars and building a common society (communal tensions notwithstanding) since 1948; the Palestinian Arabs had done it later—but today they have a generally recognized political authority in the form of the (not so democratic) PLO and they have joined in a common social and political destiny since the same year of 1948.

But how can we ever solve the second difficulty, the geographical ambiguity of the right to national self-determination? One way out, of course, is separation. Everything can be split, even atoms. Why not a country? Indeed, this solution has been on the Israeli/Palestinian agenda since 1937 (or 1922 if you think of the establishment of Transjordan). But is it a good solution? I am afraid that this country is just too small to be divided if you want to give the peoples living on both sides of the border a sense of security. Partition along the armistice lines of 1949 (this is the political proposal we have to deal with) creates more problems than it can possibly solve: Jerusalem; the Arab minority in Israel; Tel Aviv in the range of not even very sophisticated Arab weapons; the economic viability of the West Bank/Gaza State; the impossibility of settling substantial numbers of Palestinian refugees in the new Palestine etc.

And there is something even more important in my view, something that Judah Magnes mentioned in July 1946 when he opposed partition in talking to a Zionist audience in New York: On both sides of the partition border, schools will teach hatred to the children of the seperate nations.

Is the other approach to a solution of the geographical problem of national self-determination, so completely unrealistic and dangerous as most people seem to think? This is the approach to a domestic political solution, a peace process between Jewish Israelis and Arab Palestinians leading to a situation of co-existence (and, hopefully, co-operation) of the two peoples in one and the same country. I have tried to trade the historical roots and the political chances of such an approach, in my book *Jews and Arabs in One Country* recently published in German.

The theoretical blueprint is as follows: the "peace process" among governments (Israel/Egypt for the time being) must be supplemented by the establishment of a peace-connection between Jewish Israelis and Arab Palestinians. For this, a fundamental change of outlook is needed: instead of claiming rights (however legitimate) and legal titles on the international level, the representatives of the two peoples must define concrete *interests*. They must organize for the defense of those interests and develop the political will to *compromise* in a common framework. There is indeed a fundamental theoretical difference between a policy aimed at the fulfilment of rights and a policy aimed at a compromise between interests.

There is a paradox: one might expect a better chance to obtain fulfilment of a right, in a situation of domestic politics; rather than international relations which de facto consists very often in a search for compromise. But this is a superficial paradox only. The essence of all domestic politics is compromise, or an agreement to disagree and still use the facilities of a single house in common. Indeed insisting on rights and claiming rights in a domestic situation is only possible when agreement on a common legal system and submission to its sanctions has already been achieved. This is an indicator for a developed form of co-operation in domestic politics. When the basement has still to be built up, no court of law can sit and the claiming of one's right leads nowhere.

Are there any *visible practical bases* for the domestic peace approach to the "Jewish–Arab Conflict over Israel/Palestine" (this is the correct name, in my opinion)?

I can see *two* of them. Unfortunately, one only applies to the Jewish party and the other one to the Arab party only. To interrelate these two bases for a domestic peace process constitutes (in my modest view) the main task for domestic peace makers and it is an extremely difficult task.

Base no. 1 is the political and intellectual tradition, among Jews (including Zionists and Jewish Israelis), of searching for exactly this form of domestic peace with Arab neighbours. There is a tradition of *not* ignoring the "Arab question" (as it was called in the times of the British Mandate), and of approaching it in a spirit of readiness for practical compromise. Of course, an alternative Zionist tradition also exists: that of ignoring the existence of Arabs in Palestine, of claiming Jewish right over all of Eretz Israel and claiming it mainly in the international arena. Anti-Zionist forces all over the world, today are working hard to enhance this second tradition, as the only real history of Zionism. Not only PLO publications, but many academic studies by different (including Israeli) authors depict a history of Zionism which is "ethnically exclusive," colonialist, interested only in obtaining the land from the British etc. True, such a course of Zionist history can be documented. But there is equal documentation for the other tradition *within Zionism*; and I think whoever wants to promote peace among Jews and Arabs, should work equally hard to dig out the remnants of this tradition of "the other way" as Ahad Ha-Am would have said.

It is important to see that this tradition is not only confined to the idea of a bi-national state. Certainly this is the core concept for all who searched Jewish–Arab compromise in the days of the Mandate. But many variations have always existed. Ben Gurion never used the term "bi-nationalism," but preferred to speak about "parity." This is not exactly the same concept, but it belongs to the same traditional line. Secondly, it is important to know that he tradition of seeking compromise, was not confined to a tiny dissenting minority among Zionists. The "bi-nationalists" stricto sensu were a small (but respected) minority: parity and compromise were in the minds of the large majority and of the political leaders of the

Jewish people in Israel. Thirdly, it is important to remember that this tradition was not confined to one wing of the political spectrum: it was neither a purely leftist nor rightist idea (not even an exclusively Jewish idea), but shared by Hashomer Hatzair and Brit Shalom which means by Socialists and Liberals alike.

Obviously, no strong continuity of this tradition could be expected in Israel after 1947. The concrete Arab neighbours disappeared more often than not (if they were evicted, or fled voluntarily, is of secondary importance). The Arab states waged wars against the State of Israel and Israel had to rely on international alliances rather than on domestic compromises, if it wanted to survive. The remaining Arab minority in Israel, for many years, showed a submissive face to the conqueror, as Arabs had learnt to show to all conquerors in history.

The astonishing fact is that the intellectual tradition of bi-nationalism, of parity, of looking for a compromise with the Arab citizens of Israel, of questioning the Israeli government about the real content of "equal rights" for Arabs, this tradition did not die out completely in Jewish Israel. It did not, because Jewish Israel remained a democratic society in the western style (where human rights have practical meaning), because Israeli Jews remembered the long history of persecution of their ancestors, and because the Jewish religion has something to say about the spiritual value of peaceful co-existence with neighbours ("love" in the biblical language).

On the Arab side, this tradition has no equivalent. I do not know enough about Islam to discuss the spiritual side. But I found out that those individual Arabs who dared to speak about possible compromise with the Jews, always were dissenters within their people and sometimes (they) did not live long enough to practise what they had been talking about; I refer to Palestinian Arabs here, not to the absentee landlords who sold land to the Jewish National Fund, not to King Abdallah and not to President Sadat.

But there exists a "base no. 2" for domestic peace" in the Arab people of Palestine today. This is, in my opinion, the powerful quest for modernity. The young generation of Palestinian Arabs in 1979 (mainly "Israeli Arabs")(does) already live in a more modern world than did their fathers. But they want more of it, they want the full measure of Western "quality of life," and they want equal opportunities in this (brave?) new world. I put in these brackets because I know that the value of modernity has become doubtful in the West itself. We have learnt the bitter lesson that economic progress does not solve all problems. However, we are not allowed to ignore the fact that enormous masses of people in the Third World do see positive values in Western modernity. They are struggling to elevate themselves and thus they do not understand our own fear of pollution, of being bored by too much leisure etc. This trend to economic modernity is pushing the whole Third World (including China!) closer to the West and this very trend is pushing the Arabs of Palestine closer to their Jewish neighbours. At least, it could do so if only one condition were fulfilled. Arabs (at least their political leaders) must learn that certain forms of social and political organisation necessarily go together with economic modernity. Phrasing it very shortly and simply: No people can have an industrial society without political democracy and without the rule of law. It just will not work, the real needs of the people will not be expressed, the "elite circulation" will function badly and so on. I cannot go into detail here, but anybody can ask the Russians. For Arab Palestinians, the existing Jewish society of Israel could be a model, or at least a sort of signpost on their march into modernity—provided of course, that Israel itself remains a Western democracy, a modern industrial society and a nation open to peaceful domestic co-existence and co-operation with its Arab neighbours.

Now, how can this be done? I have no constitutional blueprint for the future of the one country Israel/Palestine. I have not even a strategy for the transfer between the two bases for a domestic approach that I think must be a priority. This must be worked out on the spot and by the people directly concerned.

It only makes sense, for an outsider, to do two more things: to search out the work of eminent theoreticians who have published books of general importance on the subject. The Dutchman Lijphart is one of them, and what he calls "consociational democracy" probably has some importance for the practical solution of the Near East conflict. I know that in Lebanon such a system has just been destroyed; but that does not prove anything. We know that similar ideas were discussed among Social Democrats in the old Austrian-Hungarian Empire (Otto Bauer, Karl Renner); the Empire fell apart, but Bauer's and Renner's books are still worth being read. After all, Marx did not succeed in bringing the Socialist Proletarian Revolution to England, but many people still discuss his thoughts.

Secondly, one can point out that similar problems (although not identical) exist in other parts of the world and that domestic "peace processes" are seriously being discussed there. The most important example at present is the Republic of South Africa. Perhaps politicians in South Africa have jumped too quickly to the level of constitutional blueprints. Students of the "Israeli–Arab" conflict, are advised to look closely at the South African situation. The dangers of wrong solutions, the dangers of racism, of systematic ignorance of the neighbour's needs are open visible there; and South

Africa can offer some consolation to the people of the Near East, because the difficulties of co-existence of not two, but several people in one country are much greater there. At least Jewish Israelis and Arab Palestinians are roughly equal in numbers and originate from the same ancestor.

References

Anspranger, Franz: Juden und Araber in Einem Land; die politischen Beziehungen der beiden Völker im Mandatsgebiet Palastina und in Staat Israel. München u.Mainz 1978, 335 pp. (Reihe "Entwicklung und Frieden," Wissenschaftl. Reihe 15).

Lijphart, Arend: Democracy in plural Societies, a comparative explanation. London 1978, 248 pp. (and earlier writings of this author).

Bauer, Otto: Die Nationalitätenfrage und die Sozialdemokratie. Wien 2nd ed. 1924.

Hanf. Theodor et al.: Südafrika: Friedlicher Wandel? Möglichkeiten demokratischer Konfliktregelung, eine empirische Untersuchung. München and Mainz 1978, 489 pp. (on the South African case) (Reihe Entwicklung und Frieden, wissenschaftl. Reihe 16).

International Negotiations
and Mediational Mechanisms:
Some Theoretical Observations on
the Negotiating Experience of Egypt and Israel

Jacob Bercovitch

International conflicts, like other types of social conflicts, manifest themselves in a process of escalation or de-escalation and are then terminated. The termination of one conflict can set the stage for the beginning of a new conflict and the precise demarcation point may be very difficult to locate. We do, though, assume that each conflict terminates and has a specific outcome. Three basic types of outcomes can be distinguished; withdrawal, imposition and compromise.[1] Of these three outcomes, compromise is the commonest form of terminating international conflicts. It is also the only mutually-acceptable and most peaceful outcome.

As a desired international outcome, a compromise may be attained through formal, or informal termination processes and mechanisms. Formal termination processes engage the parties in a direct, explicit transaction whereby the parties decide (or accept such a decision) what each shall give and take (e.g., peace conference, arbitration, adjudication). Informal processes seek to achieve a settlement and terminate a conflict in a more implicit, indirect and less procedural manner. Whichever process, or mechanism is utilized, a compromise represents a shift from coercive to accommodative behaviour and this can only be achieved through a process of negotiations.

International-negotiation is a conflict termining process implying an interaction between two, or more, complex social systems seeking to reach, on the basis of some rational and reciprocal calculation: 1) an acceptable compromise, 2) to determine what each shall give and take, 3) to provide some guidelines for future transactions between the parties. As a peaceful conflicting terminating

171

process, international negotiation has been embedded into the normative structure of the international system[2] and is the cardinal purpose of all diplomatic intercourse. It is also the only appropriate process for pursuing national objectives whilst preserving international peace and security. Successful negotiations can 1) de-escalate the level of violent behaviour, 2) facilitate the attainment of a compromise, 3) encourage the development of cooperation between the parties and 4) initiate and reinforce norms of constructive behaviour.

The importance of international negotiation has naturally attracted a considerable degree of scholarly attention and produced a concomitant body of scholarly output which abounds with stimulating observations, speculations and historical evidence.[3] The proliferation of research investigations employing diverse approaches and concepts has made it difficult to keep a coherent focus on the process, or to infer the importance of various dimensions and variables in reducing the frequency and intensity of international conflicts. This paper purports, therefore, to offer an exploratory paradigm for the study of international negotiations and suggest the relevance of a mediational mechanism[4] to international negotiations and the reduction, or termination, of violent behaviour. Although our efforts are primarily related to the recent negotiating experience of Egypt and Israel, the observations below are asserted at such a level of generality as to make them relevant to other settings and contexts of international negotiations and mediational mechanisms.

International negotiation has traditionally been treated as a competitive process in which two units with contradictory interests substitute verbal contact for violent action. A compromise outcome could be attained through an explicit exchange of proposals until some minimum convergence, or identity, of interests can be found and a limited form of collaboration or compromise can be established.[5] This conception of the negotiating relationships assumes a continuous series of bids and counterbids affecting the relative gains and losses of each party until they have "split the differences" in a manner which reflects their strategic positions and notions of fairness. In postulating an inexorable movement towards the "middle grounds," this conception ignores many of the intractable conditions of international negotiations, the social-psychological factors which separate the protagonists, the dynamics of the on-going process itself and the sheer complexity of international issues.

Modern international negotiations is an extremely complex process.[6] The issues being negotiated about can not always be narrowed down to clear-cut alternatives, nor is it always possible to gauge the parameters of the "middle grounds." The nature and size of conflict issues (for instance, issues of national security) and the number of official views that must be accommodated in the negotiating process make it quite impossible to carve up issues into improvised proposals at the very outset of negotiations. Moreover, some issues may be little understood and others are so complex as to be practically unknowable. International negotiators must contend with complexity, and that affects both the style and content of their neogtiating behaviour (e.g., rational choice, full information and accurate evaluations concerning proposals, positions and middle ground are not naturally built-in the process, but are, rather, intermediate objectives which the negotiators seek to achieve).

International negotiation should be seen as a response to external conditions of complexity, uncertainty and anxiety which international conflicts produce. Such complexity and uncertainty naturally affect the parties' perception, or definition, of the situation and thus, their expectations, evaluations and inclinations to exchange proposals. The complexity, uncertainty and the lack of an agreed definition of the situation make it very unlikely that negotiators can begin by trading concessions and delineating the area where their interests converge. A reasonable conclusion from the effect of complexity on negotiating behaviour, is to regard international negotiation as an adaptive, learning process between two conflict units whose main preoccupation is the management of their external system, the establishment of a tolerably predictable range of external behaviour and the attempt to contain, or preclude, the destabilizing aspects of external uncertainty. As an adaptive, joint decision-making process, international negotiation produces a desired outcome by first ordering the values, principles and guidelines which determine a common "definition of the situation" and creating a perspective within which choices and proposals can be assessed and subsequent interactions over more detailed matters can be indicated.

The prominent characteristics of international negotiations have the following features:

1. At least two conflict units are involved.
2. Their interaction is dominated by their conflicting interests.
3. They are temporarily brought together in a joint decision-making context.
4. Their activities concern learning to adapt to their external environment.
5. These activities involve developing a more simplified cognitive structure, a common perceptual framework and an agreed upon principle which can define their interactions and which may facilitate a subsequent presentation, or evaluation, of demands, proposals and other specific items (the formula-detail approach).[7]
6. International negotiation is a sequential pattern of activities

representing a meshing of personality variables, cognitive differences, background conditions and situational factors. It can only be comprehended by a model which incorporates all of these elements.

The social-psychological model developed by Sawyer and Guetzkow[8] integrates all the variables considered above and provides a framework for extrapolating the role, relevance and effectiveness of a third party. The social-psychological model of international negotiations emphasizes the perceptual, background and situational[9] forces which can impede an agreement, or a compromise and it also provides the broader perspective within which the efforts of a mediational mechanism can be located.

A mediational mechanism is an informal device or strategy for helping the parties to manage their interactions. It has a broad persuasive basis—the purpose of which is to produce feelings of trust and cooperation and focus on mental and material resources which the conflicting parties can not attain by themselves.

Mediational mechanisms exert personal and organizational pressures to reduce, or moderate, the impact of different perceptual, background or situational factors. As conceived in this paper, a mediational mechanism is an input to the initial negotiatory position of the parties designed to counteract the negative impact of the factors which interfere with the achievement of a compromise and establish a pattern of behaviour which will project the parties on a course towards a compromise (e.g., achieving shared objectives, a common perceptual framework of the situation, more accurate perception and an agreed evaluation of various proposals and outcomes).

As noted earlier, cognitive and perceptual differences, caused by variations in national characters are likely to impede attempts by negotiators to reach a compromise. While certain negotiators can be pragmatic, issue-oriented and compromising, others may well be principled, idealistic and abstractionist. Such differences intensify conflicts and are even more difficult to resolve, or reconcile when the parties' conflict behaviour has escalated to the level of violence, or when they refuse to deal directly with each other. A mediational mechanism can introduce a variety of strategies to reduce the saliency of the cognitive and perceptual differences. The most effective range of strategies include increasing the amount and type of contact between the parties (proximity and intensity of interactions provide a less-distorted perception), challenging the parties' underlying assumptions and their evaluation of the situation, helping to clarify their goals, building private channels of communications and sensitizing the parties to their common interests, principles or superordinate goals. Effective and competent third parties induce pressures towards cognitive and perceptual similarities and the adoption of a common conceptual understanding of the conflict. Such pressures heighten the preferences, and responsiveness, of negotiators to a joint decision-making effort and to some convergence of expectations concerning their external environment.

While perceptual and cognitive differences are quite difficult to counter, a mediational mechanism can be most effective in countering or reducing the impact of the personal-situational factors of international negotiations. International negotiation, it must be borne in mind, is carried on by negotiators occupying official government roles and accountable for their behaviour to their domestic polity. As representatives of government policies, international negotiators are not always free agents, or initiators of policy: more often than not they are charged with the responsibility for representing their government position and are expected to display loyalty and commitment to such position and to advocate them as competently as they can. The consequences of their role obligations are such that international negotiators are most unwilling to yield or abandon a government posture, while the dynamics of the negotiation process and the need to reach a compromise require that they do just that.[10] The pronounced pressures against making concessions and appearing to be losing a "public image" or a "public position" increase the competitive behaviour of negotiators and is likely to impede any progress towards an agreement. Such pressures are best decreased by third parties providing, in essence, an ideal "facing saving" mechanism[11] for dissolving some of the representational constraints on negotiators and enlarging their latitude of decision. The presence of a mediational mechanism exerts intangible pressures which ensures that the logic of the situation, the need to make concessions and to respond to the other party will win over the need to respond to one's own "public." In increasing mutual situational responsiveness, a mediational mechanism facilitates progress towards an acceptable compromise.

The situational factor of international negotiations refers to the actual conditions and setting under which the process takes place. The characteristics of the situation impinge both on the 1) context and the 2) on-going interactions. The complexity and characteristics of the situation can be manipulated by a mediational mechanism and conditions conducive to the attainment of a compromise can be created. Mediational strategies associated with influencing or manipulating the contect of negotiations, and reducing the pressures stemming from situational complexity, ideological blinders and emotional overtones include; determining site-neutrality, formality or informality of meetings, length of negotiations, time constraints, level of representation and the presence of legal or military experts.

The on-going process of negotiations can be substantively influenced by a third party determining the scope and order of issues on the agenda,[12] introducing "periods of reflection," to get the parties to negotiate in "good faith," reducing irrationality by eliminating personal animosity and recriminations, eliciting information, reinforcing norms of constructive behaviour (e.g., "fairness" and "equity") offering proposals and exerting pressures towards a compromise.[13]

The background conditions of international negotiation which can be considered as impeding the prospects of a compromise refer to the stresses and tensions experienced by negotiators due to the type of interactions. These too can be influenced by the presence of a mediational mechanism. A mediational mechanism can be effective in relieving the sense of personal inadequacy (arising out of lack of information or need to make concessions) or reducing the stresses and tensions through conciliatory strategies and inducing personal cooperation between negotiators. A mediational mechanism can control overreaction and/or provocations and prevent deterioration of a negotiating relationship. The stresses and tensions of the process can be reduced by evoking some symmetry in concession rates and maintaining the relationship on as informal a basis as is possible.

A mediational mechanism can guarantee the secrecy and privacy of the negotiating process. Maintaining a degree of secrecy (about the process, not about the outcome) and preventing premature disclosures or leaks keep the domestic public sufficiently ignorant of the dynamics of the process to allow negotiators to make concessions without the fear of public loss of face or public criticism.[14] Full information on the deliberations of negotiators could affect the proceedings quite adversely by producing a mutual reluctance to concede and a tendency to be seen as "firm" and "resolute." The result of such behaviour can be a deadlock. Negotiations conducted formally and publicly tend to degenerate quite quickly into an occasion for blurting propaganda and shifting responsibilities. By maintaining the secrecy of the process and controlling the flow of information to an outside public, a mediational mechanism is effective in producing acts of accommodation and concessions which are essential in achieving an acceptable compromise.

All the descriptive statements offered above underline the importance of a mediational mechanism in facilitating a more cooperative and productive pattern of international negotiations. counteract the impact of the cognitive, personal, situational and background differences—differences which can only impede the process towards a compromise. A mediational mechanism is effective in reducing the inherent complexities of international negotiations to more manageable levels and in coordinating between the various factors, processes and positions to which international negotiators are subjected. A summary of the effects of a mediational mechanism suggests that it is in a sense, a device for reducing the inherent ambiguities and uncertainties of international negotiation and a device for structuring human skills and helping to adapt them to the demands of a complex environment. A mediational mechanism can match and coordinate the attitudes and perceptions of the person, his role-dispositions and obligations with the requirements of the situation. As such, it is the most promising and effective mechanism in resolving the dilemmas of international negotiations.

• • •

In analyzing the origins and dynamics of the negotiating experience of Egypt and Israel, it is essential that we keep the observations above very firmly in our mind. There can be little doubt that, but for the strenuous and competent intervention of a third party, the entrenched positions of the two parties could not be abridged. President Carter and his team of advisors recognised the complexities of the conflict and the immensity of the issues, but were convinced that some progress could be made through a joint psychological learning drive challenging complex issues and controversial problems and providing a more comprehensible framework concentrating on the parties' mutual interest to reduce external complexity. In the immediate aftermath of the upheavals in Iran, the predicament of Lebanon and the dramatic events in Afghanistan and South Yemen, the political consciousness and diplomacy of Israel and Egypt sustained a mutual wish to contain regional instability and uncertainty and reverse the spreading trend of disequilibrium and disruption. This principal thread behind the negotiating experience of Israel and Egypt was smoothed over by a third party, whose global interests were much in line with this policy, and given a general expression in the "Framework of Peace." A framework which was to permit each party to adjust itself, respond to the complexities of their environment and share a more detailed discussion over themes and concerns in subsequent interactions.

In describing the American intervention in the conflict terminating efforts of Egypt and Israel, it is well to bear in mind that the starting point for much of the literature on the Middle East conflict concentrates on constructing desired outcomes. The terms of such outcomes are envisaged as pertaining to territories and security, the nature of human rights and self-determination and the de-escalation of violence. The conceptual premises guiding the American intervention brought about some substantial changes in the parties' attitudes and behaviour because they were related to the nature of the conflict-terminating process. The context, type and nature of the process can often determine the emerging conditions of a desired outcome. It is, therefore, as important to concentrate on *how* to achieve an acceptable outcome, as it is to focus on *which* outcomes are likely to prove most acceptable.

Various interventionary devices have been tried in the Middle East since 1967 in an attempt to terminate the conflict and reconcile the differences between the parties. Such devices included, inter alia, the mediatory efforts of the UN Secretary-General or his Special Representatives, the Rogers Plan, the interim step-by-step approach and the continuing attempts to convene a conference in Geneva to deal comprehensively with the manifold aspects of the conflict. Such devices (all of which represent a structural extension of a dyadic negotiation process) have two things in common: they have all had little success in their pursuit of conflict termination and they have all promulgated some ideas, or schemes, about what the outcome should look like. By comparison, the third party role which President Carter implemented was predicated on a vigorous endeavour to restructure the *process* of conflict termination. The determination to generate, encourage and supervise a process of "constructive confrontations" resulted in the endorsement of an acceptable outcome.

As a mediational mechanism, President Carter's third party role broke new grounds and provided the inpetus for reducing misperceptions and hostilities by presiding over the process of conflict termination, rather than becoming engaged in promoting specific outcomes. Its influence-related strategies engendered a sense of cohesion and comprehension which challenged the conceptual confusion, multiplicity of meanings and general ambiguity about the nature and scope of the conflict. Within the broad social-psychological perspective of conflict interactions, its influence in establishing a set of generic and common concepts from which guidelines and relevant dimensions for future interactions can be deduced, was consistant and persuasive.[14] A corollary of the development of a conceptual framework concentrating on areas of mutual interests was to predispose the parties to segment the complex problems, deal with them in a pragmatic, issue-oriented manner and thus produce the requisite conditions for an Egyptian— Israeli peace treaty.

The strong influence of a mediational mechanism directed the process of negotiations, emphasized the commonalities, rather than differences, and set the stage for achieving a desired outcome. What is now needed, is to enlarge the operational basis of the mediational mechanism by insisting on the Soviet involvement in the conflict-terminating process. The drive towards a more general agreement in the Middle East is obviously complicated by the regional and global rivalries between the US and the USSR. The latter's annoyance with its own series of extraordinary miscalculations and setbacks in the region and at being left out of the entire process, soured the US–Soviet relations and provided the nucleus of a political grouping embracing all the Arab states rejecting both the process of direct negotiations and any compromise outcome. This fragmentation of the region has effected an undeniable erosion in the viability of the compromise and the saliency of the mediational mechanism. If the dreams and possibilities suggested by the peace treaty between Egypt and Israel are to bear fruit and bring about a long overdue state of regional stability and normalcy, then the quest for more efficient and resourceful processes of conflict termination must overcome all the obstacles which are so heavily stacked against it. There is a great deal of merit to the view that a more subtle and cautious Soviet–American cooperation, undertaking joint mediational efforts can remove some of these obstacles. The fragility and dangers of the Middle East impose an emphatic responsibility on both superpowers to enhance and support all processes of conflict termination and jointly commit their resources towards the attainment of a peaceful and lasting, compromise outcome.

References

1. The terminology adopted from Kreiesberg, L. *The Sociology of Social Conflicts*. New Jersey: Prentice Hall. 1973.

2. Article 33 (1) of the UN Charter enjoins all members to resort to international negotiations—or variants thereof—to settle or terminate their conflicts.

3. In their critical examination of the process of bargaining and negotiations, over 1000! studies are cited by Rubin, J. Z. and Brown, B. R. *The Social Psychology of Bargaining and Negotiations*. New York: Academic Press. 1975.

4. By a mediational mechanism I mean the presence of an exogenous third party seeking to promote an agreement or compromise between the belligerents in a non-coercive and non-judicial manner.

5. See, for instance, Iklé, F. C. *How Nations Negotiate*. New York: Harper & Row. 1964; Lall, H. *Modern International Negotiations: Principles and Practice*. New York: Columbia University Press. 1966; and Northedge, F. S. and Donelan, M. D. *International Disputes: The Political Aspects*. London: Europa Publications. 1974.

6. On complexity in international negotiations, see, Winham, G. R. "Negotiations as a Management Process" in *World Politics*, Vol. 30, No. 1, 1977.

7. For a more complete account of the formula-detail conceptions of international negotiations, see, Zartman, I. W. "Negotiation as a Joint-Decision-Making Process" in Zartman, I. W. (ed.), *The Negotiations Process: Theories and Applications*. California: Sage Publications. 1978.

8.   Sawyer, J. and Guetzkow, H. "Bargaining and Negotiations in International Relations" in Kelman, H. C. (ed.) *International Behaviour: A Social-Psychological Approach*. New York: Holt, Rinehart & Winston. 1965.

9.   The manner in which these factors impede an agreement is examined by Druckman, D. "The Person, Role and Situation in International Negotiations" in Herman, M. C. (ed.), *A Psychological Examination of Political Leaders*. New York: The Free Press, 1977.

10.   This is described as the "inherent paradox" of negotiations by Stevens, C. M. *Strategy and Collective Bargaining Negotiation*. New York: McGraw-Hill. 1963; and as "boundary role-conflict" by Walton, R. E. and McKersie, R. B. *A Behavioural Theory of Labour Negotiations*. New York: McGraw-Hill. 1965.

11.   The need of international negotiators to save face and the way in which a mediational mechanism meets this need has been studied by Pruitt, D. G. and Johnson, D. F. "Mediation as an Aid to Face-Saving in Negotiations" in *Journal of Personality and Social Psychology*, Vol. 14, No. 2, 1970; and by Poddell, J. E. and Knapp, W. M. "The Effect of Mediation on the Perceived Firmness of the Opponent" in *Journal of Conflict Resolution*, Vol. 13, No. 4, 1979.

12.   Dealing at first with smaller issues which are easier to resolve serves the parties well when coming to deal with the larger and more complex issues.

13.   These third party functions are cited by Walton, R. E. *Interpersonal Peacemaking: Confrontation and Third Party Consultation*. Mass.: Addison-Wesley Publishing Co. 1969 and Young, O. R. *The Intermediaries: Third Parties in International Crises*. New Jersey: Princeton University Press. 1967.

14.   The importance of maintaining privacy and secrecy in international negotiations is pointed out by Iklé, F. C., op. cit.

15   The "Framework for Peace" provided a clearer definition of the situation and a set of issues and definitions which could be operationalized, assessed and discussed at a later stage.

The Political Economy of
a Middle Eastern Peace

Jacob Reuveny

A peace treaty is a legal document reflecting an accord reached at a definite period. Since peace is essentially a process, the nature of the relations that evolve as a result of the peace treaty are crucial for its viability. The economic consequences of the accord are a crucial part of any peace process. Positive economic results may consolidate the peace process whereas negative economic consequences may have a disruptive effect.

The history of both the First and the Second World War and their aftermaths may support this proposition. At Versailles statesmen were not adequately aware of the crucial significance of the economic aspect for the viability of the peace agreement. The seeds of the Second World War were latent at Versailles. By the end of the Second World War the lesson was self evident. The Marshall Plan reflected the natural response to past mistakes. It stimulated the recovery of the European economies hit by the war, of all belligerent parties of Western and Central Europe. The Marshall Plan was a contributing factor towards the healing of past wounds and the establishment of a new economic, political and military alliance which cuts across old animosities.

In many respects, the Camp David Accord and the subsequent Israeli–Egyptian peace agreement of March 26 1979 could be supported by positive economic processes, ensuing as a direct or indirect consequence of these agreements. The reduction of tension and the subsequent limitation of military expenditure may prove beneficial for the economies of both states, which have been drained by excessive allocation to military purposes. Defense expenditures could be diverted for investment and consumption. Both parties may benefit from the normalization of economic relations, mutual trade, tourism and exchange of skills. A massive aid program by the industrialized states of the west (A "Middle Eastern Marshall Plan") could be a major factor in bolstering the peace process.[1] However, in some major respects, the relevance of the European experience to the

Israeli–Egyptian case may be limited, and the very comparison between both cases may be misleading.

The Relevance of the Marshall Plan Experience

The partial irrelevance of the Marshall Plan experience to the present Middle Eastern peace process is due to two major factors: the difference in economic dynamics between the Middle East and post-World War Western and Central Europe and the difference in regard to the possible weight of the economic factor within the broader matrix of forces which dominate the current historical processes of the Middle East.

It is now commonly accepted that Marshall Plan concepts are inappropriate to the Third World. The countries which benefited from the Marshall Plan were former industrial societies with a modern human and industrial infrastructure. The reconstruction, after the Second World War, did not require basic structural transformation of the economies, cultural changes and other prerequisites of modernization faced by Third World countries.

It is for this reason that foreign aid policies to developing countries based on the Marshall Plan experience have proved counterproductive.[2] The economic difficulties of both Israel and Egypt, respectively, though affected by the military burden, stem from different causes than the difficulties of post-World War Europe. Assuming that an appropriate policy could be designed to provide effective economic benefits of the peace process, the economic component could not be conceived as an autonomous factor. In non-Western countries, there is an intricate mechanism which governs the relation between economic, political and social processes, a mechanism which differs radically from its counterparts in Western societies. The possible effect of economic benefits on propensity for peace and war could, therefore, be examined only in terms of broad theories of social change which present a systematic interrelationship between social change, economic development and international relations.

W. W. Rostow's Theory on War, Peace and Economic Development

A comprehensive theory on the way economic social and political processes may impinge upon propensities for peace and war has been presented in W. W. Rostow's *The Stages of Economic Growth* (1960).[3] Rostow maintains that there are five stages of economic development:

1. The traditional Society (the primitive, pre-scientific pre-industrial stage, characteristic of agrarian communities; subsistence agriculture, and hierarchical social structure).
2. Preconditions for takeoff (emergence of modernizing elites, the rise of nationalism in reaction to foreign intrusion).
3. The Takeoff. (the crucial stage of dynamic transformation, industrial revolution).
4. The Drive to Maturity (Spread of modern technology, advanced industrialization), and
5. The age of high mass consumption (increased economic resources are allocated to consumption, welfare and security).

At the second stage — the preconditions for takeoff — wars arise from the initial intrusion of a colonial power on a traditional society and efforts of colonial peoples to assert their independence of the metropolitan power. The type of wars common in the contemporary Middle East take place between the second and third stages and are defined by Rostow as "Regional Aggression."[4] They occur as part of internal political dynamics of transition. Rostow maintains that policies appropriate for achieving independence rarely suit the subsequent need for completing the preconditions and launching the takeoff. Whereas reactive nationalism serves as a unifying factor in supplying the developing society with an ad-hoc coalition, this coalition tends to disintegrate, after independence.

At this stage, the developing society is faced with a number of alternatives: should nationalism be turned to assert power and dignity on the world scene? Should the major focus of attention be directed towards social and economic modernization or towards the consolidation of power of the central government? The choice is very difficult, since modernization tends to raise divisive issues. Rostow concludes that:

> Historically, it has proved extremely tempting of the new nationalism to be diverted on to external objectives if these objectives looked to be accessible at little real cost or risk.[5]

Rostow classifies the Arab–Israeli conflicts in the fifties under the category of "Regional Aggression." Regional aggression is necessary for building internal cohesion at the early stages of the takeoff. At later stages, after past humiliations have been avenged, the leadership tends to adopt an inward looking policy, aimed at social and economic modernization.

Assuming that Egypt has entered the takeoff stage, and that the 1973 war has provided the country with a proper redress for past humiliations, Rostow's theory would imply that Egypt is ready for an inward looking, development oriented policy. Hence the economic component may have a crucial role in supporting the present peace-process, as far as Egypt is concerned.

We should, however, consider the fact that Rostow's theory is very controversial, and that some aspects of this controversy directly impinge on its applicability to the Middle Eastern conditions. Rostow's theory has been criticized for its unilinearity, its "economism," for the way it relates nationalism and other poltical factors to economic development and for its overemphasis on endogenous factors.[6] For example, such exogenous factors as inter-Arab relations, the fact that hostility towards Israel is a unifying factor in the Arab and Moslem world, and that this factor is significant due to the chronic political instability in the region, do not fit into his model. In our case, inter-Arab relations are not mere epiphenomena. They have potential economic consequences as they may affect aid and investment by oil-producing states in the Egyptian economy.

There are a number of additional factors which may limit the possible benefits of economic normalization of relations between Israel and Egypt. The very contact between Israeli and Egyptian citizens through tourism, technical cooperation and Israeli economic presence in Egypt may stir up nationalistic feelings.[7] Both the radical left as well as Islamic fundamentalists may use the Israeli presence as a source of agitation against the Sadat regime, for different reasons. Some popular theories of imperialism, widely accepted among students and the educated class, may reinforce negative attitudes.

Egypt's capacity to divert resources from the military establishment to the non-military sector seems questionable, in view of the structural characteristics of the Egyptian economy as well as the problems of employment of the educated class. It may be paradoxical that since the Camp David accord, most the United States' financial aid to Egypt has been directed towards the modernization of the Egyptian army. On the Israeli side, a major part of the US aid was allocated for the construction of airfields in the Negev Desert. In the short term perspective, Israel's economy has been adversely affected by the peace agreement.

Conclusion

The problem to what extent economic benefits may enhance the Israeli–Egyptian peace process does not lend itself to a simple answer. The answer is largely contingent upon our interpretation of the nature of the historical process the Middle East is currently undergoing. Some dominant theories of modernization have failed in explaining and predicting current trends. The case of the Islamic revolution in Iran is one significant example. A major difficulty has been the inability to relate the economic and the political dynamics. Whereas an economic analysis may lead to optimistic conclusions, a political emphasis may focus on the volatility and unpredictable nature of the Middle Eastern situation. Economic concepts are rational and systematic whereas the relevant political theory is elusive and non-structured. Unfortunately, it is the political dynamics which has the final word, and political dynamics often puts aside the economic logic. A valid theory which could provide realistic answers to our problem could be defined as a "Political Economy of Peace." Such theory should provide new insights into conditions where economic and political dynamics would converge or diverge and some forms of "rates of exchange" between economic and political values.

Within the foreseeable future, the economic factor in the processes supporting the Israeli–Egyptian peace seems extremely limited. "Normalization of Economic Relations" is itself dependent on lasting political good-will.

Notes

1.   Edgar L. Feige, "The Economic Consequences of Peace in the Middle East." *Challenge.* Jan.(Feb. 1979, pp. 2–32.

2.   Robert A. Packenham, *Liberal America and the Third World* (Princeton, NJ: Princeton University Press, 1973), pp. 32–42.

3.   W. W. Rostow, *The Stages of Economic Growth* (Cambridge: MIT University Press, 1960), ch. 1–6.

4.   Ibid., pp. 108–111.

5.   Ibid., p. 113.

6.   For criticism of Rostow's stage theory, see P. T. Bauer, *Dissent on Development* (London: Weidenfeld & Nicolson, 1971).

7.   Some new insights on the problem of nationalism are presented in Selig S. Harrison, *The Widening Gulf* (New York: The Free Press, 1978).

Economic Difficulties in the Transition from War to Peace

Fanny Ginor

It is possible to predict the difficulties of transition from war to peace by comparing a model of a peace-time economy with the present state of the economy in Israel. To construct such an economic peace-time model, certain assumptions have to be made as to the kind of peace to be expected. Shall there be peace with one of our neighbours or with all our neighbours, or with the whole Arab world? Shall there be a full peace or only a cessation of hostilities and how long will the transition period be?

At present it seems that it will be a lengthy and slow process until normal relations can be established with all our neighbours, and eventually with the Arab world.

It would, therefore, be best to think of two peace-time models: one for the more distant future, when peaceful relations are established with all Arab countries, the goal to be attained, and another for the near future given peaceful relations with Egypt.

In the first case we can assume the abrogation of the Arab boycott, the opening of the borders to trade and tourism with all our neighbours and eventually with all countries of the Middle East and North Africa, and, perhaps a controlled flow of capital and people to and from them. In the near future peace-time model with Egypt only, it can be assumed that the Arab boycott will be weakened, that the borders to the south will be opened to trade and tourism, and that there may be some controlled flow of capital and people between the two countries.

The feasibility of economic cooperation in various fields such as the efficient use of water resources and the possibility of joint power works with our neighbours to the north and the east, and the opening up of connecting railway lines and efficient motor roads with all neighbours has to be examined. Cooperation in the field of transport and tourism may include the mutual granting of port facilities and landing rights, and joint arrangements of group tours. Further possibilities of economic cooperation are sub-contracting

187

arrangements in the field of industry to utilize surplus labour in certain areas, and the exchange of know-how, especially in agriculture. The programming of technical assistance will have to take into account sensitivities and psychological difficulties after long periods of enmity. In spite of Israeli leadership in the development of agriculture and water resources, economic cooperation in this field should be a two-way street. For instance, in the field of cotton-growing, much can be learned from Egyptian research and experience.

Cooperation in the field of science and cultural exchange, apart from their economic impact, will also be important for the creation of human contact and the promotion of understanding and friendly feelings.

The transition from the present situation in which Israel is cut off from all connections with her neighbours, to one in which such connections will be gradually formed (or restored, since they existed before 1948), will, of course, have its influence on all branches of the economy. We can envisage cheap imports of certain agricultural and industrial products which may require adjustments and structural changes. Production may decline in various branches. On the other hand, the expansion of exports will lead to increased production in other branches. As the transition is expected to be a long drawn-out process, because of the slow progress of peace, these structural changes may be part of the general changes required to achieve the gradual reduction of the balance of payments gap.

The economy in its present state is not exactly a wartime economy, but it has many of its features such as an extremely high defence budget and, in its wake, a government deficit, strong inflationary pressures and full employment. A major difference between this situation and an "ideal" model of a wartime economy is the continuation of "business as usual" in the civilian sector of the economy. In spite of the high security expenditures even during the intermittently acute war periods, investments in the civilian sector have continued as has housing construction, and the standard of living of the population has continued to rise or was at least maintained. Usually, in war periods, investments in the civilian sector are dramatically cut or even stopped and the standard of living of the population declines, as the war effort needs increasing resources. The prolonged situation of no war and no peace with acute war situations in between and the fact that Israel has other tasks to perform apart from the battle for survival—the absorption of immigrants within an expanding economy—lead to this special situation.

The decline in the burden of military expenditure and the transfer of resources from defence purposes to civilian goals seems to be the expected first phase in a transition from an economy geared to security needs, to that of a peace economy. In such a case it is expected that the discharge of people from the army, and from the plants producing military equipment, and the reduction of the period of military service will at first create a labour surplus. The danger of unemployment will then become a severe problem. Though there are many jobs to be done: housing for all those living in crowded and low-standard housing, telephones for those waiting for years, the expansion of export industries, the improvement of the transport system, and so on, there would be the organizational difficulty of transferring manpower from one sector of the economy to other sectors, and the question of the additional capital required in these sectors to match the additional labour.

Since a decline in the capital import from the usual sources has eventually to be expected (though a peace situation may bring capital imports of a different kind), the structural changes necessary for the reduction of the balance of payments gap will become more urgent, i.e., increased production for exports and for import replacement, which would have to be part of the general restructuring of the economy. This means,i n the main, that the share of the employed in industry will have to be increased at the expense of the services, in which, for various reasons too high a proportion of the labour force is at present employed.

As matters now stand, however, no such straight transition can be expected from a war-time to a peace-time situation in the sense that more and more resources are directly diverted from defence to civilian purposes. High security standards have to be maintained in view of the attitude of our neighbours to the north and the east. The high costs of the geographical rearrangement of the security system connected with the peace treaty in the south will even raise defence expenditure in the coming years. The transition will, therefore, at first not mean a decline in the use of resources for defence purposes, and the first difficulty will be this increased diversion of resources (capital, manpower, building materials) to the defence sector which, at a later time, will increase the difficulties in restructuring the economy for the peacetime situation.

At the present juncture, when the goals set by government policy are already competing for scarce resources, this will increase the difficulties the economy is experiencing now.

The two most important problems of the economy at present are the balance of payments deficit and inflation. In 1978, the balance of payments deficit—the import surplus—accounted for one quarter of all resources for domestic use (for 16%, if direct imports for defence purposes are excluded). After a substantial improvement during the two years 1976 and 1977, the import surplus rose by over 30% in

1978. As much of the rise was caused by increased imports for defence purposes, the civilian import surplus rose less, but still by 22%. Part of the deterioration in the balance of payments has to be attributed to increased inflation (prices rose over 50% in 1978), as inflation increases the demand for imports and the high internal demand reduces the incentive to export. Higher imports, however, contributed also to a rise in the gross national product by 5%, after it had almost stagnated for two years. But higher imports and higher production led to increased consumption and raised investments but little. Private consumption in real terms rose 8% (5½% per capita) in 1978, public consumption increased by 11% (civilian public consumption by 5%) and local gross investments only by 4%. A closer look shows a more favourable picture; investments in fixed assets rose 7%, and fixed investments in industry, agriculture and power rose more than 15%.

Inflation was sped up by rising costs and by increasing demands in all spheres which gained momentum by the expectations of rising prices and the rise in real incomes. The most spectacular development in 1978 was the large rise in real disposable incomes which rose almost 8% while the gross national product rose only 5%! (Real disposable income from internal sources rose about 6% and transfers from abroad raised the increase to 8%). This explains the great rise in private consumption (the purchase of durable consumers' goods rose about 18%) and the rising demand for homes and apartments.

The government's budget deficit must be seen as a main cause for the rising inflationary waves. Further causes were the expansion of bank credit and the increase in credits from abroad, which were exchanged for local currency and used for local purchases. We cannot analyze here in detail the developments which led to the present situation, but will only point out the connection of the great rise in real disposable incomes with the government deficit. The fact that real disposable incomes rose more than the gross national product was caused by the decline in the net tax burden in real terms. Government's net transfer payments to the public in real terms (social payments and interest payments) rose considerably more than direct taxes. Furthermore, the large rise in subsidies caused a decline in net indirect taxes. The government's index-linked borrowing from the public and its unlinked or only partly linked lending to the public was a further inflationary factor increasing the government's deficit.

The situation in mid-1979 shows an acceleration of inflation and a further deterioration of the balance of payments, reflecting apparently the first impact of the expected rise in defence expenditures.

Obviously, the simplest measure to improve the situation would be to change the Government deficit into a surplus, by cutting public expenditure and raising taxes. This would reduce all-over demand. But can it be done? There is no doubt that only unpopular measures can lead to a turning point in the inflationary development and in the balance of payments deficit. To raise taxes and to cut down public expenditure requires certainly unpopular measures, and a special campaign is necessary to persuade the people of the necessity of such steps.

For instance, improvements and expansion of health and educational services and of the social security system are believed to be important for the improvement of the social situation, and it is, therefore, difficult even to freeze them at their present levels. Any reduction of these services is very difficult to conceive. Furthermore, the improvement of the housing situation is regarded as equally important for the same reasons and a reduction in public investments in housing will, therefore, also be difficult to achieve.

Because of the heterogeneity of the population, there is great sensitivity to any deterioration in the relative situation of the weaker social strata and to any increase in the inequality of incomes. Inflationary profits tend to increase social disparities, but full employment reduces inequality. Data available show that there was some increase in inequality since 1977, after it had declined steadily since 1967, apart from a small rise after the 1973 war. Hence, a decline in social transfer payments would be detrimental to the social situation.

The immediate difficulty is to be seen in the conflicting targets of economic policy, in a very difficult situation: too many tasks in the face of very limited resources.

It is necessary to combat inflation and to prevent further deterioration of the balance of payments. The foreign debt has reached a figure of $15 billion at the end of 1979 (twice the annual exports of Israel), and interest payments in 1979 were about $860 million. Improvement of the balance of payments requires investments in export industries and in production replacing imports, and transfer of labour to these branches, as well as an increase in efficiency, which is difficult under inflationary pressures. To reduce inflation means raising taxes, cutting government expenditure and restraining the rise of wages and income. No raising of taxes is envisaged in the policy proposed in the present national budget. Instead it is also government's policy to increase expenses for the construction of housing for immigrants, for young couples, for people in low-standard housing while labour and building materials are required for the work in the Negev in connection with the rearrangement of the security system. And there is the task of immigrant absorption and the social policy of income maintenance of the economically weak.

To all this, the economic price for peace has to be added—the costs of the rearrangement of the defence system, the loss of certain resources such as oil, the expenses connected with the transfer of settlements, and compensation schemes for economic claims and counterclaims which may be forthcoming. Though American assistance will be extended, the demand for local resources will increase.

How far can local production be raised to meet the rising demand from all quarters without further considerably raising prices, wages and salaries? What will be the impact on the balance of payments? Can the rise in private consumption be restrained without any rise in taxes? A substantial reduction in subsidies will be an important step in the right direction. Can the subsidization of capital (credits, investment loans, mortgages) be significantly reduced? Can public consumption for civilian purposes be reduced or at least maintained at its previous level? Will government policy be sufficiently consistent in the pursuit of its goals, and still be elastic enough in view of changes in the situation?

As all this increases economic problems and is contrary to expectations of most people, the necessary policy measures become more and more complicated and the transition from war to peace means growing economic difficulties.

The Contributors

Dr. Franz Ansprenger is professor of political science and director of the Department of African Studies at the Free University of Berlin.

Dr. S. B. Asante is a member of the academic staff of the Department of Political Science at the Nigerian University of Calabar. He is currently working at the University of Ghana in Legon.

Dr. Rafel Barkan is a research fellow of the Israeli Institute for the Study of International Affairs.

Dr. Mortimer Becker is a faculty member of the Community College of the State University of New York.

Dr. Yacov Bercovitch is lecturing at the London School of Economics and Political Science.

Dr. Charles Saul Boasson is one-time professor of the universities of Jerusalem, Tel Aviv and Sydney. He has written several books and articles dealing with international law and peace research issues.

Dr. Ernst-Otto Czempiel is professor of political science at the University of Frankfurt and director of the Peace Research Institute of Hessen.

Dr. Fanny Ginor is a research fellow of the D. Horowitz Institute for the Research of Developing Countries of Tel Aviv University.

Dr. Leo Hamon is professor of political science at the University of Paris.

Dr. William Kluback is a faculty member of the Community College of the State University of New York.

Dr. Martin Kriele is professor of philosophy of law and director of the Institute of Constitutional Law at the University of Cologne.

Herbert Lamm, Licencié des Sciences Politiques. He is a member of the board of the Israeli Institute for the Study of International Affairs and is its representative in Paris.

Dr. Mieczyslaw Maneli is professor of political doctrines at the Queen's College of the SUNY, NY.

Dr. Mario'n Mushkat is professor of international law and practice and chairman of the Israeli Institute for the Study of International Affairs.

Dr. Olusola Ojo is a member of the staff of the Department of International Relations of the University of Ife, Nigeria.

Dr. Chaim Perelman is honorary professor and co-director of the Institute of Philosophy of Law of the Free University of Bruxelles.

Dr. Yacov Reuveny is senior lecturer at the Department of Political Science of the Bar-Ilan University.

Dr. E. Tuma is professor of economics, currently working at Davis, UCLA.

Dr. Marek Thee is research director of the International Peace Research Institute in Oslo.

Dr. Arye Yodfat is research fellow of the Israeli Institute for the Study of International Affairs. He has written several books and papers dealing with Soviet and Middle East Politics.

Dr. Alan Zaremba is assistant professor at the Fredonia College of the State University of New York.

A Forthcoming IISIA Publication

The Third World and Peace

Some aspects of the interrelationship between
underdevelopment and international security

by Mario'n Mushkat

Contents